The Bears of Yellowstone

Books by Paul Schullery

Old Yellowstone Days (editor)

The Bears of Yellowstone

The Grand Canyon: Early Impressions (editor)

The Orvis Story (with Austin Hogan)

American Bears: Selections from the Writings of
   Theodore Roosevelt (editor)

Freshwater Wilderness: Yellowstone Fishes and Their World
   (with John D. Varley)

Mountain Time

Theodore Roosevelt: Wilderness Writings (editor)

The National Parks (editor)

Island in the Sky: Pioneering Accounts of Mount Rainier (editor)

Wildlife in Transition: Man and Nature on Yellowstone's Northern
   Range (with Don Despain, Douglas Houston, and Mary Meagher)

Bud Lilly's Guide to Western Fly Fishing (with Bud Lilly)

American Fly Fishing: A History

A Trout's Best Friend (with Bud Lilly)

The Bear Hunter's Century

Pregnant Bears and Crawdad Eyes: Excursions
   and Encounters in Animal Worlds

The National Parks: A Seventy-fifth Anniversary Album
Yellowstone Bear Tales (editor)

Contributing Author

The Sierra Club Guide to the National Parks,
   the Rocky Mountains and the Great Plains

The Adirondack League Club, 1890–1990

Encyclopedia Brittanica Year Book of Science and the Future, 1991

A Living History Reader

The Greater Yellowstone Ecosystem

The Great Bear

The Bears of Yellowstone

Paul Schullery

High Plains Publishing Company, Inc.

Author's note: The first two editions of this book were written while I was not employed by the National Park Service. This third edition is written while I am working for the Research Division in Yellowstone Park. The revision has been done on my own time, but I must make it clear that the views expressed in the book are not necessarily those of any or all of the people I work for in the National Park Service; nor am I speaking for the National Park Service at any point in this book.

Published by High Plains Publishing Company, Inc.
Post Office Box 1860, Worland, WY 82401
Library of Congress Catalog Number 91-78168
International Standard Book Numbers
0-9623333-9-5 (cloth) and 1-881019-00-4 (paper)
Printed in the United States of America

Cover design by Jody Chapel
Cover to Cover Design
Denver, Co

Cover photo:"Madonna of the Wilds"—The famous early twentieth-century naturalist Ernest Thompson Seton called this photograph "the most remarkable wild animal photograph ever taken." It was taken by F. J. Haynes, an early park photographer. Haynes Foundation, #16343, Montana Historical Society.

The Bears of Yellowstone

is dedicated to my friends

Dick Follett and John Whitman

This whole episode of bear life in the Yellowstone is so extraordinary that it will be well worth while for any man who has the right powers and enough time, to make a complete study of the life and history of the Yellowstone bears.

Theodore Roosevelt, 1904

The grizzly is a massive and powerful statement of the evolutionary history of circumpolar northern environments. The grizzly symbolizes the power, dynamism and productivity of the ice ages. Grizzly bears are a well-tuned way of capturing and utilizing a broad range of available energy. But the omnivorous grizzly ultimately competes with omnivorous man, and human beings through their technology have what our primitive ancestors lacked—the power to exterminate the grizzly.

We should preserve grizzly bear populations, not because their ecological function is critical, but because of what they can do for human imagination, thought and experience.

Steve Herrero, 1976

Contents

Introduction 1

PART ONE: THE WILD BEARS OF YELLOWSTONE

1   The Black Bear: Description 7
2   The Black Bear: Food Habits 11
3   The Black Bear: Denning 17
4   The Black Bear: Mating and Cub Growth 23
5   The Black Bear: Lifestyle 30
6   The Grizzly Bear: Origins 37
7   The Grizzly Bear: Description 41
8   The Grizzly Bear: Food Habits 45
9   The Grizzly Bear: Denning 57
10 The Grizzly Bear: Mating and Cub Growth 62
11 The Grizzly Bear: Lifestyle 69

PART TWO: OF BEARS AND MEN

12 The First 10,000 Years 87
13 1872-1916: The First Park Bears 89
14 1916-1945: The Great Yellowstone Bear Show 102
15 1946-1967: Crisis and Response 109
16 The Grizzly Bear Controversy Begins 114
17 Regrouping 133
18 The Greater Yellowstone Grizzly Bear 149
19 How Many Bears Is Enough? 165
20 Don't Feed the Bears, Again 182
21 Keeping the Bears 191

PART THREE: THE BEARS OF YELLOWSTONE—
AN AMERICAN ROMANCE

22 The Bear as Person 199
23 Famous Yellowstone Bears 202
24 Hunting Yellowstone's Bears 207
25 Making Themselves at Home 214
26 Bears, Tourists, and Rangers: The Eternal Triangle 219
27 Living with Bears 232
28 Camping with Bears 236
29 Looking for Bears 248
30 A Clashing of Symbols 253

Notes 257

Acknowledgments 279

Appendix A: Friends of the Bear 281

Appendix B: Bear Statistics 285

Bibliography 295

Index 315

Introduction

I am extremely pleased to see *The Bears of Yellowstone* have such an extended life, and to have the chance to revise it for a third edition. The story of the Yellowstone bears goes on, and continues to be so eventful that a book like this becomes out of date in some respects in only a few years.

The bears of Yellowstone have long been the park's most popular animals; they may be the most famous wild animals in the country. They inhabit the world's most famous national park, and over the course of the past century have had a lot to do with that park's reputation as a place of wonder. They have also had a lot to do with the American perception of bears.

Yellowstone National Park, in the northwest corner of Wyoming (with small slivers of land in Idaho and Montana), protects more than two million acres (about 3,300 square miles) of wilderness. Elevations vary from one to two miles, but the average is more than 7,000 feet. About 80 percent of the park is covered by forest, mostly lodgepole pine but with smaller amounts of spruce, fir, and a few other species of trees. Average precipitation varies dramatically, from less than 20 inches in arid lower areas to more than 40 in the mountains. The mean annual temperature at park headquarters, Mammoth Hot Springs, is 39.8 degrees Fahrenheit. For the rest of the park, the average is about five degrees cooler.

The park includes or neighbors the headwaters of several major river systems, including the Snake, which starts just south of the park and flows eventually to the Pacific, the Madison, which starts in the park and flows to the Missouri and on to the Gulf of Mexico, and the

1

Yellowstone itself, which starts near the southeast corner of the park and flows into the Missouri as well. Almost all of the park, probably in the neighborhood of 98 percent, is undeveloped, virtually as wild as when European man first saw it.

Yellowstone and Grand Teton National Parks, the six surrounding national forests, and the complex checkerboard of other federal, state, and private lands in the area have become widely known as the Greater Yellowstone Ecosystem. Bears inhabit much of this region, which includes, depending upon your definition of its boundaries, upwards of 18 million acres of land, about 12 million of which is federal. Grizzly bears occupy more than 5,000 square miles of park, forest, and other lands at the center of the Ecosystem, and show signs of wanting to occupy more than that. The fate of the grizzly population in Greater Yellowstone rests on our ability to manage it sensibly across many administrative and philosophical boundaries.

Greater Yellowstone is one of the finest wildlife areas in North America, perhaps in the world. The park alone hosts more than 2,000 bison, 30,000 summering elk, and many hundreds of deer, bighorn sheep, moose, and pronghorn, and most of these animals are present in far greater numbers in the rest of the Ecosystem; the total elk population for Greater Yellowstone is around 90,000. With the possible exception of the wolf, these wildlands retain populations of every wild mammal that was here in 1872 when Yellowstone National Park was created, including cougar, coyote, wolverine, badger, beaver, and many others.

Much the same is true of the populations of birds, fish, reptiles, and plants, though in the case of fish and plants many additional species, some quite harmful to native species, have been introduced. One other animal, humans, also occupied the Yellowstone region for thousands of years in what Europeans call prehistoric times; we are not especially well informed on the extent to which native Americans may have affected the Yellowstone landscape and its other inhabitants.

Many of these native inhabitants have been or still are subjects of heated debate, as the American people and their governmental representatives attempt to come to terms with the challenge of managing wild areas. Yellowstone has often been in the forefront in the development of such management, and thus has been among the most controversy-ridden of parks.

Not unlike Caesar's Gaul, this book is divided into three parts. The first is devoted to natural history; thanks to many small studies

2

and three large ones, we are blessed with a vast if yet incomplete knowledge of bear ecology in Yellowstone. The second tells the story of how the bears have been managed and fought over since the park's establishment to the present, and considers the prospects for the future. The third is an appreciation—a celebration, really—of the lore and magic of the bears of Yellowstone, in which I try to suggest the reach and the power of these animals in our culture.

It is early November as I write this, and last week we had an unseasonable cold spell, with a series of sub-zero nights that probably persuaded whatever bears weren't already finding or digging dens to get to work. In a few weeks they'll all be gone for the winter, and another bear season will be behind us. The scientists will settle into their labs to analyze new data, the conservationists and other special interest groups will continue to argue over old data, and at least some of the millions of people who visit Yellowstone will occasionally pause to think about the bear they saw—or wished they'd seen—last summer or the one they hope to see next year. From this convoluted flow of inquiry, dialogue, argument, emotion, and dreams will come some direction for American society, a course of action or inaction that will eventually decide the fate of the bears and of the park they inhabit. I've written and twice rewritten this book because that process seems so important to me, and because I believe that the more we know, the more chance we have to do right by the bears of Yellowstone.

Part One

The Wild Bears of Yellowstone

Chapter 1

The Black Bear:
Description

*N*o two bears live exactly the same life. They are nearly as different in physical appearance and in personality as are people. In attempting to summarize their lives, it is easy to speak of norms, averages, and probabilities, but one of the marvels of an animal as complex as the bear is its endless capacity to surprise us.

The ecology of any animal is based on a shifting foundation of circumstances. The bear is among the most adaptable of large mammals, existing in an impressive variety of conditions. Indeed, in the course of its year, it exhibits tremendous flexibility of food and habitat use, and then closes the year with an even more memorable encore, the metabolic wonder of winter denning.

To speak of the bears of Yellowstone, when speaking to the average visitor, is to speak of the black bear. The black bear is the one most frequently seen and photographed; the one remembered from the not-so-good old days when a drive through Yellowstone turned up several dozen begging bears. The grizzly bear is seldom seen from the road, and has practically never begged there.[1]

"Black bear" is more a label than a description; the animal comes in many shades, from black to brown to almost-blonde. In the eastern United States most are black, but in the Rockies many more, perhaps as many as half, are brown.[2] The black ones occasionally have white marks on their chests, usually one small patch of varying shape. Color does sometimes change during the cub's first two years, but after that changes in color are usually just the result of seasonal fading.[3] One litter often contains a mixture of cubs, each a different shade.

The hair is shed in summer, especially July, at which time the

A black bear sow, showing the plantigrade foot. The small ears, placed well back on the head, probably do more than any other feature to make the bears face appear comic. N.P.S. photo.

coat's appearance is shaggy and uneven. Shedding is encouraged by rubbing the loose hair off against trees and other objects, but we do not know if this is done with a conscious intention to remove the hair or simply to relieve itching. Perhaps because it is almost covered by hair, and because of the interest always inspired by the other end, the bear's four to six-inch tail is rarely noticed.

The black bear, as imagined by the Yellowstone visitor, is larger and stockier than life. An adult standing on all fours is rarely more than 30 to 32 inches at the shoulder and 5-1/2 feet from nose to tail. Only extremely rare individuals weigh 500 pounds, and Yellowstone's black bears are on the average smaller than those in some other habitats, especially in mast-rich eastern areas such as Pennsylvania. Most Yellowstone males weigh 250 pounds or less, and most females 150 pounds or less. The largest black bear weighed in a study in Yellowstone in the late 1960s was 479 pounds.[4]

The legs, especially the front ones, may appear long to the visitor accustomed to animated bears and outdoor magazine artwork. The black bear quite often can be described as "lanky," especially in the spring, but many do achieve the general roundness characteristic of comic strip bears.

The bear is a "plantigrade" animal, meaning it is one who walks on the flat of the foot, like man, rather than on the toes, like dogs. The foot has nearly hairless toe pads and soles, usually dark brown or black, and five clawed toes. Black bear claws, an inch and a half long at most, are deeply curved for digging and scraping. Rear claws, used more for climbing than digging, are not so sharply curved as front ones.

It is said, usually in an attempt to differentiate blacks from grizzlies, that the back of a black bear has a straight profile with no hump at the shoulder. This is a good general rule, but individual animals will break it, especially when shoulder hair is thick and bristling.

The black bear's head is long with a flat brow—almost a straight line from top of head to nose. The brown snout ends in a pig-like nose, the pad of which extends a short distance up the snout.

The nose of the bear is legendary. Carrion is scented miles away, cubs are identified, buried materials located, and all manner of unknown commodities are investigated. The nose provides the leading sense in the search for nourishment.

Like its sense of smell, the bear's hearing is more acute than human hearing. The ears are small and rounded, set well back on the head. They also do more than any other facial feature to make the bear appear comic.

Bears are characterized as nearsighted, but sight is an important sense. Bear eyesight, so long regarded as hopelessly poor, has been reconsidered by scientists; not only does the bear have some color vision, but its eyesight is a useful tool in feeding.[5] Good, or at least functional, eyesight is also indicated by the almost dainty way in which bears have been observed feeding on single berries. Distance vision, though still considered poor, is often aided by the bear's ability to stand on its hind legs.

Standing on the rear legs is a stationary activity. Outside of circuses and television bears do not often walk about in this fashion. Even when attacking, they usually stay down until right on the target. Bear fights have been observed where neither combatant raised up at all—the teeth were the main weapon, accompanied by powerful swats from the front paws.

Black bears are strong and durable. Drugged bears have frequently (though not always) survived falls of twenty or more feet from trees. The very fact that the bear was able to haul itself up into the tree in the first place proves its strength.

Black bears are quick—they can turn or strike with alarming swiftness—and they are fast. Twenty-five miles per hour is not unusual for them over a short distance.

In the wild, the black bear often remains healthy for fifteen or more years. Twenty-year-olds are rare, though they have been known to live past thirty in captivity. Under natural circumstances the animal gradually wears out, much like a human: teeth wear down, senses weaken, and old age reduces efficiency until the bear no longer survives. Interestingly, there does not seem to be an extended period of infertility in the elder years. The system of the bear appears capable of reproduction as long as it is capable of maintaining good health.

Chapter 2

The Black Bear:
Food Habits

*A*s a forager the black bear is the consummate opportunist. It thrives by being flexible in its appetites, so it is drawn to those places that afford the greatest variety of opportunity, or to the unusual place with an especially rich food source. Black bears in Yellowstone concentrate more heavily in a mixed forest blessed with numerous open meadows, bare hillsides and watering places than in a uniform closed forest. In the Barnes and Bray study of black bears in the Gallatin range in Yellowstone Park, an estimate of one black bear per 1.4 square miles was made for the best habitat, while the concentration of bears in neighboring areas of lodgepole pine forest was much less, perhaps as low as one bear per 20 square miles.[1]

In this desirable habitat, a mixed forest of Engelmann spruce, lodgepole and whitebark pine, fir, and aspen, with frequent meadows, the bear can be a creature of edges, moving from forest to field (always near the safety of trees), from food to food, as season and food availability dictate.

The bear's feeding habits, from the time of spring emergence, are investigative. Unless some favorite and abundant food causes it to settle in, the bear spends much of its time slowly roaming. The impression this gives observers is a mistaken one. As the hunter-naturalist William Wright put it, "You never watch Black Bear when they are quite at home and undisturbed without being made to feel that they are hard put to know what to do with themselves."[2] Their seemingly aimless meandering is actually purposeful. With such a wide diet, exploration is always a promising enterprise.

The black bear is well outfitted for its diet. A fully equipped adult has forty-two teeth. Front teeth, incisors and canines, are for cutting, and rear teeth, premolars and molars, are for crushing; a standard arrangement for omnivores, who must be able to handle both vegetation and meat. The claws, described earlier, complete the bear's complement of utensils.

Vegetation

By far the most common form of nourishment for all of Yellowstone's bears is plant matter. An examination of bear droppings (known as scats) done in 1944 revealed an average of about 81 percent vegetation.[3] This was from bears who also had access to garbage feeding. Grasses and sedges made up 47 percent of the plant matter, and the rest was a variety of herbaceous plants, berries, and nuts. Though the figures vary from year to year (and this 1944 study did not include a proper proportion of spring scats) depending on the success of failure of specific crop types, the overall figure is reasonable, and is more or less supported by more recent studies in the Yellowstone area.[4] The black bear is primarily a vegetarian, taking other food when available to supplement its basic diet.

The newly emerged black bear sometimes can not be choosy about food. Succulence is important, so bears seek out moist areas, and mix the new grass shoots with roots of spring-beauty and wild onion. In digging out the roots and tubers, bears encounter rodents and rodent food caches. Both are welcomed.

Another occasional meal during the spring shortage, and even in early summer, is cambium, the tender layer below the bark of lodgepole pines, Douglas fir, and spruce trees. Bears strip the bark with their teeth to reach this soft chewy layer of wood, leaving long strips of outer bark hanging loose, and occasionally girdling the tree completely and killing it. In some parts of the country, particularly the Pacific Northwest, bear-killed trees run into the hundreds in some areas.[5] In Yellowstone, bears kill few trees, but are entitled to.

It is the unglamorous truth that black bears pass much of the summer grazing. Yellowstone's meadows are rich in white clover and grasses, so the bears, like the elk and bison, take advantage of them.

Though Yellowstone is not known for the tremendous berry crops produced elsewhere in the Rocky Mountains, some years the bears do quite well. Usually berry hunting becomes profitable in August, when small sweet strawberries ripen under the lodgepole cover. Later, in these same forests, bearberries and grouse whortleberries will also appear.

The grouse whortleberry, also called the low red huckleberry, was rated as the number one berry in availability by Murie in 1944. His scat analysis indicated it made up 5 percent of the total sample. In some years and locations the figure would undoubtedly be much higher. Bears are exceptionally fond of berries. Among the other favorites are serviceberries, snowberries, red raspberries (found on rocky slopes as early as July), and chokecherries (which may not reach their peak until mid-September or later). These last two have accounted for many a surprise meeting between person and bear in the Mammoth Hot Springs area. The dense foliage often screens fellow berry-pickers until they practically collide.

Though bears are capable of feeding neatly on single berries, and have been observed to do so in other parts of the country, their enthusiasm rarely permits it. A more common approach is to grab a branch (or several) with paws and either strip off leaves and berries into the open mouth or feed at random while holding the branches. The amount of non-berry material consumed varies with the style. Some scats have contained mostly twigs and leaves, while others were almost pure berry. Very little chewing is done; the smaller berries are often bolted whole. Bear scat is easily recognizable at this time; a runny mixture of pulp and seeds. Scientists have had difficulty estimating the importance of berries to the bear diet because berry scats, which deteriorate or are consumed by scavengers very quickly, are not as lasting as scats made of other food materials, and so are perhaps not found as often as the others.

Berries are often available well into fall, and will draw a number of bears into a surprisingly small feeding area. Even the following spring bears are on the lookout for a few remaining tidbits.

In fall the nut of the whitebark pine is a favorite of black bears. The agile black has an advantage over the non-climbing grizzly, since it can go up into the trees while the cones are still hanging. Such activity commences in August, when the blacks climb to break off branches and bring them back to the ground. Holding the cone in its mouth, the bear tears it apart with its teeth to get the nuts. Also, bears make life rough for red squirrels by uncovering carefully stored caches of nuts and gobbling down several hours' accumulations in a few seconds.

Whitebark pine is available at higher elevations in Yellowstone, above 8,000 feet. A study just northeast of the park in 1985 and 1986 revealed that black bears there also would eat limber pine seed, but preferred whitebark pine seed.[6]

The whitebark pine nut crop is very important to both species of Yellowstone bears. Black bear sows seem to have fewer cubs in a year following a poor nut crop, suggesting the nut's importance as a food source.[7]

Animals

Though vegetation comprises the bulk of the bear's diet, there are times when meat has considerable significance, and it is always of interest. The black bear eats what nature offers, from buffalo to bird egg, but there are certain meats that it has regular chances to obtain.

The meat of large mammals is most available in the spring. Bears are most apt to have it as carrion, the remains of some animal that did not survive the winter, but they will occasionally hunt standing meat, seeking out the winter weakened elk or deer.

Most of Yellowstone's elk give birth to calves in late May and early June, and black bears have long been known to take calves in their first few weeks of life.[8]

Much has been made of cannibalism in bears. To a wild animal dead meat is dead meat, so the carcass of a bear that succumbed to disease, old age, or battle is cleaned like any other carcass. Too, there are documented cases in Yellowstone of members of the same bear family, loyal during life, consuming one of their number that has died.[9] And a cub is prey of adult male bears until it is grown.

The popular literature has taken to the idea that bears (both grizzlies and blacks) prefer a rank carcass to a fresh one, as if this indicates some deficiency in the bear's appetite or character. If there is a preference, and there is little evidence to prove one, it might be based on the increased odor, and therefore increased detectability/ locatability of the putrid meat, or on the presence of maggots. The maggots in an carcass are a prize among scavengers. Even songbirds have been observed venturing into the body cavity of a dead elk to get them.[10]

Spring is also the best time to get fish. Around Yellowstone Lake, and in other areas where cutthroat trout spawn, bears find good fishing. The use of these spawning runs has increased enormously in the past twenty years since new, more strict fishing regulations allowed fish populations to recover from a collapsed state.[11] Grizzly bears have taken the most advantage of this newly restored food source. The black takes the occasional stranded trout, and may succeed in getting one from the water, but fish are not recognized as an important part of their diet in Yellowstone. Long-time Yellowstone Ranger Dale Nuss has twice observed black bears fishing in creeks, and in both cases the bears were quite successful.

The black bear's attitude toward meat, especially in great quantities, is more casual than the grizzly's. A black bear may drag meat to a more convenient spot to eat it, but blacks do not often "cache" meat, that is they do not formally hide it by concealment or burial to save it for later. When we turn to the grizzly bear we will see several examples of this contrast between blacks and grizzlies, with the grizzly generally appearing more systematic and forward-looking in its arrangements.

Most of the black bear's meat comes from small animals. It is adept at flipping rocks and logs to uncover mice. The technique has been observed: a paw is hooked underneath the near side of the rock, and it is flipped away from the bear, who is poised to grab or slap whatever dodges out. The hunting efforts of the black bear, even for these small animals, are not as determined as the grizzly's. The black bear will take a marmot it happens to catch in the open, but is not inclined to excavate the marmot's burrow. The digging bear will now and then unearth a vole, pocket gopher, or ground squirrel.

Frogs and salamanders are intentionally hunted, and must also be encountered accidentally by bears that come to water to drink, bathe, or fish.

Black bears eat practically any insect, even ones so tiny there would seem no point in making the effort. Ants are a favorite. A study in northern Montana reported ants in more than 30 percent of all spring and summer scats. It has been suggested that their acidic taste is appealing (just as some anglers claim it is appealing to trout), but for whatever reason, bear interest has inspired a charming bit of lore. Early naturalists claimed that the bear, upon discovering an ant hill, would remove its top, stick its nose into the center tunnel, and inhale the inhabitants. The real approach, as observed in Yellowstone and elsewhere, is much more practical. A quick swipe of the paw wrecks the hill, and the paw is then laid on the center of turmoil. Once a sufficient number of ants have swarmed onto the paw to "defend" their home, the bear licks them off.

Ants and other colonizing insects live in rotting and down trees. Bears use their powerful forepaws and claws to rip the trees apart in search of the insects, speeding up the processes of decay while they are at it.

Bears also frequent snowbanks, any time of the year, to lick off insects that have mistakenly landed on the snow and become immobilized by the cold. This happens often to aquatic insects, emerging from nearby streams, who are later drawn to the bright snow.

In fact, any time cold weather chills insects bears gather them. In 1935, for example, northern Yellowstone Park experienced a great abundance of crickets. Adolph Murie, hiking the ridges in the upper Lamar River valley, observed eleven bears in one day feeding on the crickets, and grasshoppers, which were sluggish and easily captured. He examined sixty-four scats, fifty-eight of which were composed entirely of crickets and grasshoppers. The most unusual part of the report was not the insects, however; it was their chosen hiding place. Old dried buffalo chips were common in the area, and bears were flipping chips to find the insects:

> Most of the crickets were picked up in the grass, but some were taken under bison chips. With a paw the chip was delicately tipped on one edge and held poised while she peered beneath to see what was uncovered.[12]

Murie believed some of these bears were accustomed to feeding at park garbage dumps, which were then regularly used by bears. He was impressed that the bears were so fond of the insects that they were ignoring the easy garbage to get them.

The diet of the bear, like that of the human, does not benefit him equally in all its parts. Though no study of the digestive system of Yellowstone's black bears has been undertaken, such a study has been done of the park's grizzlies, and is summarized later. Some of that summary can be applied, with caution, to the black bear.[13]

Chapter 3

The Black Bear:
Denning

*T*he food habits of the bear are not intended merely to maintain the body in the best condition the season will allow. Bears must eat enough in three seasons to survive without eating during the fourth. The bear is a winter denner, denning being an environmental adaptation to a seasonal shortage of food.

The bear's eating habits can be divided into three stages. First, post-denning, when bears are readjusting to feeding at all. Second, a steady summer and fall of feeding, to build up a reserve of fat in preparation for the third stage, denning. Denning is a several-months-long abstinence from any feeding or drinking.

Usually by the end of July black bears begin to store up fat for the winter. Studies done around North America reveal what really capable over-consumers bears are. From August to early November, some Montana black bears were able to average about one pound weight gain per day for two or more months. Females studied in Wisconsin gained as much as 75 pounds in this period, males as much as 130.[1]

There are three uses for this layer of fat, often four inches thick, that the bears so industriously store. The first is the one we all think of: energy to be used during winter sleep. The second is a bit less frequently mentioned but just as obvious; the layer of fat is fine insulation against the cold. The third is perhaps the most surprising since it involves the time after the bear has left the den. In those first few weeks food is often scarce, so stored fat provides energy to last until the plenty of summer.

The time of denning varies greatly over the bear's range. In some extreme southern areas, denning may not happen at all. Even in a limited area like Yellowstone there is variety, depending on elevation, the weather, the condition and the sex of the bear, and its family status. A pregnant female usually dens earlier, and stays denned longer, than a lone male. She is also more careful about preparing her den. Young bears also den earlier and emerge later than adults.[2]

Denning usually begins in Yellowstone in mid to late October. Most black bears are denned by mid-November. Adult bears, except for sows with cubs, den alone.

As the first staying-snow falls in Yellowstone, and food crops of the late season are depleted or dried, black bears begin a gradual process of denning preparation. For some, several weeks of sporadic effort go into choosing a site, gathering bedding, and even excavating a little soil to improve the fit. Others, especially lone males, let it go until late in the season. Their preparations are limited to a quick search, it seems.

A den is essentially a secure shelter. It may or may not be entirely "out of the weather"; the bear may sleep in a true cave or out in relative open. In some parts of the country bears "den" simply by bedding down in a thicket. In Yellowstone they often seek partial shelter under a log or tree root, digging it out to suit, or may adopt another animal's den.

There is an interesting difference in denning practices between the black bear and the grizzly bear. The black bear's den preparations are not usually as involved as those of the grizzly, but the black bear shows a good deal more flexibility in densite than grizzlies do. In many parts of the United States, black bears do not seek out the high, steep country favored by grizzlies, but den in the forest, finding a suitable place in a hollow tree, under a tree's exposed root system, or under a fallen tree. Some digging may be necessary to make the site right, but sometimes black bears even settle down in a thicket with no cover at all.

In Yellowstone, black bears use a variety of sites, including abandoned dens of other animals, caves, and other forms of shelter. John Mack, who studied black bears in the late 1980s just north and east of the park boundary, found that in the rocky terrain of the Beartooth mountains, bears seemed to prefer slopes, mostly those facing north:

Fifty-eight percent of 33 den sites were associated with moderately steep (20-40 degrees) rock or talus outcrops. Mean slope and elevation of den sites did not differ between sexes or between years. . . . Most (61%) dens were located on northerly (northwest, north, northeast) aspects. . . . Thirty percent were located on southerly aspects and 3% each were located on east, west, and flat aspects.[3]

In most of the Rockies, north slopes hold snow longer and deeper than slopes on other aspects, which probably leads bears of both species to prefer the better shelter found on the north sides of mountains. The park has far more non-rocky slopes than the Beartooth, so probably a lot fewer park black bears den in rock caves and crevices than do in the Beartooth. But John's study does reveal the local adaptability of black bear populations.

When the time for hibernation approaches, the bear may visit the den site many times in a few weeks, showing a degree of premeditation most people do not associate with the seemingly easygoing black bear.

It is not yet established for certain what finally causes the bear to den up. Food shortage is a factor, as is severe cold, heavy snow, or a glutted bear who is no longer hungry. It may well be that all the factors listed, as well as metabolic mechanisms not entirely understood yet, contribute to the decision to move into the den.

Bears in cartoons are portrayed in spacious dens, some with several chambers. It is to the advantage of the bear to have a den only slightly larger than body size, since it will hold heat better. Bears do not normally use what is known as the classic hibernation position: "a curled up position with the top of the skull pressed against the bedding and the nose near the tail."[4] Denning bears sleep in a variety of positions, but however they choose to sleep it is clearly to their advantage to keep as compact as possible to conserve heat. Just as mittens keep your hands warmer than gloves because the fingers share their heat and have less surface exposed, the curled-up bear concentrates his heat by joining body and limbs in one close unit.

For some years the term "hibernation" was not popular to describe bear denning because the bear did not seem to hibernate in the way "true" hibernators did. Unlike some small mammals, like mice, ground squirrels, and marmots, the bear can be easily awakened. Its sleep is not the coma-like torpor of the others. Recently, however, studies of denning bears have encouraged the use of the word hibernator to describe the bear.[5]

The typical small hibernator drops very quickly into its dormant state. Reduced heart rate, slight oxygen use, and a deep unconsciousness are the result. However, these animals frequently revive (every two to ten days for some mice). During their short waking periods they feed, drink, urinate and defecate. They store food for the waking period, or they go and forage.

Bears, on the other hand, take as much as several weeks to get into their dormant state. Remarkably, they then stay in it for as much as six months. We have grown up hearing about bear denning, and are perhaps dulled to the real wonder of it. The undisturbed Yellowstone black bear sleeps, without eating, drinking, or passing any substance through its system, for four or five months. This is the equivalent of getting up from Thanksgiving dinner and taking a nap until Easter. And maybe giving birth in the meantime. We must be impressed, if not awed, by such an achievement.[6]

Shortly before the bear enters its den it stops feeding. In some cases it appears lethargic for a few days prior to denning. There have been reports that the bear will eat fibrous materials at this time in order to form an "anal plug" at the bottom of its digestive tract; such plugs have occasionally been found in the abandoned dens of all three species of North American bears. It now appears, however, that the plug actually forms during hibernation as the bear's digestive tract passes not only remnants of food but dead cells from inside the tract. It remains unclear if this plug has any physiological value.[7]

The summer sleeping heartbeat of the adult bear is about forty beats per minute. In the deepest winter sleep that drops to eight. The decline from forty to eight takes three or more weeks, and is subject to change if the bear is disturbed.

Body temperature also drops, from four to seven degrees Centigrade below normal. The body temperature of the bear will fluctuate along with the temperature of the den. It seems, however, that the black bear's body has some mechanism for preventing its temperature from dropping below a certain point.[8] The lowest measured body temperature is thirty-one degrees Centigrade, a drop of slightly more than seven degrees.[9]

Combined with these lethargic characteristics is, naturally, a decrease in oxygen use, sometimes as much as 50%. The metabolism of the bear truly gears down. It appears also that blood circulation is lessened to some parts of the body. The front of the body (brain and chest) gets a higher than usual proportion of blood, while the lower body and limbs get less. Winter fat provides the only source of the liquid essential to keep water content of the blood normal. In fact, it seems that the lean underbody changes little; the fat is the key to successful hibernation.

Black bears have been observed abroad in Yellowstone in the winter.[10] Their roaming at this time, though not typical, is revealing. They are occasionally roused; perhaps the den caved in, perhaps their fat layer was inadequate, or maybe the den was appropriated by a larger bear. Usually they will den up again quickly, as there is little or no food for them after December.

There is a longstanding legend that bears suck sustenance from their paws. It may have originated from observations of curled-up bears, who hold their paws near their mouths, but it has an unusual twist. Bears sometimes shed the outer layer of skin from their footpad while in the den, and one study (not in Yellowstone) revealed that these pads are occasionally eaten by the animal before it leaves the den area in the spring.[11]

The post-denning period is a time of gradual adjustment. The bear begins to stir as warmer temperatures reach into the den. Snow is not necessarily a factor in how soon the bear leaves the den, because it can wander to lower elevations, but of course a thick snow blanket will insulate the den and cause it to stay cold longer, thus allowing the bear to sleep longer.

In Yellowstone, emergence can be expected in early April, with young bears and sows with young coming out as much as a month later.

Hunters have often remarked that newly emerged black bears appear fat and healthy, but that the fat is "spongy" and contains little oil. More scientific observations show that the black bear loses from 15 to 25 percent of its weight before emerging, whatever its appearance may be. Also, both hunters and researchers agree that the first few weeks of activity thin the animal down considerably.

The bear, even given the opportunity, does not gorge itself like a starving man at first emergence. There may be several short exploratory jaunts, over a week or two, establishing daybeds near the den, and light feeding, before emergence is complete. As noted, spring is not a good food time, so it is suitable that the bear is not immediately ravenous. Usually in about two weeks the digestive system is functioning well and the bear is building up energy for that other big event in its metabolic schedule, mating.

Chapter 4

The Black Bear:
Mating and Cub Growth

*A*dult bears customarily live alone, disinclined to the sociability of the other large vegetarians. When they do keep company it is for mating. Though breeding often becomes a biological possibility (for both males and females) at age three and a half, females rarely mate successfully before four and a half—their fifth summer.[1] The male black bear's reproductive system begins to activate late during winter denning. His gonads become active, and production of sperm begins. He is fully potent both prior to and after the female is able to mate with him.

The female's ovaries also become active in March and April (follicular growth begins in April or May), though it will be two months before her system is prepared for estrus. The duration of estrus (the popular term is being "in heat") is up to two months. An unusual observation was made in Yellowstone of mating black bears in September, but the peak of activity is late June and early July.[2] Barnes and Bray observed the most mating activity in Yellowstone between June 8 and June 22.[3]

Promiscuity, mating with more than one partner, is often quite common. When Yellowstone's bears were concentrated near dumps and along roads, the likelihood of multiple encounters was probably even greater, but even in the wild it appears that a few dominant males may manage to take care of fertilizing most of the available females. On the other hand, it has happened that a male-female pair may travel together throughout the mating season, evidently concentrating only on each other. Dominant males are more than willing to defend females from other males.

At the height of the breeding season the female is the least affected. She will follow more or less normal daily habits of feeding, travel, and resting, while the male follows her, awaiting her acceptance. He eats less, and will spend much time attending her, nosing her, and generally hanging around. He is, in short, distracted.[4]

There is great variation in the number of times black bears copulate. The chance meeting, or one-time encounter, may occur, where the bears spend only a few hours or less together, but more often there are extensive preliminaries.

Most of the "courtship" is during the period that the female is unwilling to mate. The male follows her closely, nosing or licking her genital area, emitting low grunts, and even attempting to mount. If she is not ready, she may drive him away or simply sit down. The two can travel for some days this way, in relative peace and good humor, but when she is at last receptive copulation occurs quickly. The male mounts from the rear, staying mounted for as long as 30 minutes. During copulation the male intersperses pelvic thrusting with resting, sometimes letting the female support most of his weight. He might gently bite her about the ears, and she in turn bites at him. It is awkward, but coupled pairs do move around, the female even grazing.[5]

To those offended by the female's seeming indifference to the male's advances it will be some comfort to know that the arrangement is biologically sound. The male must travel to her, while her primary role is to keep fit and fed for the term of her pregnancy. Thus she continues to feed through the courtship.

If a strong enough bond has been formed the pair may remain together until the female is no longer in heat. The male may then seek out other females. It seems likely that promiscuity in bears, who do not reproduce very quickly or frequently, is a trait that helps guarantee that all available breeding stock will be taken advantage of.

The male has no further involvement in the lives of the pregnant sow or young bears. He has no role in cub-rearing and will even pose a threat to his offspring when they emerge from the den with their mother the following spring.

Bear pregnancy is adapted to the long winter dormancy. The cubs are born in the winter den, so the mother must be prepared to nurse them for two months without any nourishment for herself. This set of circumstances has generated in bear physiology the remarkable phenomenon of delayed implantation, or "embryonic delay."

The principle is beautiful. After fertilization, the embryo develops only slightly, to what is known as the blastocyst stage. At this point growth either stops or is retarded to imperceptibility until November. At that time one of two things may happen.

If the sow has not had a good year and is in poor condition or has not put on enough weight to nourish herself and her cubs through the winter, her body will abort the blastocyst to ensure that at least she survives the winter to breed again in future years. But if her condition is good, the blastocyst implants in the uterine wall and resumes normal growth. In this case, though the total gestation of the bear is between 200 and 220 days, only about half of that time is devoted to fetal development.[6]

This retarded prenatal growth is the key to successful winter birth of young bears. The embryo has only been growing normally since November, so the cubs are tiny at birth, only eight to ten inches long and weighing from ten to twenty ounces.[7] Here is the advantage of delayed implantation. Had the cubs developed through a full pregnancy, they would weigh ten or more pounds each and would require a great deal more milk than their mother could provide them during two months in a snowed-up den. Born the size of a squirrel, their needs are manageable.

As noted, the pregnant female is among the first to den up and among the most careful in her den preparations. She will also be among the last to emerge the following spring. We know relatively little about what pregnancy does to affect her sleep, and little about her exact physiological state at the time of birth. In late January or early February, seven months after conception, she gives birth. A first pregnancy is likely to result in only one cub, but after that the litter is most often two. Three is not unusual, but four is rare. There is one reported case of six cubs in one litter in all of North America, but such an event is extraordinarily rare.[8]

The cubs are helpless for weeks. They can crawl enough to find their mother's nipples (there are six of these), but little more. They are blind, have no teeth, and almost no hair. It must be assumed that the mother is semiconscious, or her tremendous bulk would be fatal to such fragile creatures. We do not know how many die from being crushed or suffocated, but it seems to be very few.

Nursing is done by the mother lying on her side. When the cubs are larger she can nurse them while on her back or sitting, perhaps propped against a tree.

Growth in the den amounts to several pounds per cub by emergence time. After five weeks their eyes are open (though they may not be well focused), their first coat of real hair develops, and their first teeth appear. They still are not strong enough to walk, but crawl with some authority.

When they follow their mother from the den they weigh about five pounds. They are wobbly, but can both run and climb. As soon as she leads them from the den, and even before she has readjusted to normal activity, the cubs have embarked on an intensive survival training course.

There is no way to write about bear cubs that does not reflect their playful rambunctious character. The coldest, most thoroughly scientific monograph, no matter how technical (or dry) the language, evokes for the reader the same lively image; bear cubs are frolicsome eager young animals. The naturalist who dreads anthropomorphism—the equating of animal behavior with human character traits—will become hopelessly entangled in his own language, for the similarities between child-rearing and cub-rearing are too great to be ignored. A misbehaving cub is swatted by a not-quite all-enduring mother, a frightened cub runs to mother for protection, and a mother bear's devotion to her young, though overrated in the popular literature, is legendary. Certainly restraint is in order when discussing wildlife, but anthropomorphism is less of a concern now than it was a few decades ago. Humans seem to be more willing to acknowledge their own animal nature, and so are less defensive when compared to their fellow creatures.

The cubs' immediate concern is food. Newly emerged cubs can eat small solids (buds, or maybe insects), but prefer their mother's milk for several weeks. There is evidence of a remarkable, instinctive food-finding ability in cubs. A cub taken captive (not in Yellowstone) while still in its den was released some months later in the forest. It demonstrated an uncanny ability to locate succulent roots in several inches of soil, smelling them out and digging directly to them.[9] Studies in Michigan revealed that some cubs as small as eighteen pounds (five-and-a-half months of age) could survive to adulthood with no additional guidance.[10] Fall hunters in some states are asked to not

The mother bear is teacher, disciplinarian, and guardian of the cubs until they are more than a year old. N.P.S. photo.

kill cubs, even if they have killed a mother. The cubs may well survive.[11]

The role of the mother is to coach the cubs in feeding (without her guidance they may not develop such wide tastes, especially if there are unusual techniques she has herself learned with difficulty) and to protect them.

Teaching seems to be a process of example. The cubs watch her flip rocks, or tear apart wood, or feed on vegetation. At first they may only play at such activities, but after a time the lesson takes hold. Non-feeding activities, such as swimming, also may be taught by example.

27

The mother's best defense of the cubs is to send them up a tree. This the sow will do at any risk, even if it involves a stay of several hours. She might also do it to allow herself a leisurely and worry-free feeding spree. Sow black bears in Yellowstone in the 1960s were known to leave their cubs up trees for two hours or more while they begged along the roads.

In Yellowstone the cub has few natural enemies. The most dangerous is the adult bear, both the grizzly and the black. A recent review of known black bear cub mortalities concluded that bears are the most frequent predators on cubs, and saw some interesting reasons for this:

> Biologically, both sexes could benefit through prudent cannibalism. By killing genetically unrelated cubs, an adult male could eliminate another male's offspring and at the same time create a potential breeding partner for dissemination of his genes. . . .
> Females would benefit from killing other female's cubs because this would increase the habitat resources suitable for her offspring.[12]

A small lone cub may fall prey to other predators, such as coyotes, cougars, and eagles, but as long as the mother is near the chances are slim.

Cubs spend many of their waking hours playing—with each other, with their mother, and with inanimate objects or small animals they might capture. Social encounters of comparable frequency and intensity will be limited when they are adults, but bears are not the uncommunicative hermits they have often been made out to be. Studies of captive black bears in the southeast indicate that the bears develop a surprisingly sophisticated communication system to serve them during cubhood, involving sounds, facial expressions, and body postures, all of which express some basic attitude to family members and to anyone else they encounter. It is not a language, but it is a significant means of expression that bears have never been given full credit for in the past.[13]

Adoption, of lost or orphaned cubs, has long been a subject of interest to Yellowstone naturalists.[14] Some observers thought they had witnessed it, others were skeptical. As we will see later, adoption has occurred among grizzly bears, and so it is probably possible among black bears as well.

As the summer passes the cubs learn to feed on everything the mother does. By late fall they weigh up to forty pounds and have learned most of what she can teach them. The family dens together, again entering the den earlier than mature loners. In the spring, usually shortly before mating season, she abandons them. Sometimes this is not easy, as they tag along after she has lost interest in them. It may not finally happen until an adult male appears to court her. He might even chase them off himself.

The lone yearling is the most vulnerable of bears. A Montana study showed as many as half of the yearling age group succumbing to a variety of natural causes. The annual attrition (disappearance by death) from any adult age group is less than 15 percent.[15]

Black bears continue to grow in stature for two or three years after they reach sexual maturity, and in some circumstances may continue to put on weight after that. By fall, yearlings have often doubled their weight from the previous fall, though yearling weights vary greatly; a Vermont study reported a weight ranged of dressed yearling black bears from 50 to 138 pounds.[16] Thus it is difficult to give a good "average" weight for two- or three-year-old bears. These young animals fare so differently from one another that their sizes and personalities are widely dissimilar. However well or poorly they do, though, they are entered into the lone life and challenging world of the wild bear.

Their mother, too, continues. She is capable of rearing a new family every other year for as long as she remains healthy.

Chapter 5

The Black Bear:
Lifestyle

I actually mean, by that rather trendy title, that this section of the book will suggest how the various components already considered—physical capacities, denning, mating, cub rearing, and so on—add up to a pattern of movements and habitat use.

Except during mating, a black bear's habits are primarily the result of diet. The search for food directs its movements, leading it as far as necessary. Terms like "range" and "territory" must be used carefully with bears. Their range is flexible, so that in poor forage they may travel many miles in a day, but in a good berry season may spend a week in a two-acre space. The many studies done in North America show great variations in range. In some areas the bears roamed over an area with a rough radius (the areas are not round, of course) of fifteen miles. In others the radius was only two.[1] The Barnes and Bray study in Yellowstone revealed some interesting things about bear movements in the park.

Adult males were more mobile, even twice as mobile as adult females. (Males are the mate-finders, remember, and the females often have cubs.) Some males traveled as much as twenty miles in the course of the summer from the point of original live-capture, but most stayed within ten miles of their original capture site (capture/release/recapture studies are often used to determine movements of wild animals that are difficult to observe steadily). Females moved about half as far as males. Such figures are only the roughest sort of information, they define the movements of only a few bears, some of whom were also affected by the availability of garbage and roadside food sources.

Depending upon how great the danger, the mother black bear may send or accompany her cubs up the tree, and is willing to stay there for hours if necessary. N.P.S. photo.

For many years it was believed that black bears are not territorial in the sense that they did not seem to defend a set of boundaries. More recent research has suggested that bears may be aware of some territorial limits at some times, however, so it isn't yet possible to speak with total confidence about this. Recent research on bear-marked trees, for instance, suggests that a sense of territoriality may have something to do with this well-known bear activity. Adult black bears studied in Minnesota have been observed chasing immigrating younger bears from the adult's known range.[2] Another study, in northern Montana, revealed a subtler form of territoriality, if that's what it may be called. Young bears, once separated from their mothers, were seen to adopt portions of her range as their own and then gradually expand from it. An intriguing result was a kind of "group territoriality" that resulted in all bears in a given area, say a large drainage, showing hostility to strange bears that wandered in but showing tolerance to other resident bears in the area.[3]

As mentioned earlier, black bears do not spend much time in the lodgepole pine forests that dominate much of Yellowstone. The bears favor a mixed habitat. Yellowstone, therefore, has only a limited supply of truly first-rate black bear country. Within this country the black bear's habits develop. In many areas black bears are nocturnal, but in Yellowstone the black bear seems to choose its hours to suit the circumstances. We already have the example of the early-morning insect-eaters, but a more vivid (if somewhat disheartening) example was the beggar bear. Until the 1970s, dozens of Yellowstone black bears lined the park road during the daylight hours chowing down on candy wrappers and kosher dills. They were demonstrating their versatility to the wrong audience. Day-night activities are affected by many things, not the least of which may be the presence of grizzly bears, who generally are avoided by the blacks. When grizzlies and blacks share a range, the blacks may adjust their own habits to avoid contact with the bigger bear. During the past twenty years, both roadside feeding of black bears and dump feeding of grizzly bears have been largely eliminated from Yellowstone and the surrounding country. Both bear populations have gone through a redistribution in response to the loss of these artificial food sources, as well as in response to some restored natural food sources that will be discussed later. The result may be a completely different kind of compartmentalization than occurred before. Bear management specialists in the park suspect, based on sighting records from the last decade or so, that black bears are now occupying parts of the park of least interest to grizzly bears.[4]

Like many other animals, bears "shade up" on hot days. Resting periods occur in most weather, as the bears establish day beds or just plop down in a likely looking spot. Pregnant females rest less than lone males, probably because the former have greater nutritional needs. Younger bears rest more than old ones, and often nap in trees.

Two non-feeding activities which must not be passed by are rubbing (already discussed in the chapter on physical description) and bathing. Rubbing, besides removing hair, is also done to relieve itching and, I assume, because it feels good. Bears do, indeed, back up against a tree and go at it, but many other approaches are popular. Among the most novel is belly-scratching, done sometimes by walking over a very small tree, bending it until it goes underneath them and springs up behind.

Bears in Yellowstone, as elsewhere, are fond of water. Bathing both cleans and cools them. Black bears have been observed swimming in Yellowstone Lake, miles from shore.[5] They also have shown fondness for park thermal features, resulting in some of the stories included in Part III of this book.

One of the most fascinating aspects of bear movement is their homing ability. It is more developed in adults, who can return across seemingly new country to their familiar haunts. The whole process poses important questions. How well do bears remember terrain, and how sophisticated is their innate sense of direction once they are removed from familiar range? It appears their memory does play a role in homing, for an older, more experienced bear is much more adept at it than a young one. At the same time, their sense of topographical orientation transcends simple familiarity with specific features.[6]

Bears regularly use certain trails in their home range, even stepping in the same footprints until a double rut is created. This would appear to be in contrast to other bear traits. For one thing, it differs from the meandering habit mentioned earlier, but that is probably not an important difference, because bears like cows, ducks, people, and many other animals, are at times going somewhere purposefully and at other times just wandering around. Well established bear trails in Yellowstone have traditionally been associated with park dumps; bears on those trails were not looking for random food sources, they were headed toward a specific known food source.

That several bears use the same trail does not suggest that they are maintaining exclusive territories of their own, but it does not prove they are not. Territoriality may be a seasonal instinct, as during mating or during the peak of some food crop, and a given bear trail probably leads to some communal food source where there is more food than one bear could reasonably defend (or eat). Usually when bears concentrate at a food source, whether it is a dump, a salmon stream, or a berry patch, real or imagined competition for food results in a hierarchy of privilege that serves the same purpose that territoriality would elsewhere. The biggest and most aggressive bears get the most food, though the biggest may not always be the most aggressive. Fights occur, but much more common are showdowns of bluffs, and fatalities from fights are rare.

Bears do not "hug" their prey to crush it. The bear may hold an animal with its forelegs during a struggle, but reliable records of bears using such a grip to crush the animal do not exist. It appears that a black bear may "hug" an opponent in an attempt to bite it.

One of the most fascinating and still mystifying elements of bear behavior is the famous "bear-tree," supposedly scratched or bitten by a bear as a mark of territorial claim. Legend had it that bears would reach as high as they could in order to show other passing bears, by the height of their clawmarks, just how large they were. That part of the story may not be true, but marking is clearly an important form of communication between bears. A recent study in Great Smoky Mountains National Park showed that marked trees are both visual and chemical (scented) signs, which give bears a fair number of options for reading the message, whatever it is, that has been left on a tree. It remains unclear exactly what all the messages may be. Among the suggestions: a warning system so that bears know where other bears are and avoid them; a sort of reassurance to the bear making the mark that his (most marks are made by males) chosen area is secure; a means of orienting a bear that is still learning an area and needs a few personal landmarks; some communication system between bears during mating season.[7]

The last one may help explain why, in Yellowstone, several bears have been observed marking the same tree from time to time with no noticeable regard to other marks. It could be that these "community" trees serve as signs of belligerence only a few weeks of the year (the study in the Smokies showed that marking was particularly common during mating season), and as some other communication sign the rest of the year.

Trees have another important function for bears, as refuges. There are two common climbing techniques. The most popular relies on the front legs to grasp the trunk while the hind legs, pushing in unison, move the bear upward. The other involves a "walking" motion, wherein all legs grab and lift in the same order as they move in walking. Descent, usually accompanied by "walking," is made head-up, even among inexperienced cubs (who, it might be added, climb with no apparent training).

The relationship between black bear and grizzly bear is not constant. A photograph taken during a black bear study in Yellowstone in the late 1960s shows a large black bear confronting an equally large grizzly in a dump. N.P.S. photo.

Another part of adult bearhood is play. We have seen how it figures in the education of young bears, providing instructive social interaction, but it is evidently part of the life of adult bears, though in a more controlled way. There are even popular writers who claim the bear has a sense of humor (science has not gone quite that far yet).

The relations of black bears with other animals have been discussed in the chapters on food and cub growth. About the only serious natural enemy of an adult black bear in Yellowstone is another bear, either a larger bear or a grizzly. Blacks avoid grizzlies as a rule, but the rule is not ironclad. Large black bears, whose temperament allowed it, have been known to chase grizzlies from food.[8] The black bear does not know it is not supposed to be as aggressive as grizzlies, nor does the grizzly bear know its reputation.

There are other natural enemies of the black bear, but they are much smaller than the bears. Bears in Yellowstone are attacked by ticks, mosquitos, lice, and other small pests, but rarely is a healthy bear seriously hurt by them. In the natural history of the grizzly bear I will discuss a number of other parasites that infect Yellowstone bears.

Most of those that attack grizzlies also attack blacks, but on the average the blacks apparently are not as seriously affected.

Bears produce several vocal sounds. Though not a true vocalization, the "jaw-popping," or teeth snapping, that often accompanies bluffs is an intentional bear noise that heightens the effect of the presentation. Sounds, at least in adult bears, are usually associated with actions; part of a communication system we need to study more. Perhaps the most often written-about bear sound, next to the cries of cubs, is the sudden expulsion of air that frequently occurs when the bear suddenly senses danger. Whether it is used to chase cubs up a tree or to warn an intruder, it is usually described as a "woof." It could be the result of surprise. In any case, it has often been mentioned by surprised hikers as their only warning of the bear before it fled or attacked. Sounds and other social behavior of bears are being studied nowadays for the very practical reason that the more we understand the way they communicate the better we will be prepared to react to them.

The aforementioned bluff is perhaps the most misunderstood trait of the black bear. The false charge, accompanied by growls, woofs, feet-stamping, and jaw snapping, is used against other wild animals and man. Bluffing often serves the bear's needs. Most bear-to-bear encounters can be settled by this sort of energetic conversation. Bear populations are rarely large enough to survive wholesale physical combats, and vocal showdowns are an acceptable alternative. One should not assume, however, that the black bear is a "coward," or a phony, because it pretends to do something it doesn't really plan to do. Not only can the bluff turn into a real charge, but bluffing itself is a fascinating and specialized activity, almost the equal of the birds who pretend to have a broken wing in order to lead predators from a nest.

People are inclined to judge wild animals by their own standards. A slow, fat, nearsighted individual is ridiculed, and so, at first glance, the bear is treated the same way. The black bear is slow for a good reason, and fast when it needs to be. It has equally good reasons for its other characteristics, and is, in fact, much better suited to its world than humans are to theirs. Furthermore, it is able to adjust itself to the human world and to survive the ceaseless spread of that world over its range. That adjustability may be the biggest single difference between the black bear and its entirely unlaughable cousin, the grizzly.

Chapter 6

The Grizzly Bear:
Origins

*T*he bears of North America all developed from one common ancestral species, *Ursus etruscus*.[1] *Ursus etruscus* was Asian, and not terribly unlike the modern black bear in appearance and habit (though probably larger in its later forms). *Ursus thibetanus* (the Himalayan black bear of today) and *Ursus americanus* (our black bear) seem to have formed distinct evolutionary lines from *Ursus etruscus* more than 2 million years ago. Fossil remains indicate that the ancestors of our black bear have been present in North America (presumably having crossed the Bering Straits on an ice- or land-bridge) for about 250,000 to 300,000 years.

The modern grizzly, *Ursus arctos*, also developed from *Ursus etruscus*, probably about a million years after *Ursus americanus* did so. About the time the black bear was beginning to fill its present range in North America, a distinct ancestral form of modern *Ursus arctos* was living in China, but it did not cross to North America until relatively recent times. The continental ice sheet blocked its southern migration until the end of the last ice age, about 10,000 years ago.

In this way Yellowstone got its two species of bears, but this travelogue does not answer the question of why they are different.

It has to do with trees. *Ursus etruscus* was a forest animal, a climber. So, customarily, are *Ursus thibetanus* and our own *Ursus americanus*. The ancestors of the grizzly bear, by contrast, branched from *Ursus etruscus* much more dramatically than did the ancestors of the black bear. When *Ursus etruscus* moved to new forests it became the modern black bears of Asia and North America. When it moved out of the forest, it became *Ursus arctos*, an open-ground animal that

Telling Them Apart.

Park visitors are not the only ones who have trouble knowing if what they're seeing is a grizzly bear or a black bear. Hunters accidentally shoot grizzlies near the park now and then. In order to tell one from the other, look at several features of the bear: claws, back profile, massiveness of head, and overall size. These pictures suggest some of the pitfalls and perspectives you may encounter. Usually, if you can accumulate enough information, it will be obvious which bear you are seeing. Just keep your distance and don't get close enough to ask.

Shape and massiveness of head usually distinguish black from grizzly.

Most guidelines for telling bears apart show you a nice profile, but chances are you won't get that view right away. This is a grizzly, and your best clues are the claws and the distinct hump over the front shoulders. Black bear claws never look this big.

And this is a black bear; the claws are much less prominent and there is virtually no shoulder hump. From this angle there is relatively little difference to be seen in head shape between these two bears, so keep looking until you find at least one of the distinguishing characteristics. N.P.S. photos.

38

At first glance, this black bear appears to have a shoulder hump, but the hump is mostly hair. Also, the claws are too short for a grizzly. N.P.S. photo.

gradually lost most of its dependence on trees and developed a whole different nature as a result.

For black bears, trees are security. Young and adults seldom wander far from the forest haven. Grizzlies, having adapted to hunting food in the open (better digging equipment, for example), learned to find security in other ways. A sow black bear sends her cubs up a tree in a time of danger, and may even join them if the danger is great enough. A sow grizzly, whose cubs may retain their tree-climbing ability only for a couple years, has no such refuge, so she has become an aggressive defender of her young. She cannot send them anywhere, so she protects them where they are. They learn to do the same.

The distinction has numerous implications. The safety of trees may explain why black bear cubs are weaned as yearlings while grizzly cubs stay with their mother for two or three years. Over much of the grizzly's range the cubs cannot rely on trees and need her protection. It certainly helps to explain the size differences. Black bears need a body that can climb. Grizzlies lost their dependence on climbing and so could develop other abilities, which required greater size and strength.

Grizzly bears are much more feared and respected, by wild animals and man. Their options in an encounter are limited by the lack of an "absolute security" refuge. They are, therefore, more likely to defend young or possessions aggressively. The presence or absence of security must pervade the consciousness of an animal; witness the lengths to which sows go to find isolation while they raise their young. The overall effect of the stress of cub vulnerability—a constant nagging concern—is a change in the character and behavior of the grizzly mother. And her behavior is firmly imprinted on the cubs.

And so black and grizzly bears are adapted to different environments but often share common ranges. We have seen ample evidence of the flexibility of both species. Neither can be pigeonholed; "oh yes, the black bear—it lives in the woods." Bear life is too complex, and natural opportunities too diverse, for such simplifications. Yellowstone lacks the vast Asian arctic tundra that first changed a drifting population of *Ursus etruscus* into *Ursus arctos*, but the modern grizzly makes the best of it. Grizzly bears successfully use a good part of the Yellowstone wilderness. And their smaller, less demanding, cousins the black bears cautiously share that part and eagerly exploit the rest.

Chapter 7

The Grizzly Bear
Description

*T*he grizzly bear, *Ursus arctos,* did not come to the notice of European settlers as early as did the black bear. Variations on the name began to appear in the late 1700s when accounts of a "grizzled" or "grizzle" bear were brought from what is now western Canada. It would appear that the first naming was inspired by the animal's coat colors rather than by its personality. By the time of the Lewis and Clark expedition, 1804-1806, partly because of that expedition's reports, the term "grizzly" had taken on its double meaning: grizzled hair and grizzly (often interchanged with grizly or grisly in the nineteenth century, all meaning gruesome or gory) character.[1] The dictionary definition of "grizzled" includes such terms as "streaked," "flecked," and "mixed with gray."

The grizzled hair of the bear consists of dark brown fur with long "guard hairs" extending beyond the mat of fur. The guard hairs, whose tips are pale, give the coat a grizzled, or mixed, appearance. For this same reason the bear is often called the silvertip. This coat is not a predictable pattern, however, because grizzlies may be anything from almost-cream to black. Darker colors predominate, and quite a few bears are not uniform. They have lighter, grizzled, patches variously placed on the face, shoulders, saddle, or legs.

As with black bears, a sow grizzly may give birth to three different-colored cubs in one litter. Steve French, of the Yellowstone Grizzly Foundation (who have been conducting behavioral research on Yellowstone's grizzly bears since 1983), tells me that, "we have only seen two litters that had the same coloration and marking out of several hundred observations of family groups."

Spring shedding, new growth, and the effects of climate cause noticeable change in an individual's color over a season. A dark new summer coat will often fade, another reason for pale shoulders and saddle. On the other hand, as the new coat grows and thickens, it may darken, so that a single bear might begin the season dark, shed its winter coat and appear lighter, then grow a new coat and darken again. As important to the observer, a bear's color may seem to change dramatically (you almost have to see this to believe how dramatic it is) with light (strength, direction, and quality), and because of other factors, including whether or not the bear is wet or even damp.

Adult Yellowstone grizzly bears stand 3-1/2 to 4-1/2 feet at the shoulders on all fours. The average nose-to-tail length (that is, over the contour of the back) of 55 adult male grizzlies measured by the Interagency Study Team was 77.4 inches; the average of 55 adult females was 70 inches.[2] The back profile of a grizzly has two high points, one about midway between the tail and front shoulders, and the other directly over the front shoulders. The shoulder hump, sometimes called the roach, is the result of a muscular arrangement that is different from that of black bears. It is prominent on most grizzly bears, and is a good means of identification.

Yellowstone grizzly bears were of larger average size when the population was feeding regularly at dumps in the park. Pope, writing in 1923, reported a male Yellowstone grizzly weighing 916 pounds, and the heaviest grizzly handled by the Craighead research team in the 1960s weighed 1,120 pounds. The average weight of 65 adult males handled by the Interagency Study Team was 425.2 pounds, and the average weight of 63 adult females was 296. The largest male weighed 715, and the largest female weighed 427.

Males get a lot bigger than females, as females, once they reach adulthood, invest energy that might otherwise go to growth in reproduction and cub rearing. Males continue to get heavier until they are fifteen or older.

The grizzly's front legs appear longer than the hind ones. The body of the bear is smaller in diameter behind the front legs and grows thicker toward the belly, which seems almost to sag, giving the bear a bottom-heavy appearance.

The grizzly is plantigrade, walking flat-footed. The claws extend prominently beyond the hair of the feet, being especially visible on the front feet. Claws, rarely less than two inches long, curve sharply to

The size of an adult grizzly bear is more easily appreciated when compared to these people preparing it for relocation. N.P.S. photo.

serve in digging. Claw size is another distinguishing feature between grizzlies and blacks, whose claws are not easily seen from a distance, but a grizzly bear can significantly reduce the size of its claws if it does a lot of digging.

First-time observers are often impressed with the size of the grizzly's head, which has a massiveness unlike the black's. The popular literature frequently refers to the "dish-shaped" profile of the grizzly, meaning that, when viewed from the side, the line from the brow to the nose is concave, with its low point in the middle. This is an unreliable indicator of species, as head shape varies from a very concave curve to a straight line similar to a black bear. Size, back profile, claws, and general massiveness are better guides to identification.

The nose, ears, and eyes benefit the grizzly about as they do the black. Under favorable conditions Yellowstone grizzlies are able to scent a ripe carcass from several miles away. The grizzly's ears are usually smaller and more rounded, in proportion to its head, than are the black bear's.

43

The grizzly has forty-two teeth, which take about two-and-a-half years to completely arrive in the head of a young bear.

The bear's tremendous complement of muscles permits amazing quickness and speeds in excess of twenty-five miles per hour. Bursts of such speed are useful to the adult animal both in hunting and fighting. Movement is on all four feet, and standing occurs only to improve vantage point or reach.

The strength and durability of the grizzly became legend in the nineteenth century, partly as a result of the primitive firearms of the day and partly because the bear is, indeed, very strong. Many stories have been told of grizzlies that "took a lot of killing," some even involving Yellowstone bears. Later we will turn to some of the stories, but for now we confine ourselves to natural examples. Grizzlies drag adult elk hundreds of yards, up and down rugged terrain. Their forelegs are powerful enough to break the neck of a steer or elk with one swat. And the bear is, in turn, strong enough to withstand those swats when directed at it by another bear. Perhaps the most stunning film I've ever seen of a grizzly bear is footage shot by the Yellowstone Grizzly Foundation recently, of a big male climbing a nearly vertical cliff face as if he were walking up a ladder.

Grizzly bears frequently live fifteen to twenty years in the wild. It appears that survival requires a level of health that usually includes the mating capacity; as with the black bear, and barring injury, once the animal no longer functions reproductively it has probably also lost the physical abilities it needs to live much longer. A European brown bear lived 47 years in captivity, but a Yellowstone grizzly 25 years old would be rare. The oldest bears reported by the Craigheads and the Interagency Study Team were 25.

The grizzly bear is superbly adapted to its world. None of its formidable equipment goes to waste. The animal is such a spectacular evolutionary achievement that it will always be regarded as one of Yellowstone's most exciting inhabitants. There is always the danger, in studying just one animal, of unconsciously removing it from its context. That danger is probably at its greatest with an animal like the grizzly. In the following account an effort has been made to resist glorification. The bear does not need to have its existence dramatized, and those who are interested in it will appreciate it best when it appears, in place, as part of the great Yellowstone wilderness.

Chapter 8

The Grizzly Bear:
Food Habits

*B*ear food habits are inextricably bound up with bear habitat; bear use of available habitat is in great part the result of food availability, keeping always in mind the bear's need for certain kinds of shelter. Here I will concentrate on food for the moment, and turn to habitat use in the "lifestyle" section, but ecologists don't have the luxury of separating food preferences and habitat use so conveniently. One of the most revealing elements of modern grizzly bear research is that so much of it has concentrated not on studying the bears themselves but on painstaking study, including a careful mapping of the entire grizzly bear habitat in and around Yellowstone, of where the bears live.

Changes in management in Yellowstone have altered grizzly bear food habits in many ways. I've already mentioned that the closing of the garbage dumps (the largest were closed by 1971, and several smaller ones near the park were closed during the 1970s or early 1980s) deprived the bears of a food source they were quite accustomed to. But the closing of the dumps was only one part of an overall change in management that will be discussed at length later in this book. Various elements of the Yellowstone wilderness setting were permitted to seek what are believed to be natural balances with their surroundings, and in several cases these other changes are affecting grizzly bears. The trout population of Yellowstone Lake was in a collapsed state in the 1950s and 1960s; stricter regulations have restored those fish to something more approaching historic levels, and huge numbers of fish are now available to bears in the spring when they move into the lake's many tributaries to spawn.[1] Elk numbers were suppressed for many years in Yellowstone; throughout the 1960s the northern elk herd was kept to 5,000 or less most of the time. That herd has been allowed to grow in an effort to restore it to some natural equilibrium with its range, and since 1970 it has increased more than threefold. Current bear research in Yellowstone shows that grizzlies are preying on elk—adults through the year, and calves especially in late May and June—and making heavy use of winter-killed elk carcasses in the spring.[2] Bison, for many years also kept to a low number, have also increased, and grizzlies make good use of bison carcasses in the spring and after the summer rut as well. A natural fire policy was adopted in Yellowstone in the early 1970s (though the public seems not to have become aware of it until 1988) that has great promise for maintaining grizzly bear habitat in the Greater Yellowstone Ecosystem.

The point of listing all these changes that have occurred in the last fifteen years is to make it clear that in many ways the grizzlies of Yellowstone are not yet in a stable relationship with their environment. Though the research of the Interagency Grizzly Bear Study, since 1973, of the Yellowstone Grizzly Foundation, since 1983, have provided a wealth of useful information, more than we have on any other grizzly bear population, the portrait of the bear is not a finished one. The elk are still adjusting, and land management changes outside the park are providing this migratory herd with new winter range. The fish population, though vastly restored, is perhaps not wholly recovered. The bison may have reached their practical limit, but other animal and plant populations are in flux, and indeed always will be, as climatic and other environmental factors continue to vary over time.

This is an important point. These bears, after all the years of research, continue to surprise us with new behavior. They continue to display new feeding habits, suddenly showing a previously undocumented interest in some food or other. They are amazingly versatile animals, and I think they will continue to teach us as long as we are willing to learn.

As important, human use of the Yellowstone area is changing. As various pieces of the habitat are improved or degraded (alas, this is the more common event), things will continue to change for the bears.

The summary of bear habits that follows is therefore somewhat tentative. Scientists have a pretty good idea now of what

Yellowstone's grizzly bears do and how they live, but scientists are cautious about suggesting they have all the answers. There was great scientific disagreement over just what closing the dumps did to the bear population, and there is bound to be continued uncertainty over just what the new conditions—no dumps, more elk and bison, more fish, and so on—will bring to the grizzlies of Yellowstone. But, thanks to all the studies that have been done, and especially to the two just mentioned, we do know a lot.

The Yellowstone grizzly is primarily a vegetarian.[3] Some years more than 80 percent of its diet is plant matter, and it could probably survive on even more. Most of the year it is the location of various preferred plant foods that will dictate the location of the bears; sometimes a single plant food can have a tremendous effect on the movements of most of Yellowstone's bear population.

After a week or two of gradual adjustment to renewed activity upon leaving the den, bears often seek out carrion or the first few available plants. Succulence is the key factor in bear choice of plants, so bears are drawn, at each season, to plants at that stage of growth when their succulence is greatest. Ecologist Douglas Frank first acquainted me with the concept of "growth pulse," that is, the movement of peak growth uphill across the landscape in Yellowstone. As the plants experience their peak growth, bears and other animals may follow that most desirable growth stage.[4]

This interest in succulence has a number of implications, one being that as the growing season for plants ends, bears are drawn to the last fresh vegetation, which may be in areas of greater moisture, such as river banks, seeps, marshes, and springs. Another is that in dry years, bear foods may experience substantial reductions in quality and quantity.

One safe generalization about bear diet is that their choices increase as the season goes on. The Interagency Study Team has found that diversity of food types in the grizzly bear diet increases from emergence in March or April until September, when it begins to decrease slightly until denning.

Depending upon where the bear had denned, its first feeding will vary greatly. It may settle into Pelican Valley for a few weeks of feeding on freshly thawed (or still frozen) bison carcasses, or it may be in the Firehole Valley feeding on elk carcasses, or it may be taking advantage of some other opportunity.

Grizzly bears share spring carrion, such as this elk, with other scavengers, including magpies and coyotes. N.P.S. photo

Yellowstone is blessed with an abundance of animal life, and it is in spring that the large mammals—elk, bison, moose, deer, sheep, and pronghorn—are most often available to bears. The animals provide essential protein to bears in several ways during this season. A harsh winter results in hundreds of dead elk and fewer (but larger) dead bison. The grizzly is only one of many scavengers who compete for this carrion. In some years, the bear's survival may depend in good part on this carrion supply, and in others the bears may ignore carrion in favor of an unusually good crop of some favored plant.

As with the black bear, grizzlies do not seem to prefer a rank carcass, but it will perhaps be easier to find. If a rank and a fresh carcass are found side-by-side, the grizzly may use the rank one first because it will have the added attraction of maggots (the condition of the meat does not appear to be a major factor in the bear's decision). Yellowstone Grizzly Foundation researchers have several times seen grizzly bears pass up available carcasses to seek out live elk.

Winter-weakened elk and newborn elk, bison, and other ungulates, fall prey to bears, sometimes in good numbers. A study of bear predation on elk in a western portion of the park showed that some years grizzly predation there accounted for as many as half of the spring elk deaths. Of course it isn't long before the elk that are too weak to recover are all gone, and the calves are either lost or grow strong enough to escape, so the bears have only a short time to get their share.

Grizzlies can be determined hunters. Individuals or pairs can chase a herd at an easy lope, identifying, and then taking, weak stragglers with a sudden burst of speed. Elk driven into deep snow or water are often too weak or frightened to resist. In some cases the elk is so weakened from the winter or the chase, that the bear has only to walk up to it and kill it. Grizzly killing methods have been described by Glen Cole, who studied them in the early 1970s:

> Bears pulled down running elk by rearing on their hind legs, grasping an animal on or over the rump, and apparently allowing their weight to collapse the elk's hindquarters. Bears then grabbed and vigorously shook the elk's neck with their jaws, rolled the elk over on its back, and opened the abdomen. The neck was grabbed and shaken again if the elk continued to struggle.[5]

Another approach was observed early one spring near Lava Creek, by a snowplow operator who surprised an elk and bear in mortal combat:

> The two combatants were fighting at close quarters, the elk fighting for his life, the bear endeavoring to kill, probably for food. The bear had the elk gripped around the neck with his forepaws and was endeavoring to throw the elk, after the fashion of a rodeo performer bulldogging a steer. The elk in turn was endeavoring to get free and by so doing was shoving the bear backward along the road. Thus from my vantage point I had thought that the elk was being led by someone.
>
> I stopped the snowplow and taking my camera started to try and photograph the incident. This action on my part disrupted the battle temporarily, for the elk broke loose from the bear and started running away. He seemed partially stunned from his encounter. The bear ran right beside him and kept reaching out his paw now and then to slap the elk on the side of the head. The elk by this time appeared to be about exhausted for his tongue was lolling out and he seemed wobbly.

The slapping action of the bear soon caused the elk to stop and fight again, this time charging the bear, which reared to his hind legs again. The bull's head struck the grizzly in the stomach and the bear then grabbed the elk around the neck. With all of his strength the elk would bunt the bear, each time raising the bear's hind feet from the ground. Shortly the elk became so tired that the bear's weight brought him to his knees.

While all of this was happening I had approached quite near the animals and suddenly the Grizzly sensed my presence. He reared up, sniffed, snorted, and allowed the elk to get up and stagger off into the woods. The Grizzly became frightened and ran away apparently suffering none from the elk's efforts to protect itself.[6]

Yet another approach was observed by William Rush while watching elk on Specimen Ridge in the 1930s. He was watching a line of elk climb the snowy ridge near a forested slope:

Without warning a great furry ball of grizzly bear hurtled out of the forest into the middle of the moving line. The terror-stricken elk tried to run but they could not. Some of them jumped to one side of the beaten trail. Their sharp hooves cut through the crusted snow and they floundered helpless, unable to go farther. Some crawled on top of those ahead in the trail, piling up in a frantic heap. Others turned and tried to go back. Panic held them in a milling throng wile the bear picked out a cow that had fallen on her side. With a swift rush the grizzly was upon her, grabbing her nose with a long-clawed paw while it sank saberlike teeth into her neck and ripped open her belly with the other front paw.[7]

Surprisingly, the bear then deserted its kill and carried off a calf, leaving the terrified elk to go on their way.

From these examples it is obvious the procedure varies greatly. An adult grizzly is strong enough to kill with blows from its forepaws, but more often it employs both teeth and forepaws.

The most effective hunters observed by Cole were young adults, not because they are more agile but because older, dominant bears have learned to wait until the younger ones have made a kill and then chase them from it.

Since the closing of the dumps and the increase in the elk population, many instances of grizzly bear predation on elk calves have been observed. Both the National Park Service and the

Yellowstone Grizzly Foundation have conducted fascinating observational studies of elk calf predation, something quite a few visitors get to see in early spring in Yellowstone. One report summarized the techniques as follows:

> Grizzlies used 3 techniques to hunt elk calves. In May and early June, when newborn calves are extremely immobile, bears were observed locating newborn calves, apparently by scent, in calving/bedding areas (9 of 70 hunts, 6 successes). Adult elk retreated as bears approached these areas. Bears then moved through the sagebrush in a zigzag pattern, occasionally rising onto their hind legs. Calves that had remained bedded and were detected by bears were killed....
>
> The most common hunting technique observed (59 of 70 hunts, 18 successes) was similar to that described by Cole (1972). Bear(s) approached cow/calf groups at a loping pace while in the open, apparently not using vegetation or topography for cover. Elk were aware of the bear's presence, and reacted by bunching into tight groups while intently watching the bear. After the initial approach, the bear(s) made a series of charges that tended to separate confused calves from the group. The chase then concentrated on these calves. Elk calves could generally outdistance bears in a straight run, but were often caught when bears cut to the inside of calves changing direction in an effort to rejoin the herd....
>
> The third style of hunting observed (2 of 70 hunts, both successful) involved the use of cover. Bears used tree cover to approach elk grazing within 50m of the forest edge. Each of these hunts lasted less than 20 seconds and covered less than 137m. In each incident the elk suddenly became alert and closely monitored the forest edge before a bear rushed from the trees and initiated chase. Due to the high efficiency (short chase, high success rate) of this type of hunt, it may occur more frequently than observed.[8]

The Yellowstone Grizzly Foundation research project has produced some stirring footage of these hunts. As the grizzly bear gets a visual lock on a calf and pursues it, cows sometimes cut in front of the bear to try to break the lock or distract the bear; sometimes it works. It is plain that both bears and elk are constantly learning how to deal with each other in these complex interactions.

Other large animals are also included in the bear diet. Mature bison and moose have relatively little to fear from Yellowstone

Grizzly bear investigating bison carcass. N.P.S. photo.

grizzlies, but are occasionally taken when weak or old. There is one reported case in Yellowstone of an adult bear killed by a bison, presumably the result of an unsuccessful attack by the bear.[9] Encounters of this sort are probably rare, as the animals would more often steer clear of one another.

We can assume that mule deer are occasionally taken (at least one successful stalk has been observed in Yellowstone[10]), but bighorn sheep and pronghorn are probably rarely available to grizzlies, and would have little to fear if pursued. Sheep take refuge in cliffs, and pronghorn are much too swift to be caught in the open by bears. Any of the above would naturally be consumed as carrion, and their calves, lambs, and fawns would be a special treat for a bear who found one.

Grizzlies often save food for later, dragging a partially consumed carcass to a suitable location and covering it with brush or digging a hole and burying it. On rare occasions such "caching" involves quite a lot of work, as the hole may be several feet deep and the pile on top of it may be several feet high.

Once the spring meat-feeding has ended, the bear's protein diet is replaced with one more heavily based on carbohydrates. As May progresses, bears, which have been aware of early plants such as springbeauty, turn more exclusively to plant foods. Grasses are the most important of these, and it comes as a disappointment to many of the grizzly's more romantic admirers that the bear spends most of its time grazing. According to Steve Mealey's 1973-1974 study, grizzlies prefer "dense stands" at least three inches tall.[11] Other favorites are clover, horsetail, dandelion, and biscuitroot.

Throughout the season bears show great interest in whitebark pine nuts, an especially important food in the fall but one of interest to them whenever they can locate the nuts, whether in small mammal caches or when the pine cones disintegrate in October and November and the nuts are most available.

In fact, small mammals cache a variety of bear foods, including the pine nuts and an assortment of roots, corms, and forbs, that bears find in the process of their routine grazing and digging. The bear's good fortune is sometimes compounded when they find not only the cache but the animal that made it.

Throughout the summer bears also eat insects, especially ants and grasshoppers. All sorts of special opportunities present themselves, ranging from licking numbed insects from snowbanks where they mistakenly landed to concentrating on heavy emergences of moths, an activity that has been observed more in recent years in Greater Yellowstone and is now being studied. It appears that the army cutworm moth, which is found on steep talus slopes at very high elevations, is a significant food source for many Yellowstone grizzly bears, though this feeding activity has only recently undergone study.

Small mammals are highly prized by grizzlies when they can get them. Passing over such occasionals and accidentals as birds (and eggs), frogs, snails, and small bears, we come to a few favorites. The yellow-bellied marmot, or rockchuck, is a sizeable morsel. Marmots live in rocky burrows, but a grizzly may spend an hour or more excavating hundreds of pounds of earth and stone to get at a family of the chubby little animals. Smaller rodents, such as voles and pocket gophers, are another benefit of the grizzly's devotion to meadow grazing. The presence of the rodents, which rarely make up more than 3% of the bear's total diet, is enough to attract and hold grizzlies to an area as long as the succulent plants are common. The bear feeds on the plants while hunting the rodents, which serve as little more than an occasional treat. An enthusiastic grizzly will dig up thousands of square feet of ground if there are enough rodents to keep his interest. The "grazing" grizzly is actually an open-minded shopper.

In early June grizzly bears begin to concentrate along the tributaries of Yellowstone Lake to take advantage of one of the park's great protein concentrations, the spawning runs of cutthroat trout. Literally hundreds of tons of trout move into these streams much as salmon do into many rivers of Alaska where bears also concentrate.

Fishing behavior of bears has been studied in various parts of North America, so that some of the traditional beliefs have been disregarded. Bears rarely slap fish from the water, as they are often depicted doing in outdoor artwork. Slapping has been observed in Yellowstone but more often bears use their front feet to pin the trout to the bottom of the stream. Bears, unlike some animals, will use both paws and mouth to secure their food, and though large Alaskan salmon may be caught by bears using only their mouths, Yellowstone trout require quick stepping. The fish, usually less than eighteen inches long, are trapped by a quick paw (either on the bottom or against the bank) and then grasped with the mouth. An interesting sidelight of one Yellowstone study was that cubs seemed as skilled at fishing as adults, which is different from most other studies which reported that cubs go through an awkward training period.[12] Bears will kill and eat an extraordinary number of fish; one adult female averaged about 100 fish a day for several days.[13]

Usually the trout have returned to the lake by the middle of August and bears have moved on to other foods or returned to the staples mentioned earlier. In August berries start to assume a more important role in bear diet. Yellowstone is not known for the quality of berry production of some other parts of the Rocky Mountains, but some years bears benefit from sugar-rich strawberries, huckleberries, buffaloberries, and grouse whortleberries.

By September and October, with the decline of succulent vegetation and the increased availability of pine nuts, grizzlies concentrate on the latter. Not since spring, when the meat of ungulates was the dominant food item, have the bears concentrated so single-mindedly on one type of food. The pine nuts are very important to the bears, not only for the fat that will help prepare them for denning but because in years when the pine nut crop fails the bears amble off to find other food and frequently get in trouble with people. A direct correlation has been noticed in recent years between man-caused grizzly deaths in a given year and the quality of its pine nut crop. This isn't a simple thing; the bears don't leave the pine-nut areas and immediately go looking for human garbage. They just move into areas where the likelihood of encountering people or their property increases, and whether they ever even find garbage or not, they are at greater risk.[14]

The fires of 1988 burned something more than 20 percent of the whitebark pine in Greater Yellowstone.[15] Whitebark pine is a slow-maturing tree that doesn't even produce seeds until it is 100 years old or so. One of the key questions to arise following the fires, as far as bear management is concerned, is how the reduction in available seeds will affect the bears. With so many variables in the bear's diet, and with the diet changing as it does, it will probably take many years of monitoring to get a fair idea of just what the effects of the loss of pine seeds will be. Predicted changes in the global climate may seriously reduce whitebark pine even more; global warming might drastically reduce available habitat for the whitebark pine, thus having a significant effect on grizzly bears.[16]

Though primarily herbivores, bears are not able to use plant foods as efficiently as are elk or other grazers. They cannot get as many nutrients from the plants, nor can they use as much dried material, as can elk, bison, and so on. The bear's answer to its lower efficiency is increased consumption: running a great quantity of material through its system to satisfy its needs. And, of course, supplementing its diet with more highly digestible animal material. The key to the "success" of the Yellowstone grizzly as a feeder is its flexibility. As long as there exists an ample supply of the succulent vegetation that serves as the foundation of its diet, the bear can fill in nutritional gaps from the smorgasbord of plant and animal foods Yellowstone provides in such great variety.

Though I'll pay more attention to bear movements and habitat use later, it's worth pointing out here that grizzlies, even in the best of feeding conditions, seem to have some interesting tendencies to look around. Like the black bear, it pays for the grizzly to keep moving, and unless the food is a carcass, or a particularly easy trout stream, or an exceptional berry crop, the bear may move on after a while. Dean Graham's 1975-1976 study of grizzly food habits in Pelican and Hayden Valleys in central Yellowstone reported other evidence of this mobility:

Eighty-four percent of grizzly sign was associated with feeding activity. Although some dig sites were quite extensive (up to one-tenth hectares), most feeding sites covered less than 45 square meters. Bears would dig, grub and graze in these microsite locations and then move to an adjacent microsite or to a site a considerable distance away before resuming their feeding activity. On two occasions I observed a bear feeding in a clover patch of less than 35 square meters. After foraging about thirty minutes, the bears left the site which still supplied an abundance of readily available and highly nutritional clover. They traveled about 100m into a *Festuca idahoensis/Deschampsia caespitosa* habitat type where they began grubbing for yampa roots.[17]

This urge to move, even though the next pasture is no greener than the one being abandoned, has been reported for bears in other parts of North America. Like all other parts of the bear's food habits, it is perhaps best characterized by a descriptive phrase David Mattson, of the Interagency Grizzly Bear Study Team, used while talking to my grizzly bear ecology and management class at the Yellowstone Institute in 1991. After running through some of the main points of how many ways the bear's food choices might go at any time, and might then go next, he smiled and said, "Variation on variation on variation."

Chapter 9

The Grizzly Bear:
Denning

*T*he grizzly bear's food habits are designed to prepare it for several months of fasting. By fall the bear is putting on a layer of fat that approaches eight inches in thickness in places. The fat serves as it serves the black bear. In fact, grizzlies follow essentially the same course as blacks in the whole denning process—weight loss during denning, further loss in early spring, and then a summer and fall of feeding and weight increase until shortly before denning. In terms of the basic metabolic processes involved, grizzlies differ little from blacks in the character of their winter sleep. There are several differences in the actual practice of denning, however, and so it is well worth the time to examine the winter denning of the grizzly.

Grizzlies put a great deal of work and advance preparation into winter denning. Grizzlies are usually burrowing denners in Yellowstone—they create an entire cave to suit their purposes.

The first denning preparations have been observed in summer in some northern areas, but in Yellowstone bears do not begin to dig their dens until much later. The Interagency Study Team reported that the average entrance date of seventy radio-collared Yellowstone grizzly bears was November 9, the earliest being a pregnant female who denned on September 28 and the latest being a three-and-a-half-year-old female who did not den until December 21. This female, incidentally, provided an unusual record of denning behavior:

> This female denned with another slightly larger bear, possibly her mother. We are not aware of any documented precedents where

57

2 bears of this age denned together or where a bear was 4 years old before estrangement.[1]

The Craighead study reported that grizzly bears seemed to den almost in unison during snowstorms, suggesting that among other things this helped obscure their location, but the Interagency Study Team's data suggested that bears were denning more individually. Pregnant females denned earliest.

Grizzly bears spend anywhere from one to three weeks near the densite. Bears often seem to return to the same general area each year to den; site selection might be an instinctive process, but it appears that younger, less experienced bears are less able to locate a good site.

Dens are usually dug into slopes, most of which are between thirty and sixty degrees. The slope site has several advantages. First, it is easier to remove the dug-out material because it just rolls downhill. Second, a moderate slope provides the bear with the easiest way of putting a reasonably thick "roof" over its head; digging a cave on level ground would require a much longer entrance tunnel, and digging on a very steep slope would be difficult because of the awkwardness of approach. Third, the sleeping chamber can hold its heat better if the tunnel does not rise from the chamber. Some bears actually build the entrance tunnel so that its mouth is lower than the sleeping chamber, thus creating a "heat trap," but only six of twenty-eight dens examined by the Interagency Study Team were of that type.

There are no absolute rules about where a bear will put its den, but generally they prefer northern exposures with at least a moderate tree cover of whitebark pine or subalpine fir. A few grizzlies in Yellowstone have used natural caves or even hollow trees. Dens have been observed at many elevations from 6,500 feet to more than 10,000 but most fall between 8,000 and 9,000.

Grizzlies are energetic diggers, not only in feeding and in caching of food but in denning. Unlike black bears, who are opportunists about denning, grizzlies rarely take advantage of some other animal's burrow that they can modify. Even after the den is completed, the bear sometimes goes through a "ritualized" digging, arranging its bedding or just straightening whatever seems out of order. This apparent need to dig has been seen as an instinctive necessity, as has the grizzly's reluctance to reuse the same den, though that reluctance is probably also partly the result of the number of dens that cave in during spring thaws.

Den diagrams of grizzly bears. (All measurements in cm.) Courtesy of Interagency Grizzly Bear Study Team.

About half the time the bear digs its den under the roots of a tree, using the spreading root system as a sort of roof support. About the same number of dens are simply dug into slopes with no roof support, and a few are dug under fallen trees. The chamber of a dug den is usually just a little larger than the bear. Typically there is a small opening (perhaps between two tree roots), a short passageway (1 to 5 feet in length), and the chamber itself. The average size of ten chambers measured in the Craighead studies in the 1960s was 56 x 53 x 37 inches. The Craighead team determined that, though digging may go on intermittently for weeks, the biggest part is done in a short stretch of a week or less.[2]

Once the den is completed, and the hundreds of pounds of soil and rock have been removed, final preparations include gathering of bedding. Spruce and fir boughs, mosses, and grasses are used to line the den floor. These materials are more than just an added comfort to the bear. They add warmth. Just as the air in loose pockets in thermal underwear hold small amounts of warmed air, the openings in the boughs hold air warmed by the bear's body, part of a very shallow "microclimate" that surrounds the bear in its den.

The metabolic changes that occur in the system of the grizzly do not differ significantly from those that occur in black bears. The bear ceases to consume, and heart rate, respiration, and body temperature are all reduced. Sleep is deep, but the bear can be roused.

Even in a subject where great variations in scientific findings seem to be the rule, the observations of weight losses by denning grizzlies are remarkably variable. Biologist Albert Pearson recorded losses of from 30 to 43% in southern Yukon grizzlies (who den a month or more longer than Yellowstone bears).[3] A much lower percentage weight loss, more in agreement with figures already given for black bears, may be more typical for Yellowstone grizzlies. Unquestionably, much additional weight is lost in the first few weeks of post-emergence activity.

Length of denning time of grizzly bears varies by almost 100%. Radio-collared grizzlies in the 1970s stayed in the den as short as 86 days and as long as 211 days. The average for males was 113 days. For single females and those that denned with young it was 132 days, and for females who gave birth in the den it was 170 days. That means that males emerged first, usually in late February or the month following. Females with new cubs usually didn't appear until April. Though other studies have suggested that snow depth at the densite had a direct effect on when bears emerged, the most recent Yellowstone study does not show any such connection.

One interesting aspect of bear hibernation is that they are the only mammal known to maintain bone mass despite an extended period of inactivity, when all bones are freed from bearing any weight. When humans endure this condition, they invariably suffer loss of bone strength, known as osteoporosis. Some metabolic process allows bears to avoid this problem, and current research may reveal how. As one scientist has put it, "It is ironic that despite man's apparent complacency with the slow demise of the grizzly, the great bear and its cousins may ultimately contribute more to relieving human suffering than any other animal in history."[4]

Emergence from the den should be of special interest to Yellowstone visitors because the springtime grizzly bear, the carrion seeker of magnificent appetite, is also the most visible grizzly bear. If you can get to the park in April and May, and if the snow will let you drive through, you have the best chance of seeing a grizzly in Yellowstone.

Though they seem devoted to expending lots of energy in constructing a den, grizzly bears sometimes do reuse an old den. Of thirty-five dens examined by the Interagency Study Team, ten had been reused. In two cases the den was used by the same bear two years in a row, in one case it was used by different bears in different years, and in seven cases there was no way of knowing if the same or different bears had reused the den.

Chapter 10

The Grizzly Bear:
Mating and Cub Growth

*G*rizzly bears in Yellowstone mate from late May to mid-July, with most activity occurring in June. We can assume that the same biological preparations take place in grizzlies as in blacks. Reproductive behavior of grizzlies has been studied in several places, but perhaps nowhere as exhaustively as in Yellowstone, so we have a wealth of information on the proceedings.[1]

Female grizzly bears may first mate successfully at age three and a half, but more mate at four and a half or older. The grizzly bear is probably an induced ovulator, meaning that ovulation does not take place without some sexual stimulus. A sow that does not encounter a boar, even if she is not accompanied by cubs, might not ovulate at all. The male bear seems to most often take the initiative, seeking out the female and pursuing her until she is ready to mate or until he is chased off by another male. Males may accompany a female for a few days, or they may remain together throughout the entire estrus cycle of the female.

The estrus cycle varies, with older females apparently remaining receptive for a longer period of time—a few days for young females, and two to four weeks for older ones.

When given the opportunity grizzly bears are promiscuous. In circumstances where bears are concentrated by food, such as at a dump or a salmon stream, both sows and boars may mate with several bears. Since the dumps were closed, Yellowstone bears are less often concentrated during mating season than they used to be, and for this reason a lengthy pair-bond is generally the rule, because other mates are less easily found. Only about one-third of the adult females are receptive in any given year, the others having cubs or yearlings to take care of.

The receptive female, having attracted a mate who in turn has proven his ability to defend and breed her, exhibits certain behavior toward him. His approaches in the courtship stage include rubbing, licking, and smelling, and physical contact is evidently quite important to him, even if only to rest quietly at her side. The behavior of both male and female may seem extremely rough to human observers; she may actually injure him if he attempts to mate before she is ready.

Once she is receptive and he has become fully aroused, his behavior is predictable. Maurice Hornocker, who studied grizzly mating habits during the Craighead study, has described the male's activity:

> Sexually aroused males were easily recognized, even at a distance. Some variation in behavior existed, but generally they exhibited a characteristic stiff-legged, swaggering walk. When approaching another bear this walk was exaggerated, the neck was bowed and the head was held low. They salivated profusely and frequently urinated on the belly and hind legs.[2]

There has been great variation in observations of the female's response to the male. In the Hornocker study, the female's response involved a demonstration of submission, usually accomplished by cowering—lowering of the head and shoulders in an obviously subordinate stance, not unlike scolded dogs behave. In the longer and more extensive Yellowstone Grizzly Foundation study, this submissive behavior has not been observed. The females are often quite dominant or aggressive, biting at the male and even throwing him off.

Actual copulation has been measured from five minutes to 65 minutes, with an average between fifteen and twenty minutes. The boar, mounting the sow and grasping her sides with his front legs, may stay motionless for some moments. Nibbling and biting exchanges take place, sometimes quite aggressive ones.

It is helpful to remember how near these bears are to enmity. The mating season tolerance is a shaky contract; it works but it must not work too well, for the sow needs a sharply developed antipathy to the boar if her cubs are to survive.

If the pair has joined for the duration of the female's estrus, the boar leaves as soon as she has gone out of heat. Until then he attends and even herds her, usually sacrificing his appetite for food to his greater urge to mate. Sows seem to be able to keep producing young as long as they remain healthy. The Craighead study reported a Yellowstone sow giving birth at age twenty-two-and-one-half. The Interagency Study Team reported a sow giving birth to one cub at age 25.

Grizzlies are very slow to reproduce. A grizzly bear population is more easily hurt by heavy mortality than a black bear population because grizzlies are slower to replace themselves. Black bear sows can rear another family every second year while many grizzly sows keep their cubs with them through two winters.

Upon completion of the mating season, the sow is once again alone. Embryonic delay occurs, and the sow carries the free blastocyst until November, at which time it implants in the uterine wall and normal fetal development resumes. The sow probably is in her den by the time the fetus begins to grow. As noted, pregnant sows den a few weeks earlier than lone adults, and take special care to provide soft bedding.

Unlike the black bear, the first litter of a sow grizzly is more often than not two cubs. They are born in late January or early February, not much larger than black bear cubs, less than a foot long and weighing about a pound or a pound and a half. They appear naked but in fact are covered by very fine short hair. Their eyes are closed, and stay closed for five or six weeks. In most respects the pre-emergence life of black and grizzly cubs is similar. The mother provides warmth and nourishment while the cub passes through its most helpless stage.

The average litter size in Yellowstone has varied over the years. During the 1960s, when the bears had access to the garbage dumps, it was 2.24. From 1973 to 1980, it was 1.9. From 1981 to 1990, it was 2.4.[3] Climate may be the single most important factor in influencing the foods that determine the reproductive rate of the grizzly bear population. There is one reasonably well documented case of a sow with five new cubs in Yellowstone, but two is most typical.[4]

Cubs weigh between five and ten pounds when, in April or May, their mother leads them from the den. Sows often establish daybeds near the den, and make forays to and from it for some days, taking the cubs along on gradually increasing trips.

Cub life is full of adventure and surprise. The cubs follow their

Young grizzly bears occasionally have a "collar" of lighter-colored hair. N.P.S. photo.

mother's lead, striking off on small explorations of their own, tumbling into all sorts of mischief. Cub education was described for the black bear, as a training by example and experience. The scene is heartwarming and charming. The cubs play, fight, climb, and grow, stopping now and then to nurse contentedly (a humming noise has been heard from nursing cubs). The family association, with all its lessons, is at the heart of the adult bear's character. The sow's feeding habits become the cubs'. Her job is to find food for the whole family, and presumably each new food she introduces them to is a lesson for their future.

The cubs take quickly to a partial diet of solids, generally copying and learning from their mother's feeding behavior almost from the time of emergence, though relying heavily on her milk. In fact most cubs are not entirely weaned until sometime during their second summer. It seems that no feeding takes place during this second denning, but the sow is able to produce some milk the following year.

65

Yellowstone Grizzly Foundation observations include a sow who nursed her cubs during her third year, after she had mated; the cubs returned to her once the male was gone.

Grizzly cubs frequently stay with their mother for two winters, going on their own in the spring of their third year. The Craighead study showed that about 50% of Yellowstone's grizzly bear cubs remained the extra year with their mother. This obviously has some effects on the cubs. Cubs staying that extra year with the mother are going to be larger, when weaned and abandoned, than cubs left on their own a year earlier, since they have the advantages of mother's milk and her help with foraging. Too, an extra year of experience with the sow might make them better food-finders. One would expect, therefore, that the two-and-one-half-year-old weaners would dominate the population after a few years. It does not seem to work that way, perhaps because the sows who wean their cubs at one-and-one-half years are capable of breeding more often and therefore keep producing more cubs than the other sows can. In recent years, 50% of those bears weaned as cubs did not survive to adulthood.

There are other effects on individual cubs. A one-and-one-half-year-old on its own is likely to be less assertive, more wary, than the larger two-and-one-half-year-old, and can be expected to retain that trait for some years. Subtle differences like these are hard to measure, but we do know that an aggressive sow usually passes that trait along to her cubs. It also seems that a sow with only one cub forms a closer bond with it (and in fact serves as a playmate for it) than that same sow would if she had two or more cubs.

Yellowstone grizzly cubs have little chance of surviving if they are orphaned. Some may make it through their first winter alone, but very few will survive the yearling year.

The sow-cub bond is weakened by the time the cub becomes a yearling. As the young bear becomes more independent and self-sufficient, the sow is less solicitous and protective. The final separation is often still quite a strain on the cubs, and sometimes is only accomplished when a courting male arrives and chases them off.

Adoption and interchange of cubs, though not common, has been observed in some bear populations. Sometimes the cubs of two sows will have the opportunity to play together (not a common opportunity in Yellowstone now), and actually mix, leaving with the wrong mother (it has been seen, for example, along Alaskan salmon streams, where

By the end of their first summer, grizzly cubs begin to lose some of their cub appearance. N.P.S. photo.

the mothers are busy fishing). One case of this sort in Yellowstone resulted in one of the two sows assuming responsibility for all cubs. Now that grizzlies do not learn to tolerate one another as they did at dumps, such an event is unlikely, and even then it was not typical. Orphaned cubs have been physically rebuked by strange sows they tried to follow.

Weaning and abandonment occurs in the spring, about a week before mating season begins. The cubs are often reluctant to part company with one another, so they may spend that summer together and even den together. One unusual case in Yellowstone, of a pair of cubs living together for eight years, was reported by naturalist Milton Skinner in the 1920s.[5]

By their first fall, the cubs will weigh between 60 and 70 pounds. The following fall, their weight will have more than doubled. The average of 11 two-year-old females was 186 pounds, and of 19 males was 217. The average weight of eight four-year-old females was 255, and of 14 four-year-old males was 339.

It appears that in the present grizzly population in Yellowstone the most dangerous time for a young bear is between the time it is weaned and the time it reaches four years of age. Its first year or two it has the protection and help of its mother. Once on its own it is without an established range of its own and is also without the savvy and experience needed to take care of itself as well as it should. The bears that survive those first two years alone are the ones who avoid getting into trouble with humans, bigger bears, and other predators, and who have best learned their mother's lessons about food and shelter.

From the time they are five until they enter their teens, Yellowstone grizzly bears are at their best. After age twelve their odds of not surviving a given year are greater. Very few reach their late teens.

Chapter 11

The Grizzly Bear:
Lifestyle

G rizzly bears spend almost all of their waking time searching for and consuming food. Though to the casual observer the bear's feeding behavior may appear random, it is not. Yellowstone offers the bear many foods in many places and at many times, and all the offerings vary from year to year. A mild winter means fewer winterkilled elk. A dry summer means a failed pine nut crop or a poor berry crop. Bears, through a combination of experience and instinct, have adapted to take as full advantage of their varying menu as possible. A grizzly bear may not know at some given time just exactly what it will be eating in an hour, but it is where it is that day for a very good reason, the reason being that the feeding opportunities are the best there of anywhere in its range.

The size and shape of a grizzly bear's range, that is, the area of land it uses in the course of its life over several years, is the result of nutritional need. When there were dumps in Yellowstone, grizzlies had far less need to move great distances in search of food. When the dumps ceased to contribute to the bear's nutritional budget, the bears had to move more. The average adult male grizzly bear range as determined by the Craigheads was about 90 square miles; the average adult female range was about 28 square miles.[1] These numbers were based upon a relatively small number of bears, 23, most of whom were radiocollared for only a year or two in a row in a pioneering study.[2] It is now clear that the longer the animal is observed, the more variation there may be in its range, and, as a consequence, the larger the known range will become.

The Interagency Grizzly Bear Study Team radiocollared 97 bears between 1975 and 1987, and radio-located them 6,299 times in a much more comprehensive study. The average home range of adult males was 1,450 square miles, and of adult females was 341 square miles. As important, the Team determined that the grizzly bear's flexibility makes it difficult to speak with assurance about the "completeness" of any bear's range, because the animals do not establish a range and then invariably stay loyal only to that country:

> Total home range size could apparently be estimated for some females after six consecutive years of monitoring with a minimum 40 locations per year in the Yellowstone area. However, total home range size was obviously not achieved during the 13-year study period for several females monitored six or more years. It is entirely possible that some individual females never attain a maximum home range size within the Yellowstone population, particularly given the unpredictable food sources (Mattson et al., 1991). After ten years of food habits data collection, new feeding strategies continued to appear annually in this population. Males monitored during this study never attained maximum home range size or even stabilized range location as they sought to enlarge breeding opportunities. The largest male home range documented in this study was the largest recorded in North American grizzly bear studies; the largest female home range was the second largest recorded. . . .[3]

A grizzly bear with a big range, say one of over 1,000 square miles, is not necessarily an unusually large bear; it is important that bear needs are not confused with human ambition for territory. It is just as likely that the bear with the largest range is one that must look the hardest in that range for good things to eat. In terms of survival chances, it is often the case that the bear with the small range is the best off; it obviously is finding what it needs to get along without having to travel great distances and increase the chances it will run into enemies or accidents. It is able to feed, sleep, reproduce, and den without as much risk-taking as the more mobile bear.

Females with cubs of the year tended to have the smallest ranges, though young females with their first litter of cubs had larger ranges than other females with cubs, probably because they had not yet established their own range or weren't fully aware of the need to keep isolated from other bears while caring for cubs.

And, as has been discussed in previous chapters, climate, especially precipitation, has an important effect on the bears:

> Annual range sizes and indices of movement tended to be largest during years of below-normal precipitation. A substantial portion of the diet of Yellowstone grizzly bears is graminoids, which are preferred when succulent and high in protein content. . . . The driest year during this study was 1977. During that year, a dramatic decline in volume of graminoids in scat contents was documented . . ., the largest annual female range was recorded, and spring and fall indices of movement for females were the greatest observed during the study period. Also, virtually no whitebark pine seeds were available during that fall.[4]

The selection of ranges by bears, and the competition between bears for the best spots, have the attention of managers because they affect what bears are most likely to come into conflict with humans and their property. It is now fairly clear that Yellowstone Park, at the center of the Greater Yellowstone Ecosystem, is at its carrying capacity for grizzly bears; bears are moving into country outside of the traditionally recognized grizzly bear ranges of 15 or 20 years ago.[5] This probably means that the bears in the park are partitioning themselves in no more space than they absolutely must have, which in turn means that the most dominant bears will get the best spots, which in turn means that less dominant bears are sometimes forced to go places, or to feed at times, that are higher risk. David Mattson of the Interagency Grizzly Bear Study Team has considered this at some length in a recent paper, as follows:

> . . . adult males apparently more often have the prerogative to use native foods farther from humans. . . .
> Given the very likely pivotal role that adult males play in habitat selection, adult females and subadult males are probably more often left to use sites less secure from humans for feeding on human or rich native foods. Also, these bear classes probably have the motivation to feed in areas less secure from humans; not uncommonly, adult females, females with young, and subadult males have been observed to forage nearest to humans, especially when rich native foods were at stake. The nearness of humans may serve as a refuge from adult males, especially for subadult males and females with

young; and where black and grizzly bears coexist, the nearness of humans may also serve as a refuge for black bears.

This disportment of bears has had and continues to have consequences. Because adult females and subadult males seem to more often end up feeding near humans out of necessity or by default, these classes more often comprise bears habituated to humans. . . . This is a generalization, given that adult males are known to habituate to humans. . . . Still, in many regions, proportionately more adult females and subadult males come into conflict with, or are perceived as risks by, humans because of habituation.[6]

This has brought the management of Yellowstone's bears to a new and peculiar state of affairs, worth an aside here even though this isn't a chapter about management. The park now experiences any number of grizzly bears who are not interested in or accustomed to garbage but who, perhaps for the reasons Dave outlined, are willing to hang around really close to developed areas. They don't meet the traditional definition of a "problem" or "bad" bear; they've just developed a tolerance for humans nearby in order to eat natural foods.

The restoration of trout populations in Yellowstone Lake has led to the increase in spawning runs in several small tributary streams near the Lake Hotel and other developments, which has led in turn to the use of those streams by grizzly bears, some of which are habituated enough to humans to feed in broad daylight. The result is, from the perspective of any manager who wants to keep bears and people apart, a kind of madness: wild grizzly bears, interested only in natural foods, wandering among the early season traffic to fish at all hours of the day and night, while rangers frantically try to keep the fascinated public at a reasonable distance.

It is an explosive situation, one that, being the result of a success in restoring the bear, does not have easy answers. Demands by conservationists to simply close the hotel until the spawning run is over are reasonable only if you aren't one of the many people wanting to stay at the hotel or if you aren't somehow dependent upon the hotel and associated businesses in the development for an income. Needs conflict, tempers rise, and now and then a bear is removed, not because it has done anything wrong, but because it has just become too easy to approach so closely that someone is bound to get hurt. It is all fertile ground for an environmental ethicist, and all proof that, even when managers get something right, it's almost certain to turn around and bite back a little.

The Interagency Study Team's many reports on bear activities have revealed some important general patterns in bear habitat use.[7] Bears tend to use gradually higher elevations as the spring and summer progress. They traveled farthest in dry years, and least far in wet years. They were less mobile in spring and fall, and most mobile in summer. These general rules fit their food habits nicely. In spring, many bears emerge from their dens to find carrion, a food that requires less travel than most vegetation types (many bears now are selecting den sites in areas of spring carcass concentrations). In fall, once again bears concentrate heavily on a few food types, especially pine nuts, and once again they are set loose to wander great distances if those few food types are in short supply. As summer wears on, bears seek out succulent vegetation, which they find at progressively higher altitudes. Dramatic failure—or unusual success— of any given food can alter the movement pattern. For example, when pine nuts do not materialize in sufficient quantities, the bear's flexibility as a feeder is its best hope for survival on a day-to-day basis.

The daily habits of the bear are not as simple as is often reported in the popular literature. Grizzly bears have often been characterized as meadow animals that favor fairly open habitat. They do indeed favor meadows, but in a certain way. What bears often prefer most is a fairly small "mosaic" of habitat types that gives them regular access to non-forested habitats while keeping forested habitats close. Ecologists used to refer to this as the "edge effect," that is, a mixture of habitats that provides a richness of borders between contrasting types. For the grizzly bear the most important contrast seems to be between forest and non-forest.

Various Yellowstone studies disagree to some extent on when bears are active each day. There is a general increase in daytime activity in the spring and fall over that of the summer, when bears are more exclusively nocturnal. Some interesting if not necessarily conclusive studies and theorizing have been done about the effects of various kinds of weather on bear activities. For example, high humidity may increase bear activity because the scent of food is better carried on a wet day than a dry one. Rain may cause bears to seek shelter and sit still more than they would on a clear day. Windspeed (and direction) and cloud cover are other factors that must have some effect on individual bears, but safe generalizations are slow to come about these environmental factors. Temperature variations do have a noticeable effect, however, with a peak of activity occurring around fifty degrees Fahrenheit.[8]

During their periods of activity, bears alternate feeding with resting. The exploratory nature of their feeding leads them on a twisted path; the straight-line distance from where they start the day to where they finish it may be quite short, but the distance they traveled to get there is probably quite long.

In 1981 members of the Interagency Study Team used trained bear dogs to follow the trail of a grizzly bear outside the west boundary of Yellowstone Park near Hebgen Lake. The dogs were not pursuing the bear, which had moved through the area several hours earlier. The account of the tracking is wonderfully illustrative of how Bear #15 moved through his day. He spent the night of July 15, 1981, bedded in willows near the lake. The dogs found the daybed and followed the trail for several hours. The bear had wandered through the heavy vegetation with numerous turns, settling briefly in some lodgepole pines. He then moved on, repeatedly wading back and forth across a small creek. He followed various established roads and cattle trails, then crossed U.S. 191 and took a logging road through a lodgepole forest until he came to a small community, which he did not avoid (it was at night, remember). He left the homes, crossed a shallow pond, then turned back and again crossed U.S. 191, where he was probably seen at 2:30 a.m. by passersby. He then turned south, feeding as he wandered. At this point the dogs were losing the trail, and the bear was soon relocated by radiolocation, about two-and-one-half miles from where the dogs lost him. Had the researchers relied only on the radiolocations, they would have known only that the bear had moved at least four-and-one-half miles. The trail followed by the dogs was at least nine miles long.[9] This is not an unusual distance, and in fact grizzlies have been known to occasionally "light out" from one location and move dozens of miles in only a couple days.

Cover is of great importance to them, wherever they are. Radio-tracked grizzlies show high reliance on timber for much of the day, as reported recently by Interagency Study Team member Bonnie Blanchard:

Instrumented grizzly bears were located in the timber 90% of the time (1635 of 1826 radio locations . . .). The majority (76%) of the locations in timber were either in scattered timber (6%) or less than 100m from an opening at least 100m^2 in size (70%). . . . Only 1% of the locations were in dense timber more than 1 km from an opening at least 100m^2 in size.

Grizzly bears were observed in the open 191 times from 1977 through 1979. . . . The majority (75%) of bears in the open were observed less than 100m from timber cover; over half of these were less than 30m from timber.[10]

Here again we see the bear's commitment to edges. Whether in the timber or not, the bears were usually close to the forest-nonforest boundary.

Grizzly bears often maintain several daybeds in an area, and use them frequently. Their location should be of nearly urgent interest to anyone hiking in grizzly country. Of 149 grizzly daybeds examined by the Interagency Study Team, 115 were on moderate slopes. All but one were in timber and 83% were within a yard of a tree. The average distance of the daybeds to the edge of the timber was a little over 100 yards, and there was sufficient cover around the bed to conceal the bear from observers until they were within 20 yards. Bears didn't put much work into construction; the beds were usually just shallow depressions in the soil.[11] More recent observations by the Yellowstone Grizzly Foundation indicate that often the bears don't make any kind of bed at all; they just lie down for a while in a likely spot.

This assortment of lifetime, annual, seasonal, and daily movements has a strong cumulative effect on the bear. Grizzlies have a better ability to "home" in on its range than the black bear. It appears that the grizzly is a determined traveler when displaced, or when suddenly in the mood to explore some remembered food source, and it appears that its memory can be extraordinary. Their ability to return to home ranges is so strong that managers now recognize as impractical the transplanting of bears to new country if the transplanting distance is less than fifty miles, and even then the bear may well find its way home. Transplanting is still commonly used in national parks, often in the hope of getting the bear away from trouble before it becomes accustomed to a human food source, for example. But once a food source has been learned it may never be forgotten. After the Trout Creek Dump in central Yellowstone was closed and covered in 1970, one grizzly visited the site and dug for possible food every year up to at least the early 1980s.

Other Activities and Traits

A few other activities of grizzly bears are gathered here in catch-all fashion. Grizzlies have many of the same behavioral traits as already described for black bears. One interesting difference is that grizzlies seem to use specific trails much more often than blacks, especially near feeding areas. Early writers commented occasionally on double-rutted trails left by bears. Again the Trout Creek Dump is a good example. It was situated in the middle of a large open valley, and from the dump site emanated straight bear trails that ran to the surrounding forests. So well packed were these trails that fourteen years after the dump was closed the ruts had not disappeared.

Bears of both species do what they can to make themselves comfortable. Grizzlies enjoy swimming, and are known to bathe in order to cool themselves and relieve itching. For the same reasons they wallow in dust beds and rub against trees, rocks, and any other object sturdy enough to serve their needs.

A topic of great popular interest is play. Nature writers, for example, with some justification, characterize the otter as "carefree" and the beaver as "businesslike." Animal species do seem to have different capacities for enjoyment, at least the sort of frivolous enjoyment we think of as play—a term suggesting non-productive activity. Playing cubs are, in fact, learning cubs. As they frolic and scuffle they are developing coordination and social attitudes. The proof may be in adult bears, who play less often, for obvious reasons, but who are known to romp and sport not unlike cubs. Adult grizzlies, for example, have been observed sliding down snowbanks, climbing up and doing it again. Doubtless some bears never entirely lose their interest in play.

An often-mentioned character trait of bears is curiosity, which seems quite natural, important in fact, for an animal whose food habits are so exploratory. A bear is apt to investigate anything its nose can lead its eyes, claws and teeth close enough to examine.

Given the opportunity, grizzly bears are fond of bathing. N.P.S. photo.

Ferocity is probably the trait most often associated with the grizzly. Here we are inclined to subject the bear's behavior to our own value judgments. If ferocity means "might react violently if made to feel it or its young are threatened," the word applies. If it means "is by nature malicious, and usually wishes to cause pain to its fellow creatures," we have gone too far. Conscious premeditated malice is probably beyond the bear's mental capabilities. It acts as it has been conditioned to act and as it judges the circumstances. The grizzly bear is not capable of any more intense anger than, say, the blue jay. The bear, by virtue of its size and power, just happens to be able to assert itself more conclusively. Every animal acts as an individual, and no absolute predictions can be made about those actions, but the next time you encounter an enraged blue jay, imagine what he would do to you if he weighed 500 pounds.

Bears and Other Animals

Adult grizzlies are not preyed on by any other large animal except larger bears. Cubs may be threatened by adult bears, or by the other predators that also threaten black bear cubs.

If we wish to consider parasites predators, there are several rather serious attackers of the Yellowstone grizzly. Most adults, and about 50% of the cubs, carry intestinal worms. Close to half are infected by trichina worms.[12] A number of other internal and external parasites, the latter including ticks and fleas, are occasionally present. Bears hardly ever die from such attacks, but it appears that their general health and behavior can be influenced, at least by the first two. If their life functions are impaired, life expectancy may be less because the animal has been weakened.

Even though a grizzly will prey on a large animal, instances of coexistence are not uncommon. Bears are known to graze in the same meadows as elk or bison, for example. There seem to be tolerances developed by all concerned that permit a cautious neutrality at times.

Bears' behavior with other bears has been observed extensively. Under circumstances of frequent encounters a complex social hierarchy can develop, with some animals having established dominance and therefore first rights to food or mates.

In the simplest of situations, two bears encounter each other on their daily rounds. If neither is defending food or young, and if it is not mating season, there may be, literally, no encounter at all. They may actually ignore each other. If one has reason to be defensive, or for some reason wishes to challenge the presence of the other, it may become necessary for one to establish its supremacy, either by a showdown of bluffs, vocalizations, and other displays, or by actual combat.

The bluff has been discussed for the black bear. Veteran researchers, and some hunter-naturalists, have remarked that practically all charges by grizzly bears they had experienced firsthand were false. Some did not terminate until the bear was within ten feet, but it is felt that many hunters who think they are facing a killing charge are shooting bears that are either bluffing or running up to get a closer look. These same researchers and hunters do not recommend that the sportsman wait to find out, and quite often, under natural circumstances, the bear being charged does not wait either; it attacks or flees. As we will see in Part III, these two choices are not good ones for humans in the same situation.

Bear sounds include crying, snorting, growling, whining, and all the non-vocal noises described for black bears. Some figure in encounters, as do other actions such as pawing and head swinging. We do not know exactly what each action means, but there is a system to it that is consistent. Bear communication in an angry encounter can be quite intricate, with an assortment of feints and growls, snorts and stampings, reaching a climax either in one bear backing down or in actual fighting. Fighting, if it occurs, is mostly done with the mouth and front paws. Adult grizzlies, especially older males, are often scarred from battles. Serious injury is infrequent (crippling, for example), and death is rare.

Supremacy, once established, is remarkably final. In many encounters observed by the Craighead team, the triumphant bear turned his back on the conquered one and walked away. Never did the loser take advantage of his opponent's vulnerability and attack from behind. Furthermore, they discovered that long-dominant males who were accustomed to being "in charge" at the dumps disappeared quickly once they were defeated in battle. It seemed likely to the observers that the defeat broke their spirit and, though in good health, they soon died. Groupings with the intensity of the old dump days are less frequent in Yellowstone, so such complex social behavior has less opportunity to occur.

Bears and the Fires of 1988

Nature operates on many scales at once. We who view it tend to see things in our own scale, usually enjoying the daily and seasonal changes, but rarely thinking about the really large picture, of how settings evolve and adapt in the face of singular events that may not even occur once in our lifetimes. Most people think of the biggest events—earthquakes, 100-year floods, tornadoes, fires—as disasters. Ecologists think of them a little more neutrally, as disturbances. The biggest disturbances, for all the havoc and untidiness they create, seem to be crucial to many ecosystems. They give the system a jump-start, and provide opportunities for all manner of new competitions between the life forms that were dominant and those that will try to be. It isn't always pretty, to our civilized eyes, but it's always exciting.

The fires of 1988 are a lesson in the long view. Just as you can't get a full understanding of the variation and consequences of grizzly bear behavior from only a decade or two of study, you can't appreciate the richness and complexity of Greater Yellowstone without a few hundred years to watch. Fires have been occurring here for thousands of years, and are a fundamental part of the natural processes that drive and maintain the ecological system of which grizzly bears are a part.

Fire does not visit the Yellowstone country uniformly. There is always lightning, but there is not always fuel that is dry enough to burn. Most years only a few acres or few hundred acres burn. Then, in drier years, fires may grow to a few thousand acres. Then, in the rare year of extreme dryness, a threshold is crossed and the fires skip and sweep across hundreds of thousands of acres. Tree-ring studies indicate that such giant fires occurred here in the mid-1800s and around 1700, just as they did again in 1988.[13] It is too soon to know, but global climate change, as it is predicted, may increase the frequency of the big burns.[14]

The fires of 1988 killed far fewer large mammals than most of us, conditioned by Smokey and Bambi, would have expected. Perhaps 300 large mammals were killed in the fires, which affected almost 800,000 acres in Yellowstone Park (five of the seven major fire complexes, including the largest of all, started outside the park and burned in). Far more animals—several thousand—died the following winter, as the cumulative effects of the extreme drought (which greatly reduced forage), the fires (which burned some key winter ranges), and the first normal winter snowfall in six years caught up with an elk population that had been living easy for a long time.[15]

Most of the time, the large mammals simply stepped aside as the fire approached. Only when fires made fast runs across very broad fronts did elk and other animals find it impossible to escape. More than half of the 250 or so elk known to have been killed by the fires were in one large group, caught by the smoke of a fast-moving fire on the Blacktail Plateau in northern Yellowstone Park.

In 1988, 38 grizzly bears were wearing radiocollars in Greater Yellowstone, and so researchers were presented with a rare opportunity to see how the fires affected them. Here is the summary from the Interagency Grizzly Bear Study Team:

Twenty-one of the 38 radio-monitored bears had home ranges containing one or more of the 1988 fires. Thirteen of the 21 bears moved into burned areas after the fire front passed, three remained within active burns as the fire progressed, three stayed outside burn lines at all times, and two could not be located after the fires. Average annual range sizes of six individuals were larger during 1988 compared to previous years, although the difference was not statistically significant. . . .[16]

Public concerns that the fires were somehow "bad" for park wildlife were largely unfounded. These wildlife populations have been coexisting with fire for thousands of years; it is the kind of disturbance their populations are well able to respond to, even take advantage of.

The grizzly bear, of course, is of special concern because of its rarity; by law, the federal government must ensure its survival now that its population isn't as large as it was a few hundred years ago, when bears and fire managed to coexist throughout the Rocky Mountains. The fires of 1988 did many things to the life of the grizzly bears. They may have killed at least those two with radiocollars. They provided a good deal of burned elk for a few bears that found it. They, along with the drought and the winter, provided many tons of elk and bison meat the following spring. They started vegetative cycles that will affect grizzly bear feeding habits, and those of other animals of interest to grizzly bears, for many years, including the opening of forest canopies to make the forest floor more hospitable to plant communities of many kinds, and the reduction of available whitebark pine. We will probably see, or suspect, numerous effects of the fires for as long as we are willing to watch, but we don't know enough yet to pronounce the fires of 1988 "bad" for the bears of Yellowstone.

Bears and Wolves

For about twenty years now, there has been growing interest in restoring wolves to Yellowstone Park. This has been an enormously controversial issue, one that, since at least the mid-1980s (when it began to seem like something that might actually happen) has gotten more attention from conservationists than has grizzly bear protection. The polarization is extreme; some people love wolves, and others loathe them. Already there are signs of what one biologist recently called "wolf hysteria," as the most ardent (and remarkably ill-informed) opponents of wolf restoration claim that wolves will somehow kill off all the region's other large mammals, or take to a steady diet of human children.

One of the many interesting questions about wolves in Yellowstone is what would happen to other predators if they were restored here in any number. A recent highly publicized incident in Alaska, in which wolves were observed killing a grizzly bear, was used by some anti-wolf interests to try to prove that wolves were likely to endanger the park's grizzly bear population, and thus should not be restored. But it is an important question. Most scientists agree that the grizzly bear population in Greater Yellowstone is in a precarious state; it's small enough that only a modest change in the factors that affect its mortality rate could put it into decline. Grizzly bears and wolves manage to share ranges in a number of places, but that doesn't necessarily prove that Yellowstone's small, isolated population of bears can automatically handle wolves. There will be competition for prey and carrion, and there will be occasional direct encounters that could result in the death of wolves or bears.

Though scientists generally agree that this question, like most other questions relating to wolf restoration, will not really be answered until wolves are here, they also generally agree that the effects of wolves on bears will not be serious. A 1990 paper by Richard Knight and Christopher Servheen reviewed situations around the world where wolves and bears coexist, and concluded that changes in "ungulate numbers and distribution would be the most important impact of an increasing wolf population to grizzly bears in the Yellowstone area. It seems reasonable to assume that grizzly bears would adapt to these changes with little detrimental effect to grizzly numbers or survival."[17] Another 1990 paper reported the results of a poll of fifteen leading North American wolf experts, who unanimously agreed that there will be little interspecies killing, and that "Grizzly bear distribution and behavior were not expected to change if wolves were reintroduced to Yellowstone National Park,"[18] They were less sure whether or not wolves would, by their predation on park animals, inadvertently provide grizzly bears with a more consistent or larger supply of carrion than they have now.

I can imagine few more interesting developments in the story of the Yellowstone grizzly bear than the addition of another predator to its habitat. The interactions between wolves and grizzly bears should be fascinating, and I can already think of several places to go where I should be able to watch them.

Part Two

Of Bears and Men

Chapter 12

The First 10,000 Years

*B*ears and humans have interacted for thousands of years in the Yellowstone country. Primitive human occupation of the area began shortly after the receding glaciers of the last ice age exposed it, and it was the disappearance of that ice farther north that opened the way for the spread of the grizzly into the present western United States. The climate of Yellowstone has undergone several major changes in the past 10,000 years. It remained relatively moist for the first 3,000, so that the area served as a hunting ground for nomadic tribes with the simplest of weapons; they were not even aware of the bow and arrow. A grizzly was a formidable adversary, not to be attacked by less than a party of men. The climate then dried in this part of the west by about 5000 B.C. The hunters were gradually replaced by bands of foragers, gathering whatever sorts of food were available, since the climatic changes had caused the disappearance of most of the big game.[1]

If one measures human progress in terms of invention, the relative scarcity of food at this time caused some great leaps forward in the "civilizing" process. The people of the great plains and the northern Rockies, responding to the greater challenge of obtaining food, developed animal traps, and, by the time of Christ, the bow and arrow. As they progressed the climate reversed itself, the drought subsided, and large mammals again became abundant. Man now faced bear on slightly better terms, but the increasing sophistication of human culture added other dimensions to the contact. The bear, especially the grizzly, became a figure of kinship or reverence for many tribes, just as it also became a fearsome adversary.[2]

At the time of the first European visit to what is now Yellowstone (probably John Colter, a member of the Lewis and Clark expedition, who seems to have passed through what is now the park in 1807), the tribes in control of the region were the Crow, Blackfeet, and Shoshone. The only permanent occupants were a few members of a branch of the Shoshone tribe known as the Sheepeaters. Except for the advantage of an occasional horse or trapper's gun, they faced bears much as their ancestors had. Explorers in the Rocky Mountains reported that it was a much greater honor for a brave to have killed a grizzly than to have killed an enemy brave.

From 1810 to 1870 Yellowstone was visited by many whites. At first, trappers wandered the region, seeking beaver. By 1850 the heyday of beaver trapping was past, but prospectors, seeking a variety of precious metals, explored the region, eventually establishing a small settlement, the New World Mining District (present Cooke City) neat the northeast corner of what is now the park in the late 1860s. Stories of Yellowstone's geologic and geothermal wonders were taken back to the settlements, but polite society disregarded the reports of trappers and similar disreputables. It was not until the 1860s that serious progress was made in formal exploration.[3]

Many of these adventurers—trapper, prospector, and explorer—met Yellowstone's bears. We will turn to some of their tales in the third part of this book, but for now our subject is an adventure of a different sort: the 1872 Act of Congress that created Yellowstone Park, and the profound effect that act had on our concept of wildlife in general and bears in particular.

Chapter 13

1872–1916:
The First Park Bears

*T*he establishment of Yellowstone Park was one of the great milestones of early American conservation. The park's geological, geothermal, and biological riches, surviving today in remarkably good condition, are ample testament to the foresight of its founders. But much of what Yellowstone has become, including a magnificent wildlife sanctuary, was neither suspected nor intended by its creators. Yellowstone as a wilderness may have changed little, but as a concept—as an institution—it is radically altered from its original form.[1]

The Yellowstone Park Act of March 1, 1872 specified that "the tract of land . . . lying near the headwaters of the Yellowstone River . . . is hereby reserved and withdrawn from settlement, occupancy, or sale under the laws of the United States, and dedicated and set apart as a public park or pleasuring ground for the benefit and enjoyment of the people."

The greatest concern of the sponsors of the park (excluding the overriding commercial interests of some of its most effective supporters) was to preserve the spectacular scenic and geothermal wonders of Yellowstone. There was no special interest in wildlife, beyond the mandate to the secretary of the interior, who had charge of the park, to establish such "rules and regulations as he may deem necessary or proper" to protect the park, and to "provide against the wanton destruction of the fish and game found within said Park, and against their capture or destruction for the purposes of merchandise or profit." Hunting, for sport or provision, was regarded as a legitimate public use of Yellowstone Park in 1872.

Yellowstone National Park

The complex and even self-contradictory philosophies which now direct our management of national parks were not even foreseen in 1872. It was forty-four years before a comprehensive statement of modern park preservation received codification in the National Park Service Act of 1916. In the meantime, there were lessons to be learned, mistakes to be made, and, now and then, bears to be dealt with.

From 1872 to 1886 Yellowstone was administered by a series (five) of civilian superintendents. They were grossly underfinanced and received virtually no guidance from an understandably ignorant government. As a result of the inadequacies of this civilian administration, an assortment of political pressures resulted in the assignment, in 1886, of the U.S. Cavalry to the care and protection of the park. For over thirty years the army provided discipline, defense, and blessed order to Yellowstone Park. They initiated many management procedures that had lasting effects on Yellowstone's biological communities. Some were good and some were not, but most were continued by the National Park Service when that agency took over in 1916.[2]

Yellowstone was subjected to some exciting scientific research in the nineteenth century, beginning with the first government explorations and continuing through several later survey parties, but most of the work was geological or topographical. Mapping and study of the park's wonders was complemented by some excellent work on botanical and zoological subjects, the latter especially with fish and invertebrates, but very little was learned about the bear or other large animals.

In 1880, Philetus Norris, second superintendent of the park, made an attempt at describing the "varieties" of bears. Norris, an avid if unschooled naturalist, named six: grizzly bear, silver-tipped bear, cinnamon bear, smut-faced bear ("with a brackled, impish-looking face—a true indicator of the character of the beast . . ."), black bear, and silk bear.[3] All were simply individual variations on the two species we know the park contains, but at least Norris was showing some interest.

The public was showing a little interest too. In the park's first ten years about 10,000 people found their way to Yellowstone, and once there they were pretty much on their own. There were few hotels, and for some years virtually no roads. Visitors either brought provisions or shot what they needed. Many shot a lot more than they needed.

In fact, the wildlife situation before 1886 was dangerously out of control. Skin hunters, concentrating on elk and bison, ignored regulations (as well as hopelessly ineffective officials) and killed thousands of animals. Visiting sportsmen, from the east and Europe, were more moderate but just as deadly. A dawning of awareness was occurring, however, among sportsmen and nature-lovers; the wildlife of the west was not an inexhaustible resource. The park's staunchest defenders, voicing their displeasure through magazines like *Forest and Stream* urged elimination of hunting. Thus within a very few years

Yellowstone took on a new role. It became a wildlife sanctuary of unparalleled size.

In 1883, by order of the Secretary of the Interior, hunting became illegal. At first, only the grazing animals and others deemed harmless by the standards of the day were protected. Predators, including cougars, coyotes, wolves, and bears, were still fair game. Of these, bears had only three more years before their reprieve. The others faced a full half-century of additional, and increasingly intense, persecution at the hands of park managers.[4]

The ecological processes we now appreciate in a wilderness were only dimly perceived by a few naturalists before 1900. Animals, to most people, were "good" or "bad" as they fit the human plan. Judging from contemporary accounts, bears, though respected and coveted by hunters, were not considered game in the same class as elk or deer. Bears stood somewhere between the noble ungulates (elk, moose, deer, and so on) and the evil wolves. Wolves were not game animals at all—they were vermin. Additionally, bears were still annoyingly abundant throughout the west. Grizzlies still thrived in parts of the Sierras, in the Pacific Northwest, and in New Mexico and Colorado in 1880. There was little or no concern for their numbers beyond how to reduce them.[5]

Some accounts of Yellowstone's bears have suggested that bear populations, both grizzly and black, were substantially reduced during the first lawless years.[6] The available evidence, though too sketchy to be absolutely conclusive, indicates that the bears remained reasonably common until protected, In 1885, for example, a correspondent to *Forest and Stream* reported that Yellowstone's bears were "numerous."[7]

That same year the *Livingston* (Montana) *Enterprise* informed its readers that H.A. Pearson, of San Francisco, who had bagged three grizzlies and two blacks while hunting in the park, was so excited about the excellent sport that he was considering setting up a guide service.[8] Surely, if park bears were thinned out by hunting, no good businessman would want to count on them for income. It seems more likely that later writers accustomed to judging bear numbers in terms of visibility (at roadside, in camps, or in dumps) mistook a lack of visibility for a lack of presence.

When the Cavalry arrived in August of 1886 the struggling young park turned a corner and within a few years was transformed from a questionable experiment in government stewardship into a secure American institution. The strong and stable army administration responded to the most crying needs; vandals were arrested, poachers were apprehended, and haphazard fortune was replaced by regimented process. The officers who were appointed acting superintendent took their assignment very seriously. They immediately began to protect the park in every imaginable way.

Bears, in fact all animals, were brought under the protection of the 1883 hunting prohibition. Never again would Yellowstone's visitors be legally entitled to kill its wildlife (and often yet park rangers must answer the difficult question of why fish are not "wildlife"). Killing would occur, but it would be either clandestine or administratively sanctioned. In a very short time the animals began to lose their wariness. By the 1890s visitors were delighted by the sight of elk and deer calmly grazing on the grounds of park developments. Not tame, these wild animals had simply responded to protection by losing their shyness.

Bears were no exception. Within three years (1889) black bears were gathering at night at garbage piles near the hotels. Garbage disposal being a very informal matter in the park, open pits were located near all the hotels, and smaller ones occurred wherever camping was popular. The idea of open piles of decaying refuse is repulsive to us now, but then it seemed an entirely satisfactory arrangement; if the bears were willing to dispose of some of it, all the better. Just how acceptable it was became clear when the garbage and camp food attracted enough bears to cause problems. The only solution even considered was removal of the bears. Garbage was here to stay.

By 1891 there *was* a problem. Acting Superintendent Anderson reported that "bears have become very troublesome at all the hotels, camps, slaughterhouses, and other places in the Park where there is anything for them to eat. They have not proved at all dangerous, but it is impossible to keep provisions anywhere within their reach." He mentioned also capturing four, and suggested that it might become necessary to kill "an occasional one" if they were too destructive.[9]

The same year bears from Yellowstone became available to zoos, with one being shipped to Washington at the beginning of a long and flourishing relationship between the park and the National Zoological Gardens. In 1911, for example, a total of twelve bears (ten grizzlies and two blacks) were shipped to zoos in Philadelphia, Toronto, Kansas City, and Iowa.[10] A notion of "surplus" animals was established, ones that the park could spare, and another management philosophy congealed: Yellowstone could be relied on to

Acting superintendent Captain George Anderson, U.S. Cavalry, with captive bear cub at Fort Yellowstone, Mammoth Hot Springs, in the 1890s. N.P.S. photo.

overproduce its wildlife, from bears to elk to trout, so the administration was justified (later the word would be obligated) to manage this harvest.

Bears appeared at the dumps in increasing numbers. By the early

1890s the blacks were joined by a few grizzlies, who seemed more cautious about associating with man and his food.

If they needed it, bears got added protection under the National Park Protective Act of 1894, which at last put legislative teeth in the park's feeble regulations (the civilians had had little recourse to punish offenders; all they were allowed to do was expel them from the park. The army "found ways" to punish, sometimes extralegally). Stiff fines and jail sentences made would-be poachers and vandals think twice about their plans.

Quickly the dumps became a tourist attraction. Another institution, the bear-feeding grounds, was born. Tourists gathered in the evening (the bears learned the dumping schedule) within a few yards of the pits to watch one to twenty bears sort through the trash for tidbits. Of course some adventurous souls took to hand-feeding the animals, so that it seemed only a matter of time before a bear would, literally, be fed a hand.

The acting superintendents were reluctant to tamper with what appeared to them to be a harmless situation. In 1893 Anderson commented only that he suspected some bears had been taken by poachers. In 1894, though he felt they had "increased notably," he saw no need to control them; "They are not dangerous to human life . . ." Two years later Acting Superintendent Young reported complaints of bear damage from Norris, Fountain Hotel, Thumb Lunch Station, Lake Hotel, and the soldiers at Canyon, whose storehouses were raided by bears. He suggested that it would be advisable to send "at least twelve" to zoos. The following year he reiterated his sentiment, and was joined in it by at least one newspaper, whose editor objected to the practice of feeding as not only dangerous to the public but to the bears; "They have become too indolent to hunt for themselves." Expressions of concern for the bears, however muted, were rare at this time.[11]

The situation remained much the same throughout the army administration. The number of dump-fed bears increased, a few were killed, others were shipped to zoos, and the feeding grounds were formalized. Feeding by other means than dump was prohibited by Acting Superintendent Pitcher in 1902:

> The interference with, or molestation of bear or other wild game in the Yellowstone Park, by *ANYONE* is absolutely prohibited.
> The custom of feeding the bear, on the part of tourists, hotel

employees, or enlisted men, must cease at once, as this practice will sooner or later, surely result in serious injury to some individual.

The bear of the Park, while absolutely wild, are perfectly harmless, but when rendered tame by being fed—in any other way except at the regular garbage piles at the various hotels—lose all fear of human beings and will enter kitchens and camps in search of food, thereby frequently doing considerable damage to property and provisions.

For their own protection and for the protection of tourists throughout the Park, hotel managers are requested to post this circular in a conspicuous place, and to promptly notify the Acting Superintendent of the Park of any violation of the above instructions.

Whenever a bear becomes vicious or dangerous at any hotel or station throughout the Park, the fact should at once be reported, and a scout will be specially detailed for the purpose of capturing or killing it.[12]

Later that summer Mr. R. E. Southwick, from Hart, Michigan, was seriously injured while violating the new rule.[13] Again, a tradition was established. For half a century Americans would come to Yellowstone for the avowed purpose of feeding bears. That it was illegal to do so did not matter to many of them.

Injuries began to increase, but little sympathy was wasted on bear feeders. An injured hotel employee in 1904 "got simply what he deserved," according to the superintendent. Between 1905 and 1915, while visitation ranged between 16,000 and 51,000, bears invaded camps, destroyed storehouses, and were a constant headache for the soldiers. Public reaction varied. In one exchange in *Science* magazine in 1913, a bear enthusiast described the "repelling of an attack on the larder," which to him was much like "a midnight sally to rout the neighbor's cow from one's garden patch," as "great fun." His opponent, who "lost all of our grub at the Canyon," considered the bears an "outrageous nuisance," and recommended that "either 95% of the Yellowstone Park bears be killed off or soldiers must be placed on all-night guard around the chief camping places."[14]

There is a report of a bear-caused human death in Yellowstone in 1907, in F. D. Smith's *Book of a Hundred Bears*, published in 1909.[15] It involves a tourist who attempted to chase some grizzly cubs up a tree. According to the published account, he poked at the cubs with his umbrella and was then fatally mauled by their mother. My confidence

The bears were quickly recognized as efficient garbage disposals, and a remarkable degree of familiarity between people, bears, and horses was the result. N.P.S. photo.

in the authenticity of this account is not high; its author was a popular writer who heard the story from one of the park scouts, who may not have been above stringing the writer along with a tall tale. One reason for my uncertainty is that this incident, if it occurred, received no official notice, while the next reported fatality was a national news item.

In 1916 Frank Welch, a teamster with the Army Quartermaster Corps, was dragged from camp one night by a grizzly that had been raiding camps for several weeks in the Fishing Bridge–Sylvan Pass area. Welch died later of the injury, and the bear caused a good deal more trouble before it was finally destroyed. What is surprising is that even at this point, after grizzlies were a well-established nuisance around the camps, the death of Frank Welch caused great amazement among experienced bear "authorities" who believed that the killing was completely out of character for grizzlies.[16] There was a widespread feeling that the ferocity of the grizzly bear first met by Lewis and Clark had been "educated" out of the species by a century of hunting. Eighty years later behaviorists would tell us that habituation to humans is not the same as domestication, and that it is never possible, and may never be possible, to predict how any individual grizzly bear will act on the basis of what we know about other grizzly bears.

We are much better able to assess human effects on Yellowstone's bears in this second period of administration, partly because the army kept such good records and partly because there were more tourists around to record their own impressions. The bears became secure enough in the company of humans to enter developments and forage openly in the garbage. They became bold enough to break into buildings.

A lot of informal "bear management" was practiced that certainly did no good for bear-human relations. Bears that entered the permanent camp facilities (where visitors could rent tent-cabins by the night) were sometimes fed meat with broken glass in it, or sponges fried in grease. For a few years a colorful old frontier character and self-promoter named C. J. "Buffalo" Jones held the position of Game Warden in Yellowstone, and he assigned himself the job of punishing troublesome bears. He would snare them and use a block and tackle to suspend them from a tree with their hind feet barely touching the ground, then beat them with a switch. He was finally ordered to quit this practice, shortly before he "resigned" in 1905. One could almost

A very early photograph, about 1912, of a bear-feeding grounds in Yellowstone; certain formalities, such as fences and grandstands, had not yet arrived. N.P.S. photo.

wish that Jones had tried this "punishment" on a grizzly rather than on small black bears.[17] The army made a reasonable effort to prevent cruelty to the bears, and saw to it that those found guilty (usually hotel or camp employees) were punished, but in a day when bears were still regarded as little more than varmints it isn't surprising that so many people were quick to abuse the animals. The bears were, in any event, durable and patient enough to keep coming back no matter how roughly they were treated. The miracle is that more people were not hurt. Yellowstone history is a profound testament to the patience of bears.

Later writers have differed on the number of park bears before the 1930s. Some naturalists and scientists have taken the early accounts and superintendents' reports quite literally, and accept the number of bears counted at the dumps as a true estimate of the park's bear population.[18] Others suspect that the gradually increasing number of bears at the dumps were just a reflection of such things as a gradual loss of wariness after more than a decade of being hunted, a slow adjustment of a large, widely dispersed population of bears to feeding at a few sites, and a gradual increase in garbage that over the years was able to feed more and more bears. I find the latter interpretation much more convincing. There is no reason to suppose that the park was not supporting a healthy wild population of both species of bears (as was much of the surrounding country, where settlement was light), most of whom had not yet discovered dump feeding. The final proof of that would seem to be that as amounts of garbage increased so did the numbers of bears feeding. Garbage does not spontaneously generate bears the way that people once believed a pile of rags would generate mice. By the 1930s and 1940s, as visitation increased, and as the opportunity for bears to feed on human foods likewise increased, the reported number of bears in the park grew from a few dozen to a few hundred.

If we accept, as I think we should, that Yellowstone supported healthy populations of both black and grizzly bears by the 1890s, there is a lesson there for modern bear-watchers. The only place bears were seen with regularity was near the small park developments and at the dumps. Many modern visitors, traveling through the park looking for bears, assume that because they do no see the bears the bears must not be in the park. Here we have an earlier time in Yellowstone's history when black bears were known to be in the park but simply had not yet learned that it was to their advantage to be near roads.

But they did learn it, and in the last few years of the army administration bear-watching (and bear managing) took a new twist. Traditionally accepted accounts have claimed that in the years between 1917 and 1919 a black bear cub learned to beg near the West Thumb Soldier Station. This bear, who became famous as "Jesse James" and was featured in the Annual Report of the Director of the National Park Service in 1919, was in fact far from being first. My own research into early park visitor accounts, along with Dr. Mary Meagher's examination of soldier station records, reveal that it wasn't that simple. Sometime around 1900 a few black bears were occasionally reported by soldier patrols near well-traveled roads. These first reports do not indicate that the bears were actively "panhandling," and make no mention of visitors looking for bears, but evidently bears and tourists were beginning to understand what they had in common. The first tourist account I have located in which a rather bashful bear approaches tourists along a park road occurred in about 1910. Roadside begging was an extension of the familiarity already bred in the dumps and camps. Bears knew that people meant food, and as road traffic increased to the point that it was worth a bear's time to hang around waiting for handouts, more and more bears learned to do it. Some probably learned by example, some by boldness, and almost immediately they were teaching their cubs to do it. By the 1920s, bears could be seen begging at many points on the park's grand loop road, and many people who visited Yellowstone in the 1950s or 1960s will recall seeing thirty or more roadside bears in the course of their visit. It is these beggars that most people think of even yet when someone mentions the bears of Yellowstone.

Serious study of Yellowstone's bears had progressed little by the time the National Park Service was created in 1916. In 1904 Theodore Roosevelt wrote about his presidential visit to the park the previous year and noted that the bears were fascinating and deserving of some naturalist's attention.[19] In 1906 and 1908 William Wright, a well-known hunter-naturalist and the most reliable popular bear writer of his day (even better than Roosevelt), spent several weeks in the park. He took many flash photographs of the grizzlies that visited various dumps at night, and some of the better pictures appeared in his milestone book *The Grizzly Bear* (1910). Seventy-five years later, after dozen of books about bears have been published, Wright's is still among the most enjoyable and is still remarkably accurate most of the time. It is an important contribution to the literature of Yellowstone's bears.[20]

A more mundane investigation, in 1913, made a priceless suggestion that was ignored. Robert Dole of the U.S. Geological Survey examined sanitary conditions in the park, finding dangerous pollution at every turn. His report upbraided park administrators, since "in Yellowstone Park, where the avowed effort is to keep natural features as nearly as possible in their primeval state, the streams should be kept much cleaner." As an aside, he suggested that garbage should be burned or buried, and that all incinerators and dump operations "should be fenced with barbed wire to keep out the bears."[21] Dole was on the right track, but he was ahead of his time. The dump bears had only begun to entertain America.

Chapter 14

1916–1945:
The Great Yellowstone Bear Show

*T*he creation of the National Park Service in 1916 marked the formal coming of age of an almost venerable idea. By 1916 Yellowstone had been joined by a host of sister parks and monuments. Where in 1872 it stood alone, in 1916 it was part of a thriving system with an avid and growing public. Among this public, and in the structure of the infant agency, were people who foresaw many changes in the future parks. No features of the parks, especially of Yellowstone, concerned them more than wildlife.

The National Park Service Act of August 25, 1916, contained a dual mandate:

> to conserve the scenery and the natural and historic objects and the wildlife therein and to provide for the enjoyment of the same in such a manner and by such means as will leave them unimpaired for the enjoyment of future generations.

Here, the resource, whether geyser, bear, or aster, was given some preference. It could be enjoyed, but not so much that future enjoyment might be threatened or even diminished. The mandate is an eternal challenge.

The strengthening of national park goals was timely, for there was an increasing restlessness among the aware over many aspects of management. Exotic species of animals, introduced in some parks, had destroyed delicate balances. Yellowstone's primitiveness suffered most from the spread of several species of fish, but it had also been threatened with many other introductions; reindeer, chamois,

102

mountain goat, and a variety of birds were considered and rejected.[1] The notion that man can "improve" the wilderness by adding to it has been slow to die.

In Yellowstone, from 1904 to 1945, elk were fed to help them through the winters.[2] Predators were killed (between 1904 and 1935 the total was 121 cougars, 136 wolves, and 4,352 coyotes), to further "protect" the elk, deer, and bison.[3] The most spectacular manipulation of the park's animal populations occurred under water. Starting before 1900, under the administration of earlier versions of the present U.S. Fish and Wildlife Service, a massive stocking and stream "improvement" effort took place, with the expressed goal of making Yellowstone an angler's paradise. Many barren waters were stocked, and many native fish were outcompeted by newcomers. Native stocks were hopelessly mixed. A giant hatchery program was developed that, at its peak in the 1940s, was producing over 30,000,000 eyed cutthroat trout eggs a year for shipping to other areas.[4]

As late as 1911, the superintendent of Sequoia National Park recommended the general elimination of bears from that park.[5] At the same time, and later, a complaining hotel guest could cause the death of noisy woodpeckers in Yosemite National Park.[6]

The scope of the manipulation now seems almost incredible. In the 1920s, when it was widely learned that white pelicans were an alternate host for the parasite that infects many trout in Yellowstone Lake, there was active enthusiasm for an egg-stomping campaign at the pelican nesting sites on the Molly Islands. The campaign was further fueled by an awareness of how many fish those pelicans ate and therefore kept visiting anglers from catching. The campaign was nipped in the bud by public outcry, but it illustrates the mood of many managers.[7] In these cases, and in others, it was clear the visitor came first.

Why was this so? A big reason was that the new Park Service had the opposite "people problem" it has now: There weren't enough visitors. The first two directors of the Park Service, Stephen Mather and Horace Albright, were superb publicists. They realized the only way they could get adequate funding from Congress to support and enlarge the National Park system was by broadening public interest. They were fabulously successful. Yellowstone visitation went from 25,000 in 1914 to 260,000 in 1929. More people, more camps, more garbage, and more bear problems.

The scientific community had begun to respond to growing threats to wildlife even as the Park Service was being born. An article in *Science* (appropriately entitled "Animal Life as an Asset of National Parks") in 1916 stated that the "first necessity in adapting the parks for recreative purposes is to preserve natural conditions." The article urged that professional naturalists be assigned to the parks to make careful studies of conditions, so that managers would act on the basis of fact rather than supposition.[8] The same recommendation was made by other distinguished specialists. In 1921 the American Association for the Advancement of Science resolved to oppose all introductions of exotics (plants too) in parks. They were supported by the Ecological Society of America.[9]

By 1927, when research was widely regarded as essential. A good beginning was made in 1930 when a National Park Service "Branch of Research and Education" was established to direct both the gathering and dissemination of knowledge. It initiated the Fauna Series, books which dealt with wildlife problems in the parks (Fauna No. 4, on the ecology of the coyote in Yellowstone, by Adolph Murie, at last established that Yellowstone's long-persecuted predators were of only marginal influence on ungulate numbers), and between 1932 and 1940 there were twenty-five biologists working in the Park Service (Civilian Conservation Corps funding made this possible). World War II put this to an end, and recovery was slow, but that is ahead of our story of the bears.

The challenge of the Park Service Act, to preserve yet enjoy, had been recognized immediately. As one writer put it, "ice and fire were expected to consort together without change of complexion."[10] For the bears, the 1920s were just an expansion of earlier situations, but more bears in dumps prompted officials to announce dramatic population increases. Based on dump estimates, grizzly numbers were said to have gone from 40 in 1920 to 260 in 1933 (keep in mind also that until recently bears were partly or completely unprotected around the park, and bears that made seasonal migrations in to the park to the dumps were often killed when they left. We are not certain what effects this killing had on the entire population). As late as 1929 the superintendent commented "the bear population of Yellowstone seems to have reached a point where they are somewhat of a nuisance."

In 1931 bear damage cases totalled 209, and in 1932 they hit an all-time peak of 451. Partly in response to these alarming totals and the

A black bear trapped for shipment to a zoo, 1922. N.P.S. photo.

growing number of human injuries, the Branch of Research and Education suggested that dump feeding be reconsidered. Not only were dumps unhealthy for bears and a violation of park principles, they were no longer necessary for the park:

> The bear show has been one of the greatest assets of the national parks. However, it has served its greatest purpose in the period when bringing the people to an appreciation of the wonderful things to be seen and done in the parks was of prime importance. Now that the popularity of their values is established and their place secure, it may

105

be necessary to modify the old practices in the interests of the welfare of both people and bears.[11]

The idea was to have wild animals in a wild setting, independent of man's influence. "The sight of one bear under natural conditions is more stimulating than close association with dozens of bears," the report concluded.

Some Park Service officials disagreed, but in some ways the park had already begun to respond to the problem. Live-trapping techniques, for removing bears to isolated parts of the park or to zoos, were refined. Public viewing at dumps was restricted after 1931 to Old Faithful and Canyon, and after 1935 to Canyon. In 1937 it was reported that there was not enough parking space for the 500 to 600 cars that appeared every evening near the feeding grounds, and that as many as 70 grizzlies could be viewed on a good night.

Management was still ineffective. It has been noted that years of frequent bear-caused injuries were usually followed by increased bear removals, so that really little more was accomplished than temporary easing of the nuisance.[12] Starting in 1938, food at the Canyon dump was reduced to disperse some of the grizzlies to other, non-visible dumps in the park. In 1942 greatly reduced visitation due to the war allowed the park to not reopen the Canyon public feeding grounds. Dumping (and bear-feeding), combined with incineration, continued at several sites out of public view. That year eighty-three bears were killed in the park by officials; fifty-five blacks and twenty-eight grizzlies. No doubt some were drawn into developed areas by shortages at the dumps, but there also seemed to have been a smaller crop of favored natural foods that year.[13] A "ten-year average" of thirty-three bears killed (total, both species) was estimated for 1931 to 1941. The problem was getting worse, and would erupt anew at the end of the war.

Also in 1942, Miss Martha Hansen, 45, of Twin Falls, Idaho, was mauled in the Old Faithful Campground on the night of August 22. She died on August 27, and two years later President Roosevelt approved payment of $1,894.95 to her family (the species of bear responsible, a "large brown bear" by description, is in doubt). The superintendent noted "this is the first relief bill of record due to an injury to a park visitor by a bear." Actually, at least one previous House bill had been introduced, in 1929, giving "relief" amounting to $10,000 to Margaret Constable, "for injuries received by reason of bear bites while visiting

Bear damage to a car top, Fishing Bridge, 1932. N.P.S. photo.

Hundreds of people gather every night at the Canyon feeding grounds in the 1930s. N.P.S. photo.

Yellowstone National Park," but this was not a fatality. I imagine it was referring to the black bear injuries that were so common, but I do not know for certain.[14] At the time of the Hansen fatality, Congress openly criticized the Park Service for failing to solve the bear problem. The Park Service responded that it could not solve any problems until Congress gave it adequate funding to do so.

Bear study progressed between 1916 and 1940 in Yellowstone, but only through brief, informal studies by park naturalists, who wrote many accounts of the bears in the park's newsletter and occasionally published stories in magazines. In 1925 Skinner's *Bears in the Yellowstone* appeared, a rambling narrative of his many years of experience with park bears. Pleasant enough reading, and full of curious and entertaining tidbits about bear life, it apparently contributed little of use to management.

As much concern as bears were, their importance to wildlife experts could not compare with that of the Yellowstone elk, whose population, it was believed, was dreadfully out of kilter with its environment. Thus serious research projects, such as William Rush's in the 1920s and Murie's coyote study in the 1930s, were aimed at understanding that problem. Research was needed, yes, but only so much could be afforded.

At last, in 1943, Olaus Murie undertook an honest-to-goodness field research project for the bears. He learned much about their food habits, and determined that the bears, which administrators seemed to feel were so numerous because of the dump food, could survive quite nicely on natural foods. He further stated that driving bears away from food was no answer so long as the food remained available. He encouraged experimenting with bearproofing, especially the use of electricity, and made many useful comments about bear behavior in campgrounds.[15]

And here a great opportunity passed. With substantial scientific evidence to support them, the Park Service might have capitalized on the reprieve of the war years with a massive sanitation campaign, so that when the visitors returned bear feeding would be much less common. They might have, that is, had they not been financially paralyzed by war shortages. As it was, the service could not even brace itself adequately for the hordes, who, after all, were the heart of the problem. Again and again, the issue came back to the public, and the overwhelming need to make them understand that it was unhealthy, unnatural, illegal . . . that it was wrong to do the one thing they most wanted to do in Yellowstone—feed the bears.

Chapter 15

1946-1967:
Crisis and Response

A recreation boom occurred at the close of World War II. The national parks, still struggling along on paltry old budgets, responded by falling apart. Everywhere, visitor services and facilities were neglected in the most serious crisis the service had ever faced. Finally, in 1954-1955, a bold new program, Mission 66, was inaugurated, to upgrade park facilities and find ways to respond to increasing (1,000,000 in 1948; 2,000,000 in 1965) numbers of visitors. New visitor centers, employee housing, and all manner of other structures and improvements were built, in an effort that has since been seen by many in the conservation community as a mistake because it simply made the parks more usable by more people, sometimes at the cost of important habitat and other values. But the Park Service, faced with both increasing public visitation and the embarrassment of their existing facilities, saw Mission 66 in a more positive light, as a way to help them serve their growing public; remember that it was less than 30 years earlier that Mather and Albright were firmly convinced that their little agency's only salvation lay in getting more people to the parks. "To conserve the scenery and the natural and historic objects. . . ." The challenge grew imponderable.

Bear research did not resume. Yellowstone was the subject of continued study concerning elk, which had become its major wildlife problem, but the service spent little on other projects. As in earlier years, park naturalists and rangers gathered what information they could, but this was fragmented progress at best. It was not until 1959 that independent researchers, providing most of their own funding, began to study Yellowstone's grizzly bears.

A 1961 photograph of an all-too-common sight in those days: a grizzly bear making itself at home in a park campground, in this case at Old Faithful. N.P.S. photo.

In 1960 a new set of bear management guidelines went into effect, generally aimed at doing more efficiently what had been done in the past; avoid having too many black bears along the road, stop roadside feeding, and educate visitors. The approach was more systematic, involving more training for personnel in bear capturing techniques (drug-firing guns were now being used) and park management, and record-keeping was improved. Despite these things, the basic problem remained: too much food was still available, and management was still a holding action, trying only to keep the problem at a tolerable level.

In 1963 the Advisory Committee to the National Park Service on Research, while making a service-wide study, was "shocked to learn that the research staff (including the chief naturalist and field men in natural history) was limited to ten people and that the Service budget for natural history research was $28,000—the cost of one campground comfort station."[1]

That same year a far more famous report appeared, one that is still discussed and debated today: "Wildlife Management in the National Parks," prepared by the Secretary's Advisory Board on Wildlife Management. The report, known commonly as the "Leopold Report" after the board's chairman A. Starker Leopold, was a major step toward restoration and preservation of natural ecosystems in the parks.[2] The board recommended that park biotic communities should be maintained in as near a primitive state as practical, keeping always in mind that human use would prevent achievement of perfect primitiveness.

The report has been the subject of endless debate. A full spectrum of interest groups have emerged, each promoting some approach to managing parks. These range from intensive, highly manipulative management to achieve some static vignette, to nearly complete removal of human influence from the setting to allow the natural processes to make their own choices. I can think of no other document in national park history that has been used (and sometimes misused) to justify so many different viewpoints on Yellowstone management. It contained plenty of language to encourage the pro-manipulators as well as the hands-off enthusiasts, and is still invoked frequently by proponents of some viewpoint or other.

As it would turn out, however, though Starker Leopold, the chief author of the document did believe that there were plenty of times that human intervention was necessary to protect important values in a given park, he generally sided with a more hands-off philosophy in Yellowstone management in the years between the writing of the report and his death in 1983.

Starker was amused by the weight the report eventually was given in park management deliberations, saying that he would have paid a little more attention to writing it carefully if he'd known it was going to have such a long reach.

But he sold its quality, both as careful thinking and as durable prose, a little short when he said that. It contains many splendid statements of principle. For example, in recognizing that it would not always be possible to achieve or restore a fully "primitive" setting in a park that might have been affected in many ways by European man, the report still held up a high goal:

> If the goal cannot be fully achieved it can be approached. A reasonable illusion of primitive America could be recreated.

111

In recent years the most interesting discussions of this mission have involved the extent to which the parks are to preserve some particular state of primitiveness: the alternatives include the condition of a park the day it was established, or when it was first visited by Europeans, or by simply letting nature do what it wants. The tendency in Yellowstone has been to recognize that it is more or less impossible to exactly re-create any past state of nature, and that there is much more to be learned and enjoyed by letting the natural system function as it will. This is an inordinately involved issue, one I explore in some depth in another book, *Mountain Time*, and that has been explored by many other writers as well.[3] For the purposes of the present book, it is enough to say that bear management has offered us an interesting case study in the challenges of natural area management; some of the issues that were probably not even guessed at by the writers of the Leopold Report will be considered in later chapters.

Of more immediate interest was another recommendation of the report, one echoed by the committee on research mentioned earlier: the Park Service needed to do a lot more ecological homework. Furthermore, the Leopold Report urged that this "mission-oriented research" (that is, research aimed at solving specific resource management issues) should be conducted by the Park Service; it was not believed that independent researchers or researchers from other agencies would necessarily have an appreciation for the Park Service's unusual mission of preservation. The issue of independent researchers and their supposed lack of appreciation of park goals is part of the next chapter; Leopold and his fellow board members were prescient in anticipating problems.

So by the mid-1960s a general goal had emerged, to study the natural resource issues and at the same time attempt to restore conditions to as primitive a state as possible. In Yellowstone that meant many things. When Jack Anderson became superintendent in 1967, he faced a raft of resource issues that were either already hot or showed signs of getting that way. The park's fish populations were in awful condition, the great trout population of Yellowstone Lake having become totally collapsed by excessive harvest. Elk management was constantly a political problem; the public was outraged over Park Service efforts to keep the herd down to what was at that time considered a "healthy" size by killing or trapping thousands of elk (the meat went to Indian reservations, the live animals were used to restock elk ranges elsewhere in the country). The park was about to embark on a natural fire policy that would reverse an eighty-year program that had suppressed all wildfires and had thereby had untold effects on the dynamics of the natural ecosystem. The centennial of Yellowstone was approaching (1972), and the park would host an international conference of park managers and would be in a world-wide spotlight. The resource, what with the elk problems, the wrecked fishery, and the bears living on garbage and roadside handouts, was not a showcase item. Visitation was climbing, and the roads, developments, and backcountry were showing the wear. Anderson's mission was to do some serious housecleaning, aimed at the restorations recommended by the Leopold Report. People may never stop arguing over whether or not he did it right.

But as far as the bears were concerned, Anderson's deliberations had an additional element. It was apparent, after the 1967 grizzly-caused deaths of two girls in Glacier National Park, that bears were a spectacularly sensitive subject. A bear mauling was big news. It was, actually, big news because it was so rare; there were only two bear-caused deaths to that time in Yellowstone's history. It was much rarer than several other categories of fatalities in Yellowstone, but it was proving to have great media appeal. It was clear, in the excitement and aftermath of the grizzly-caused deaths in Glacier, that 1) there was an audience out there anxious to hear about bear maulings, and 2) it was politically unwise to be "in charge" of a grizzly bear that killed someone.

Meanwhile there was already underway a landmark study of the Yellowstone grizzly, a study that would have great importance, not only for the information it gained but for the controversy that grew out of it.

113

Chapter 16

The Grizzly Bear
Controversy Begins

*I*n the summer of 1959 a small team of scientific investigators, led
by Dr. John Craighead, initiated an ecological study of the
Yellowstone grizzly bear. Dr. Craighead was part of the
Montana Cooperative Wildlife Research Unit, a professor of
bioecology at Montana State University, and an employee of the U.S.
Fish and Wildlife Service. Funding for the study, which lasted more
than ten years, came from many sources: The National Geographic
Society, the Boone and Crockett Club, the New York Zoological
Society, the National Science Foundation, the U.S. Fish and Wildlife
Service (then called the Bureau of Sport Fisheries and Wildlife), the
Philco-Ford Foundation, the National Park Service, the Atomic
Energy Commission, and the Environmental Research Institute. The
funding totalled, at last, more than one million dollars.

The goals of the study were ambitious:

1. To study the population dynamics of grizzlies, determining
population density, sex and age composition, breeding age,
reproductive capacity, mortality rate, and population turnover.

2. To determine home ranges, daily and seasonal movements
and relate these to food habits, family composition and population
density.

3. To determine carrying capacity and habitat requirements and
relate these to food abundance, population density or structure and
hibernation sites.

4. To investigate the role of the grizzly as a predator and the
effect, if any, it may have on regulating the population of elk and
other large prey species within a national park.

Craighead Team members weighing and otherwise measuring a grizzly bear. N.P.S. photo.

The last goal was deleted from the study as of the 1964 project report, but the others stuck. It was a project of enormous promise.

Working primarily with grizzlies that frequented the park's several dumps, the Craighead team launched their study. They pioneered radiotracking techniques, field aging techniques, and effective systems for ear-tagging bears for field identification (using variously colored plastic streamers). Once techniques were proven, they tracked bears to dens, recorded age-sex ratios and mortality rates, determined ranges, observed social behavior, and gathered tremendous amounts of information. Theirs was the first major study of grizzly bears, and it remains one of the most exhaustive. Practically every bear study, whether of black, grizzly, or polar bears, that has followed has been indebted to the Craigheads, about whom other bear biologists have said, "They taught us how."

Over the course of eleven years they marked more than 260 animals. In eight years they made "48 instrumentations of 23 different grizzly bears,"[1] attaching radio-collars to them and accumulating over 1,000 tracking days of data. Because of their scientific work and their related work in filming and popular writing, John Craighead and his brother Frank, at that time a professor of ecology at the State University of New York at Albany, became internationally known as grizzly bear authorities. Now and then throughout their study, however, it was evident that all was not well between the Craigheads and the National Park Service. There were occasional misunderstandings and the sort of personality conflicts one would expect, but there was, from the very beginning, potential for more.

As I've already suggested, the Park Service had never taken its scientific responsibilities in Yellowstone as seriously as some wished it would. Extended scientific research on bears had been slight before the Craigheads began their work, and it seems that little thought was given to the terms of the research agreement that was set up between the team and the service. In its earliest terms, the cooperative agreement between the Montana Cooperative Wildlife Research Unit, as represented by John Craighead, and the Park Service had specified that one result of the study was to be a set of management suggestions prepared by the scientists for the use of the Park Service. According to the 1962 version of the agreement, these were called a "management plan." The provision for this management plan was deleted from agreements between the team and the Park Service after 1964, probably because the Park Service was growing more sensitive about its own responsibilities toward resource management. The Leopold Report of 1963 had specified that management-oriented research should be conducted by Park Service scientists, and perhaps park administrators felt they were giving away too much authority to the Craigheads.

Legally, they might have been. Researchers who work in parks are routinely—almost invariably—encouraged to advise managers on management, and the managers would be foolish not to take advantage of such expertise, but directing independent researchers to actually formulate policy was another thing. At the time that the "management plan" provision was removed from the agreement, there was no apparent dissatisfaction from any party, but it would eventually become clear that sufficient understanding of just what the scientists were to give the park had not been achieved. Their role in relation to management was never adequately clarified.[2]

The Park Service benefited from this study in many ways even before its results were widely published. The Craighead team taught park personnel how to trap and handle bears, and often assisted in the routine handling of problem bears. If their presence in the park was to become something of a problem for the Park Service eventually, it was also quite an advantage at times.

By the time Jack Anderson became superintendent there was widespread sentiment against any unnatural food sources for bears, and pressure was mounting to close the dumps. The dumps had been the center of focus for the Craighead study, of course, and the Craigheads were far more knowledgeable about the park's bears than the park's own managers, and so it came about that the Craigheads put together a report in 1967 entitled "Management of Bears in Yellowstone National Park." It was not a polished, final report with full presentation and interpretation of data (which they were still gathering); it was instead a sort of interim document, designed to advise the Park Service on the basis of the great amount of information that had been gathered to that point.[3]

This report was to become the subject of intense debate and magnificent confusion over the next four or five years, so it is useful to take a look at some of its major points. Already, by 1967 and 1968, an adversary relationship was underway, but here at the beginning, before the controversy got too hot, we can get a look at some of the issues that underlay the later bitterness and hostility. I'll summarize a few of the Craighead's points, and follow each one with the Park Service's response. However much you may have read about this controversy, some of this may be new to you; a great many of the journalists who followed this story never bothered to sort out the scientific and philosophical problems from the more colorful "personality" sort of news that is evidently more fun (and certainly easier) to write.

1. The Craigheads were quick to point out that this report was not really a research report. Their sense of urgency led them to present their summary and suggestions before all the data was worked up, indeed before the study was even completed: ". . . though unorthodox,

117

this procedure will permit administrators and wildlife managers to make immediate use of the information presented."

The Park Service, which now had biologists of their own in place in the park, under Chief Biologist Glen Cole, and which had the report reviewed as well by scientists in Washington, was publicly uncomfortable with management recommendations that were not supported by scientific data. They became even more uncomfortable with them when they saw to what extent the Craigheads differed from them in just how to manage the park. They must also have been uncomfortable for at least two other reasons: one, that they had specifically deleted from their working agreement with the Craigheads the provision for the report the Craigheads had produced; and two, that they had not made clear the terms of that agreement long before.

2. The Craigheads had learned that Yellowstone Park's grizzlies were not truly "park" bears. The grizzlies wandered over an area of some 5 million acres, of which the park was only half. The Craigheads recommended that a single unified management program be established for the grizzlies throughout the Yellowstone area, with full cooperation between the various state and federal agencies that would be involved.

Curiously, the earliest I can find this recommendation in the record it was made by a Park Service official, Gordon Fredine, in 1960.[4] But in 1967 the Park Service paid little attention to this recommendation. Eventually, over the course of the next fifteen years, just such interagency cooperation would become political reality.

3. The Craigheads were concerned about the welfare of the grizzly population. They were convinced that the dumps added enough to the nutritional budget of the bears to be an important part of their survival. They estimated that the average size of the population, based on their dump censuses, was 174 animals, and they believed that the population should continue to receive some nutritional supplement if its longterm welfare was to be assured. At the heart of their discussion was a zoning plan for the park, one which would limit access to various key wildlife habitats in the park as researchers and administrators saw fit, thus allowing managers to "manipulate and control animal populations with optimum efficiency."

The Park Service doubted that the grizzlies needed the dumps. In fact it seems that Glen Cole and Jack Anderson were confident the bears did not need them, and that they believed the Craigheads were underestimating the park's ability to feed bears naturally. After all, they reasoned, Yellowstone had been feeding grizzly bears adequately for many years before whites arrived. In this case they were disagreeing with the Craigheads' scientific conclusions. They went on to disagree with the Craigheads on philosophical grounds as well, saying that what the Leopold Report was suggesting was a natural population, not an artificially manipulated one. The new direction in the Park Service was toward returning parks to as near a natural state as possible, and the Craighead proposal seemed unnecessarily manipulative.

This difference was largely lost on those reporting the controversy, by the way. Most journalists zeroed in on a later step in the Craighead-Park Service disagreement, the debate over whether the dumps should be closed quickly or slowly, and were unaware that in the first place the Craigheads didn't think the dumps should be closed at all.

4. In fact, the Craigheads recommended that if the dumps were to be closed that the Park Service should bolster grizzly bears' food with surplus elk and bison. They believed that the dumps kept the grizzlies concentrated in a few isolated areas during peak visitor seasons, thus decreasing the chances of human-bear encounters, and they encouraged the Park Service to find ways to continue that arrangement for the benefit of both bears and people. If the Park Service didn't feel comfortable providing carcasses, the Craigheads recommended that at least some dumps be left open.

Here again a philosophical and scientific gap—some would say chasm—had appeared between the two sides. By 1967 Glen Cole was beginning to suspect that the notion of "surplus" animals was a fallacy of some sort. The elk management controversy, having simmered for so many years, had become a hot national issue, and the Park Service was compelled to reconsider some sixty years or more of preconceptions upon which the concept of surplus elk had been based. It was not an atmosphere in which a proposal to kill elk to feed bears was likely to be received hospitably, and within a few years additional historical research by Cole and other park biologists would convince them that the "surplus" concept was out of place entirely in Yellowstone, that nature did not "overproduce" animals in Yellowstone for the convenience of management needs.

Whether or not the dumps kept the bears and people apart was a tough question, one the Park Service wasn't prepared to answer completely, not having access to the data gathered by the Craigheads. But even had that data been available, hindsight tells us

that neither the Park Service nor the Craigheads could have conclusively won that argument. Almost twenty years later there is still disagreement over just what a dump does to bears, whether it conditions
them to lose their fear of all humans even if they see very few humans
at the dump. One would think that the Craigheads' judgment on this
question should have been the best in the world, but Cole and other
Park Service people disagreed. Yellowstone was only one of several
parks with dumps, and those parks had a wide experience with bears.
It was hard to convince Park Service people, even the most scientific,
that a dump was a good thing for bears or people.

5. As I have said, the Craigheads suggested that if the dumps
must be closed it be done gradually, so that the bears could adjust to
finding other food sources after several decades of partial
dependence on garbage. They were worried not only about bear
nutrition but about a sudden dispersal of bears to developed areas in
and outside of the park.

The Park Service was inclined to disagree, but accepted the
recommendation. At first, in 1968 and 1969, the amounts of food were
reduced rather than eliminated. I can save you some suspense on this
one and tell you that it never has become clear which approach would
have worked better. The Craighead study eventually published most
of its data, but never proved that a slow closure was preferrable. The
Park Service decided on abrupt closure in 1970, not liking the way the
slow closure was going, and though the abrupt closure did indeed
disperse bears there is no way of knowing now if abrupt closure did
more or less harm to the grizzly bear population than gradual closure
would have.

6. The Craigheads encouraged a far more systematic bear
management program. Record keeping was lax, bear management
was not as high a priority as it needed to be, and personnel needed
more training.

There were probably some Park Service people offended by this
kind of talk, but it was in good part true. Some rangers might have had
a longer experience with bears than the Craigheads, but most didn't.
The Park Service as an agency does not have a good record for caring
for its administrative paperwork, and it took several years for the park
to develop first-class records regarding bear management. This
record-keeping problem would later come back to haunt the park. At
the peak of the controversy journalists would point out the bear-
management records were incomplete, implying that records were
intentionally lost or altered. What was much more likely (and I base
this on my experience as park archivist for several years in the mid-

1970s) was that some personnel just didn't care about keeping records in the first place and did a lousy job.

7. The Craigheads urged the Park Service to improve visitor education so that people knew what to do and what not to do around bears.

The Park Service would certainly have agreed. The problem faced by all researchers and managers is in good part public ignorance of the resource's needs. The challenge is a formidable one, though, and has never adequately been addressed by the Park Service. Indeed, I doubt that the agency alone could ever perform the public relations miracle of explaining to 2-1/2 million people annually what a wild bear is for.

8. The Craigheads suggested that the black bears should be "managed to provide maximum visitor viewing with a minimum of incidents." Based on past records, the Craigheads estimated that an annual control kill of about twenty-eight bears should be appropriate to keep the roadside black bears visible but not too troublesome. At the same time, they recommended that the no-bear-feeding rule be vigilantly enforced.

Here was a case of total philosophical disagreement. Park Service administrators had a goal of wildness for the black bears; they disapproved of roadside begging as a betrayal of the principles of the National Park Service Act. If roadside feeding was stopped and the bears redistributed in the backcountry, control kills should drop to almost zero. Probably most puzzling to the Park Service was the Craigheads' suggestion that black bears not be fed along the road and yet remain visible for public viewing. Earlier generations of Park Service officials had expressed that same idea, that somehow the bears would stay there even if you didn't let people feed them. By the 1960s it was clear to managers that either you had bear-feeding along roads or you didn't. If you didn't you didn't have bears along the roads at all. They wouldn't stay unless fed.

9. The Craigheads urged that additional research be done, both by them and by others, to refine our understanding of the ecological relationships of park wildlife.

In principle the Park Service agreed, though obviously they would prefer to have the most important research projects, those that would bear directly on management decisions, done by Park Service scientists rather than by independent ones. Research was on the increase in the late 1960s, including a black bear study initiated in 1965 at the suggestion of the Craigheads. But very soon the Craigheads' research would itself become an object of controversy.

So there they were, already drawing the lines that would harden rapidly by 1970. The Craigheads had the scientific expertise, and they believed that their data, though largely unpublished, supported their recommendations. The Park Service not only wanted to see the data, they energetically disagreed with some directions the Craigheads wanted to go no matter how much data the Craigheads had. It is ironic that with so many major differences between them, so many philosophical gaps between their goals for the park, the controversy should center almost totally upon one topic—the dumps.

The Craighead study had revealed many things about the behavior and movements of grizzly bears that used dumps. From their study they certainly could have made many persuasive predictions of what would happen to the bears when the dump food is no longer available. The Park Service, however, concluded that for the Craigheads to go an additional step and suggest that one schedule of closure would cause less potential for bear-human conflict than another was to display excessive optimism in the usefulness of the data gathered during their study.

Past experiences in the Park Service dumps varied. The case of the 1941 closure of the Canyon dump, mentioned earlier, has been used to prove that bears disperse quickly into developments and camps when denied garbage. Record high numbers of both grizzly and black bears were killed the year after the dump was closed, and without question some portion of these were bears looking for another source of easy food. But the comparison is not that simple. The 1942 dispersal was accelerated by an apparent shortage of natural foods that year, which no doubt kept the bears on the move.[5] Furthermore, visitation was way down because of the war, so there was less human food available at any source, in or outside the park. World War II personnel shortages may also have complicated the situation, though we don't know how many personnel killed more bears that year just because it was simpler than chasing them out of campgrounds. In any event, the situation was not similar enough to the planned dump closures of the late 1960s for comparisons to be especially trustworthy.

There were few other examples to go by. One was in Glacier National Park, where in the 1960s the Many Glacier dump had been closed with no apparent ill effects on bears or people, but grizzly ecology is different in Glacier; the comparison is not a very safe one. There was only one known example of a gradual reduction of garbage at a dump, and it too was in Glacier, where the slow closure resulted in an apparent increase in bear problems.[6]

More than relying on any precedents, the Park Service objected to gradual dump closure in principle because it would give just that many more generations of cubs the opportunity to learn to like human foods and because it would concentrate the bears during periods of increasing garbage shortage, thus increasing the risk of bear-caused deaths among bears. These objections were essentially conjectural, but the Park Service found them more persuasive than the Craigheads' opposing conjectures.

One popular misconception that cropped up here at the beginning, and still reappears now and then, is that the Craigheads believed that the bears would starve to death without the dumps. Journalists jumped on this oversimplification, conjuring up images of faint (or bloodthirsty) grizzly bears wandering across some ecological desert in search of a little nourishment. The Craighead study had amply demonstrated that the park produced a great variety of natural foods, that indeed the bears found food to support themselves for two months in the spring before garbage showed up at the dump and again in the fall for two months after the garbage supply disappeared. The Craigheads were concerned that the loss of this nicely located food source would disperse bears in search of other easy food sources, thus causing more bear mortalities and possible human injuries. They were further concerned that in the long run the natural food supply of the park was not sufficient to maintain the population at its present level, and that eventually the population could decline dangerously, but that is a different proposition from hungry bears.

Between 1967 and 1971 the availability of Craighead data on the dumps became an issue itself. Anderson wanted to see the data that would support the Craigheads' recommendation. Letters were exchanged, some fairly impatient, about this data, and soon it became a hopelessly confused part of the public controversy. Journalists knew only that the Craigheads were the ones with all the data, and that the Craigheads believed their data supported their recommendation that the dumps be closed gradually. The Park Service complained that the data was not forthcoming. The Craigheads were, however, publishing some of their findings, and sending various publications along to the park.

Somewhere in here, the data in question, specifically the material that might support gradual dump closure, became mixed up in the public mind with all data. The result was that the Craigheads and their growing band of supporters would say that the Park Service was receiving Craighead data and was ignoring it. They were, indeed, receiving Craighead data, but none of it was useful in proving that the dumps should be closed slowly. As long as the disagreement over the closure of the dumps went on, it went on without that key data materializing.

Even without the data, however, the Craigheads were in the better position. Who knew better than they how to project the most likely behavior of this population of bears? Certainly nobody in the Park Service knew, and in fact there was no one in the world with their scientific credentials as grizzly bear authorities. Anderson and his staff, partly because they had a different philosophical goal for the park, and partly because they were not impressed with the Craighead argument, were skeptical about a slow closure of the dumps. They were put in the uneasy position of disagreeing with world authorities, and that position cost them dearly in the growing controversy over bear management. The philosophical differences between Anderson and Craigheads were totally lost in the controversy, and the issue of data availability was soon buried under additional layers of debate over new interpretations of the data that did surface.

I must say that the Park Service contributed its fair share to this initial confusion over data. I confine my discussion of the controversy in this book to material drawn from sources I can document: correspondence, publications, reports, and so on. That way, whatever else I may add to the dialogue at least I'm not adding to the misquotations that seemed to plague the story. But here I want to make an exception, and say that when I arrived to work in Yellowstone as a ranger-naturalist in 1972 it was widely thought among Park Service employees that the Craigheads had never submitted any data to the Park Service throughout the study. That is simply not true.

In fact, the Craigheads had produced numerous annual reports by 1967. They had also published a few articles and more formal papers. I know from my review of correspondence in the park archives that at least some of this material was received by the superintendent's office.

The largest remaining dump in the park was at Trout Creek, several miles southwest of Canyon Village. In 1968 the Park Service began to separate the garbage there, dumping only edible material in an apparent attempt to follow the Craighead suggestion of phasing out the dumps.[7] In June of 1969, Glen Cole reported to the superintendent on how the process seemed to be going. He started by responding to new complaints fromFrank Craighead that the dumps were being closed too fast:

> First, after only one year of separating cans and burnables from "edible" garbage as the first step in phasing out the Trout Creek dump, I don't know how we could go any slower. An unforseen result of this process appears to be that we have actually reached the final stage sooner than expected. The relatively few bears that will use the dump in full daylight are apparently able to clean up the edible garbage when it is not mixed into a large volume of burnable trash and cans. This could be part of the reason greater numbers of grizzly frequented campgrounds in 1968, but other factors, such as high rodent numbers, non-bearproof garbage cans, etc., could have contributed.

Here is one of the apparently endless number of little twists in this story. By changing the way the edible garbage was distributed, without even changing the amount, managers also changed how the bears would use it. Would the nutrition thus reach fewer bears? What would the others do?

Or, what did they do anyway? It became a common presumption that grizzly bears only frequented the campgrounds and other park developments after the dumps were closed, when in fact grizzly bears had been fixtures near and in those developments for a many decades. As Cole observed in the same memorandum quoted above, ". . . records show there have been years when substantial numbers of grizzly frequented campgrounds despite the full-scale operation of dumps. Possibly some relationship to the abundance or scarcity of alternative natural foods is involved with some animals, but it also appears that we may have developed a segment of the bear population which habitually uses human garbage instead of moving into more remote spruce-fir and subalpine regions during the summer." In Chapter 8, I quoted bear biologist Dave Mattson when he described the bear's food habits as "variation on variation on variation." In 1969, managers were tinkering with an already amazingly complex and dynamic bear diet, and even the best informed people could not be confident of what would happen next.

In the meantime the Craighead team was proceeding with the wrapup of its study. In January of 1969 John Craighead reported that the project was 95 percent complete, and that the "study should be continued on a reduced basis as the principal objectives have been realized."[8]

There was at this time considerable discussion between Craighead and Anderson over just what work should continue in the park, centering around the issue of color-marked wildlife. The Park Service wanted what they called "conspicuous" markings, such as ear tags and streamers, removed from the various elk and bears that had been tagged over the years. Anderson felt that he was getting too many complaints from photographers and other visitors who wanted to see naturally occurring animals. Craighead pointed out that very few visitors ever saw grizzly bears, that very few elk had been marked or radio-collared, and that the marked grizzly bears could be of great value to Park Service managers for years to come in monitoring bear movements. Both remained firm in their positions, but of course Anderson had the power to rule in the matter.[9]

As I look back on this, Anderson's conviction that the tags would be unappealing has always puzzled me. He was especially concerned that the park be a showplace of natural area management during the many celebrations and conferences associated with the park's centennial in 1972, but it has always seemed to me that a tagged or collared grizzly bear is just so much proof of management doing a good job by relying on scientific research for direction. Obviously, Anderson saw it differently, and this comes down to an esthetic judgment over what a park should look like. As it turned out, Yellowstone's grizzlies had a great many more collars to wear in the future, whatever happened in 1972.

Most important in John Craighead's communications to Anderson in the spring of 1969, I think, was a tone of restrained triumph that a monumental research project had been completed. In April, Craighead sent Anderson a letter summarizing the most important achievements of the project and listing forthcoming scientific reports that would result from the work.[10] It's too bad, for all concerned, that the Craigheads and the park never got to bask in the glory of this achievement together.

The disagreement over the dump-closing schedule was a topic of a meeting of the Secretary of the Interior's Natural Sciences Advisory

At feeding time, many grizzlies would gather at the Trout Creek dump. This dump was not reopened after 1970, and the dispersal and redistribution of bears that had used it is still a subject of debates over how much the bears needed the garbage. N.P.S. photo.

Committee in Yellowstone in the fall of 1969. The committee reviewed the available literature on dumps, and listened to all viewpoints. The Craigheads presented their recommendations in a two-hour session that included charts and graphs of data they had gathered. In a move that must have seemed odd to many at the time, and that signalled just how bad things had already gotten in the disagreement, the Craigheads refused to make their presentation until all Park Service personnel left the room.[11]

The secretary's committee was composed of A. Starker Leopold (Chairman), Stanley Cain, Charles Olmsted, and Sigurd Olson. Olson was ill at the time of this meeting and did not attend. Their report first summarized the goals of bear management:

1. To maintain populations of grizzly and black bears at levels that are sustainable under natural conditions as part of the native fauna of the park.

2. To plan the development and use of the Park so as to minimize conflicts and unpleasant or dangerous incidents with bears.

3. To encourage bears to lead their natural lives with a minimum of interference.

Though the committee made a number of recommendations involving research and management, it did not specifically side either way on the dump-closing issue. They agreed that the dumps must be closed, but also believed that there was no way of knowing whether one schedule of dump closing would cause more or fewer bear problems than another. They were, in short, unpersuaded by the Craigheads' presentation:

> Unfortunately, prognosticating how garbage fed grizzlies will respond to deprivation depends on judgement rather than data.[12]

The Committee's report left Anderson free to proceed as he saw fit with the dump closures. Committee members had not energetically supported rapid closure, but they had agreed with his opinion that Craighead data could not be applied to predicting grizzly behavior when the dumps were closed. In October of 1969 the Rabbit Creek dump near Old Faithful was closed and covered over, not to be opened the following year. In March of 1970 the committee met again, in Portland, Oregon, to review progress in bear management. After a briefing on the closure of Rabbit Creek and the closure of the Trout Creek dump, scheduled for the next fall, the committee approved the program:

> We feel that you are implementing the program in the manner and spirit of the mutually agreed plan.[13]

Trout Creek was the big one. All the other sizeable dumps in the park had been closed, leaving only Trout Creek and a few outlying dumps that would continue to cause problems near the park for the better part of the 1970s (the last, at Cooke City, was finally closed in 1978). At Trout Creek, where so many famous grizzly bear photographs were taken (you can recognize them because the bears seem to be standing on dirt rather than in grass or weeds), hosted as many as 100 grizzly bears some days.

In the fall of 1970 Trout Creek was closed. The grizzlies, after eighty years of garbage, were on their own. Concurrently, the Park Service had intensified its public education program, was removing black bears from the roadsides, and was bear-proofing garbage cans throughout the park. Guidelines (based in good part on recommendations from the 1967 Craighead report) were established for dealing with bears that repeatedly foraged for garbage in developments: a bear that was trapped and relocated, and then returned to a development within two years could, if managers saw fit, be removed from the population either by being killed or by being shipped off to a zoo. Many bears, as it turned out, were given more than two chances, but Park Service personnel were familiar with the concept of the "incorrigible" bear, one that will return again and again and will teach its cubs to do the same. Managers were committed to removing such animals from the population.

The Trout Creek cleanup was necessary for more than esthetic reasons. The environmental movement resulted in a host of garbage-related regulations, among them Executive Order 11507, "Prevention, Control, and Abatement of Air and Water Pollution at Federal Facilities." Trout Creek dump sat astride Trout Creek, and was a violation of both air and water standards. Dumps are inherently ugly, but this one was now a violation of federal law.

While the Park Service was making all these changes, their meaning was being interpreted in many ways. Specifically, they were being called a bad idea, and Anderson and his staff were being called worse. By 1969 Frank Craighead, who would always be more vocal and bitter in his comments than his brother John, had gone public with his opposition to the park's dump closures. His accusations went beyond disagreements over science and philosophy. They even went beyond suggesting the park was incompetent. In an article in the *Jackson Hole Guide* (Wyoming), Craighead described a "deteriorating situation," and accused the Park Service of "ill-conceived procedures."

> The number of bears that have been killed has not been accurately reported. It has been stated that the objective is to immobilize grizzlies in campgrounds when the instructions have been to shoot to kill any grizzly seen. Bears that are shot and wounded, then later killed, have been described as bears that have been killed in fights with other bears.[14]

The Park Service denied these charges, and none of them have ever been proven, but here was another layer being added to the controversy, one that had nothing to do with science or philosophy. Claims like these were made frequently for the next few years. Most came from uninformed sources (all national parks have running feuds with at least some of their neighbors about something, and all live in a rumor-mill atmosphere) such as the famous "bar-stool biologists" who happily pronounce on any subject, but some continued to come from people of greater public respect, like Frank Craighead. Many were absurd, like the claims that big pits had been dug in secret places in the park and filled with the bodies of hundreds of bears. Some were more substantial, like accusations of unreported bear deaths. There was talk of a "coverup" of bear killings now and then until the late 1970s.

I can't tell you exactly what happened. I don't think anyone can. If Frank Craighead had proof that bears were killed secretly or with distorted record-keeping, he hasn't produced it yet. Not one person has come forth since 1969 with even one solid piece of evidence, such as the skull of one of these clandestinely killed bears, or an admission from one guilty ranger, or a photograph of such a killing or such a carcass. There is some informal and often quite confident remembrance— someone saw a carcass here or there and assumed it was the result of a "secret" kill, for example—but that is hardly enough evidence to justify the sort of lingering hostility that exists. It's really easy to go out in Greater Yellowstone and find people willing to claim all sorts of things have occurred. I don't doubt some of them may be telling the truth. I have yet to hear of any claims about the alleged bear purge, however, that would stand legal scrutiny.

When I was working on the first edition of this book, I talked to a local reporter who was inclined to believe these stories. His justification was that where there's smoke there's fire. I responded that anybody who has had much dealing with the Yellowstone country knows that as you travel through it, what at first might appear to be smoke turns out to be merely steam. Yellowstone issues— grizzly bears, elk, fire—have an ability to generate a great deal more heat than light. There may be something to some of these stories of secretly killed bears. I wouldn't be too surprised if there was. But I must assume, based on my reading of Yellowstone history and how any controversy immediately sheathes the truth in a protective coating of wild rumor, that a great many more bears were killed in the local saloons than in the park. Frankly, I don't think the Park Service could have successfully carried out such a secret program. There are too many people in the park at any time willing to blow the whistle, either openly or through friends, and, considering the trouble that park managers were having just keeping track of the bears, I doubt they had the wherewithal or skill to successful hide a large campaign of secret bear killings.

I can't overemphasize how quickly this controversy became almost viciously emotional, and how ripe it was for publicity. Accusations flew, and were published, but proof never appeared. This isn't to say that the Park Service was guiltless of Craighead claims, but it is to suggest that the rule of "innocent until proven guilty" did not apply to the government. Perhaps the situation was best summed up by Wyoming Game and Fish Department biologist Larry Roop, who said that reading the Craighead account of the controversy was "comparable to reading only one side of a divorce case."

But it was just this kind of uncertainty, all of these unproven and suspected things, that made the controversy such a complicated mess. It reached the point where it didn't really matter what the Park Service said it was doing; a certain percentage of their audience was conditioned to disbelieve them. This kind of atmosphere, however hard it may have been on the bears, the Park Service, and the Craigheads, was just heaven for newspaper readers and journalists, and very quickly the noise was being heard in some important political offices. And, by the time the politicians got involved, whatever hope there had ever been for calm, rational discourse was gone.

A few stereotypes developed, and may have been unavoidable. Check your own reactions to the story as I've told it so far. When I say "The Park Service did such and such," aren't you inclined to picture a monolithic federal agency acting for mysterious but probably political reasons to get the public or the press off its back? We're all suspicious of the feds now and then, with good reason, and in the early 1970s, that mood was even more hostile than usual. Washington had a coverup a week in those days. Why not in Yellowstone too?

And so it was inevitable that the Craigheads became the beleaguered independent scientists whose work was being quashed by faceless bureaucrats. Glen Cole became a scientist-puppet whose job was to produce reports that would support the dump closures. Anderson became a sort of tyrant figure, who, for reasons that never became clear, had suddenly become commited to the destruction of Yellowstone's bear population (the destruction of the bears by park personnel—by lifelong

131

professional conservationists—was puzzling; nobody was able to explain why these people would want to do such a thing). The media, as is their wont, became the heroic exposers of all this evil and injustice.

Government bureaucracies do not welcome uninvited media events. The Park Service, however right or wrong it was on any given issue, did a terrible job with public relations through the controversy; it did not really improve at getting its story out to the public until the 1980s. Cole and other park scientists published their findings in routine ways, either in technical journals or in Park Service reports, where the public doesn't see them. Anderson and his staff weathered a terrible beating in the press, and frustrated their opponents by simply going ahead with their plans despite all the negative publicity. The Craigheads, who proved to be excellent and appealing publicists, grew ever more certain that the dump closures would hurt the bears. Anderson remained confident he was on the right track, and with the backing now of the Natural Sciences Advisory Committee he moved ahead.

Chapter 17

Regrouping

*C*ooperation between the Park Service and the Craighead team ended in 1971, in yet one more action that increased the heat of the controversy. The main study was over, but the Craigheads wanted to monitor the dispersal of the bears, which would require continuation of the techniques they had developed over the eleven years of their study. By this time there is no doubt that Anderson didn't want them around anymore, and his attitude was probably shared in both the Park Service and the Bureau of Sport Fisheries and Wildlife, judging from the terms of the new agreement that the Craigheads were offered. It was a memo of understanding between the Washington office of the National Park Service and John Craighead's employer, the Bureau of Sport Fisheries and Wildlife, and it contained two unusual stipulations.

3. All oral and written statements, including, but not limited to, progress reports, popular and scientific articles and other publications, talks, and press releases prepared by the Montana Cooperative Wildlife Research Unit concerning grizzly bear research within Yellowstone National Park shall be submitted to the Director, Bureau of Sport Fisheries and Wildlife for approval prior to publication or otherwise disseminated to the public.

4. The Bureau recognizes the National Park Service as having the responsibility and authority for all management activities within Yellowstone National Park, and the Bureau will obtain the concurrence of the Director, National Park Service, prior to making any expressions relating to the management of grizzly bears within said national park.

The Craigheads said this was a restriction of academic freedom, and would not accept the arrangement. In retrospect, No. 3 seems passably reasonable, as supervisory review is a routine matter for scientists. No. 4, on the other hand, is a bit unorthodox, to say the least. Independent researchers are commonly consulted as advisors on management. A free flow of suggestion and opinion is a matter of course under these circumstances. It seems plain that one or both of the parties to the agreement believed that the Craighead team was being too outspoken.

The restriction on public statements is not a pretty one, but it is not as absolute a limitation as it might appear. The Craighead team could continue its work, and could continue to publish material of a scientific nature with only routine supervisory control. What the team could not do was publish statements about management. In principle, and according to the earlier study agreements, the team was not responsible for management actions anyway. In fact, the team worked closely with Park Service personnel, and had a very clear and obvious interest in how management was conducted. It is safe to say that many other scientists in the same situation would not accept such an agreement. On the other hand, John Craighead's supervisor, the Director of the Bureau of Sport Fisheries and Wildlife, agreed with the restriction and signed the agreement. John Craighead did not, and so the study ended.

Immediately there was reaction in the popular press. It was said the Craigheads had been railroaded out of the park, that they had been denied the right to do research, and that the park was violating academic freedom. These are all nice oversimplifications of what was actually happening. The Craighead field headquarters in the park, an old building loaned to them by the hotel company, was torn down as part of the pre-centennial cleanup. This was seen as proof that the Park Service wanted to obliterate all trace of Craighead work. There was surely no denying that the Park Service did not grieve the ending of the study.

The conclusion of the Craighead study was generally distorted by the time it reached the public. The impression given by most popular articles was that the Craighead study had been cut short, ended prematurely before its work was done. As John Craighead himself reported, the study was essentially complete by 1970. What was cut short was Craighead efforts to monitor the dispersal of the dump bears. They had been seeking to extend the original study to gather this very important new information, but they had not been kept from finishing the original study.

That said, it was still a great misfortune that the study ended when it did. There existed right then in Yellowstone the expertise and technical equipment to monitor the dispersal of at least some of the bears and to observe just how the change in food habits affected them. This information would have been priceless for managers in other areas, and it might have gone a long way toward settling some of the disputes that were then in progress in Yellowstone.

Unfortunately, the disagreement between the Park Service and the Craigheads had gone too far for even the remotest kind of cooperation. Craighead-marked bears had both color identifying tags (these were the ones Anderson objected to) and small inconspicuous ear tags that also identified the bear for record-keeping purposes. As the Park Service handled and moved bears after the dumps were closed, they removed the color tags and either left the small ear tags on or replaced them with their own, tagging as well bears not marked by the Craigheads. Of course park personnel could have used as much information on the past history of the Craighead-marked bears as they could get, but when Anderson requested such information the Craigheads refused to send it. The Craigheads probably saw refusal as a matter of holding on to valuable scientific information. Anderson probably saw it as spite. Whatever it was, it kept park personnel from acting as intelligently as they might have about individual bears because they had no way of knowing the past history of those bears.

Bear control was a hot topic in 1970 and 1971, as the Park Service stepped up efforts to remove problem bears and as agencies on lands surrounding the park became more active in dealing with their grizzlies. In 1970 Yellowstone Park personnel killed twelve grizzlies and sent eight others to zoos. Twenty-four more bears were known to have died, either from management actions or from illegal kills, in the three surrounding states, for a total of forty-four known bear deaths in one year. The next year the park killed eight and sent one to a zoo, but the surrounding states brought the total to forty-four. Eighty-eight grizzly deaths in two years, in a population that the Craigheads reported had averaged only 174 animals up to 1967, was alarming, to say the least. But by 1972 Glen Cole and his staff had developed their own set of interpretations of the bear population's status, and they were dramatically unlike those offered by the Craigheads.[1] Again, I'll summarize some of the most important ones, Craigheads first, then Cole:

Population size

The big question, after a couple years of high mortalities, was how many grizzlies are left, and are there enough to maintain the population? The Craigheads were certain that the population was now in serious trouble, and that the fact that many bears seemed to be dispersing beyond the park boundaries, where they were even more likely to be killed, was also a serious ongoing problem. In short, they believed that by 1971 too many bears had been killed already and that the Park Service must stop.

Cole postulated the existence of a large number of grizzly bears in the Yellowstone area that the Craigheads had not counted. He suggested that they were being optimistic in assuming that all the bears in the whole area used the dumps and were therefore counted by them. The Craigheads, in their 1967 report, had specified that "almost all" of the grizzlies did indeed use the dumps and get counted. Cole pointed out that the Barnes and Bray black bear study done in the late 1960s in Yellowstone had shown, first, that there were two distinct populations of black bears—beggar bears and backcountry bears—and second, that practically none of the grizzly bears that were incidentally observed by the researchers had Craighead tags. Only one of twenty-seven grizzlies observed by these researchers had a Craighead tag, when the Craigheads assumed they had marked a much larger proportion of the population than 1/27. On the basis of this difference, and on incidental observations by Cole and his staff, Cole suspected that there were 50 to 100 more bears in the Yellowstone population than the Craigheads reported. He believed, then, that this larger population could stand the strain of the increased control removals.

Injury rates

The Craigheads compared their data on human injuries by grizzlies from 1959 to the 1968-1971 period, and found that in the earlier period the average was 1.67 per year and in the latter it was 3.33. This they blamed on the dispersal of bears into developments after the dumps were closed.

Cole responded that the Craigheads did not have complete records of injuries (I must say that as a historian who has used the park's records extensively, I am more impressed with Cole's ability to sort out historical records than I am with the Craigheads'). He further objected to lumping data from 1968 and 1969 with later years, because those two years were a transitional period with limited supplies of garbage and some unsanitized developments. His injury figures, which I found convincing enough to use in the appendices of this book, showed an average injury rate in the 1960s of 4.4 per year, with an average injury rate of .7 for the period 1970—1973.

Population future

The Craigheads predicted the continued decline of the population and much more trouble in developed areas if management was not revised.

Cole thought the high kill totals of 1970 and 1971 were only temporary and that in a very short time the control kills would drop to practically nothing. He further suspected that when the bears were redistributed in the wild that more cubs would survive to adulthood, basing that suspicion on the high cub mortality reported among dump populations compared with lower cub mortality among wild populations. He further suspected that the sows might begin reproducing at an earlier age, on the average, once away from the social pressures of the dumps. This, he suggested, explained the smaller average litter size reported among park grizzlies in 1971. In the 1960s the average litter size had been 2.2 cubs; in 1971 it dropped to 1.9. He concluded that there were not fewer bear cubs, only more families of smaller average size.

As the Craigheads criticized the Park Service for unreliable scientific hypothesizing, the Park Service pointed out that Craighead data was no longer fully applicable, and had never been complete. Cole based his position on observations of grizzly bears made by a variety of his staff, most of whom did not have the Craigheads' experience or skill at recognizing individual bears. On the other hand, there were some very skilled observers on the park staff, and Cole was rigorous and unyielding in his sifting of reports of supposed grizzly sightings. The Craigheads based their position on their knowledge of a grizzly bear population under the influence of several dump food sources. Once divorced from the dumps, the bears would use their range in different ways than when they could concentrate so much attention on one dump. This change in bear habits, and the persistent Park Service suggestion that the Craigheads were underestimating the size of the population, left a cloud of uncertainty over the data gathered by the Craighead study. It was a landmark study, yes, but did it still tell us what we needed to know about the bears?

In time, some of the suggestions of both sides would prove true. The bear population, as it would turn out, did not behave as either side predicted it would, but took a sort of middle course, which may or may not tell us something about the nature of opposing positions in a controversy. That is a bit ahead of the story, though.

Bitter words continued to pass between the contestants in 1971. Anderson wrote to John Craighead to object to statements the brothers were making about park management, and to complain that the Craigheads still weren't coming across with the data on the tagged bears that the Park Service needed to help with the relocations of problem bears:

> Here we find preliminary data from park management operations presented in a less than objective or in an inaccurate manner to force your point of view on the National Park Service. You can continue to do this if you wish, but I do not think it should be under a cooperative agreement for scientific studies. We will always welcome recommendations with supporting data, but the latter has not been forthcoming. I find that criticisms are a poor substitute for information where management decisions must be made.[2]

Craighead responded by accusing Glen Cole and Anderson of violating previous agreements. He said that Cole had "simply taken over" parts of the Craighead study, and that both Cole and Anderson had ignored Craighead data and, in fact, had said they didn't believe the data when they saw it.[3] In reading over this correspondence I am struck by how often these people aren't really talking to each other. They're talking past each other. They make good points, but they were too far apart to really communicate.

Also, they have firmed up their misunderstanding over data. When Anderson said he needs more data, the Craigheads claimed they've sent him lots and that he's ignored it. He doesn't bother to specify which data, and they don't bother to ask. To Anderson, Craighead reports on the dispersal of dump bears and the high number of killed bears didn't tell him anything he didn't know. I gather from Craighead reports and from popular articles that the high mortalities of 1970 and 1971 were widely seen as proof that fast dump closure was killing more bears than slow closure would have. That's not what those high death totals prove. They only prove that a lot of bears died when the dumps were closed fast; it's still just as possible to argue that closing the dumps slowly would have killed even more bears. That's the position Anderson took.

Actually the confusion over dead bears was considerably more complicated than most participants were making it out to be. There were many unanswered questions about the grizzly bear population, some of which were almost totally conjectural but which still should have made careful thinkers cautious about pronouncing on dumps.

For example, for many years in Yellowstone the grizzly bears had been deprived of their full share of three of their most important natural food items: elk, bison, and trout. Elk and bison management had kept the populations of those animals very low for decades, and heavy fishing pressure had collapsed the Yellowstone Lake trout population by the 1960s, so that bears no longer had access to a lot of animal protein that had been available in primitive times. Had these factors reduced the bear population, and to what extent had the dumps replaced the losses? Then, as the Park Service allowed the elk, bison, and trout to recover their prehistoric abundance, how well would that replace the loss of the dumps? (I don't mind giving you a hint here; elk, bison, and trout have all become much more important bear food sources since the early 1970s.)

Or consider this one. When I worked as park archivist in the mid-1970s, I was surprised to discover how uneven the records were throughout the National Park Service years since 1916; lots of stuff I would have thought important simply didn't survive at all, and it seemed to depend on the personality of the supervisor of each little operation here and there in the park. Rangers have been good at lots of things, but bureaucracy hasn't always been one of them. But then, record-keeping, of things like injury rates, bear mortalities, and so on, greatly improved in the 1970s (partly as the Park Service developed self-defense mechanisms to anticipated criticism). How meaningful was it to compare injury rates in different periods of the park's history when in one of those periods the people responsible for keeping the records were demonstrably uninterested and in another period they were almost obsessively careful about it?

Or this. Critics of the park's bear controls in 1970 and 1971 point to the greatly increased number of control actions—trappings or killings of bears—as proof that the bears had all dispersed from the dumps and moved directly into trouble. What we have here is a dangerous oversimplification. I don't think there's any doubt that a lot of dispersal occurred, but again, the equation is complex. After 1970, rangers who for years had casually watched bears in and near campgrounds were suddenly ordered to take action any time they saw a bear. Right there is immediate certainty that more control actions will occur. As Glen Cole had already pointed out, grizzlies appeared regularly in the campgrounds even before the dumps were closed, including bears that also used the dumps. After 1970, rangers were under orders to take care of any bear in a campground. This means that, whatever the dispersal may be contributing to the problem, there will be a great many more bear actions than in the past. What with bear management practices altered so totally after 1970, it's hard to know to what extent the increase in bear killing was necessitated by a new park policy that required more bear management activity. That doesn't let the Park Service and various other agencies off the hook for killing those bears, but it does place the role of dump-food deprivation in a different light. Even if the dumps hadn't been closed, the new policy, of keeping bears out of campgrounds, would have guaranteed a lot more management actions.

These are subtle matters, not easily susceptible to conclusive analysis. But they are also important, because they reveal how many factors park managers had to consider. They deal in unaccountable variables, and conjecture, and they remove the bear management story just a little further from scientific controversy. It got removed in a big way in 1972, when Yellowstone suffered its first bear-caused human death in thirty years.

In 1971 Yellowstone celebrated an entire year without a single grizzly-caused injury, but the celebration was short. The next summer a young man named Harry Walker, from Alabama, was fatally mauled near Old Faithful by a grizzly bear. A large book could be written about this one incident (I'm surprised someone hasn't, considering the success of the book *Night of the Grizzlies*, about the two Glacier Park deaths in 1967). The following information is drawn from park records and the court proceedings.

Mr. Walker and a friend were camped in the woods not far from Old Faithful. It was an illegal camp, not near the Park Service campground. Late at night they returned from a visit to the Old Faithful development and met a grizzly bear that had found food left lying on the ground in the campsite. The bear killed Walker and his friend escaped. Walker's parents sued the government on the grounds that he had not been adequately warned of the danger, and they won an award of $87,417.67 in damages. The Park Service appealed the case and the decision was reversed. The Walkers attempted to recover damages through congressional action, as the Hansens had done in 1944, but were unable to do so.

Walker and his friend had entered the park as hitchhikers, and so they had not received the warning literature normally given to people entering the park. They were informed by an acquaintance at Old Faithful that they were camped illegally. Being from another part of the country, they apparently had no experience with camping in grizzly bear country.

The Walker case was mostly a trial of park management. Dr. Frank Craighead testified for the plaintiff, reviewing his past criticisms of park management (as early as 1970, John Craighead had predicted that a human fatality would occur from the Park Service's program). To read the Park Service's reports of this episode, Walker and his friend were clearly negligent in several ways. To read Frank Craighead's account, they did absolutely nothing wrong. What really was at issue was park bear management; Harry Walker was an opportunity to again take the case to the public, and the tragedy of his death seemed like a minor element in the story of the court case.

But Walker was like many other Yellowstone visitors. In many other places they could behave just as he did and run no risk at all. The implications of court cases like this one go far beyond personal tragedy. At stake is just how far the parks will be allowed to have a natural setting. People stumble into hot springs, and fall off of cliffs. Other people object to too many railings and boardwalks around hot springs, and barriers that obstruct their view from cliffs. There is some small portion of the visiting public that would like to remove all danger from the parks; more than one scientist has recommended that all grizzlies be removed from Yellowstone.[4]

What makes me uncomfortable about these court cases, no matter how justified any given suit might be, is that they create park policy in a judicial vacuum sometimes thousands of miles from the park. A judge with no interest in, or experience with, wilderness and national

141

parks, can have an inordinate effect on park management, if only as managers try to anticipate where they must be most careful to avoid lawsuits. That may be good legal behavior, but it doesn't seem the best way to run a wilderness. That the Park Service technically "won" the Walker case couldn't have been much comfort to them.

A second court case, in 1973, was a little more lighthearted in its entertainment value. Late that year the Fund for Animals, a Washington, D.C.-based protectionist group, filed a lawsuit against the Secretary of the Interior, the director of the National Park Service, and the park superintendent because no Environmental Impact Statement had been prepared prior to closing the dumps and changing the bear management program. The case was nearly farcical. The Park Service, which had been working on an E.I.S. anyway, was nettled because it seemed to them that closing the dumps was solving, not creating, an environmental problem, and because there never should have been dumps in the first place. In any case, when it became known that an E.I.S. was in progress, and that a review of the park's bear management program was being prepared by the National Academy of Sciences, the Fund for Animals agreed to a dismissal of their suit, agreeing also to retract some remarkably inaccurate statements they'd made in a press release about the Park Service and its management.[5]

The most important event of 1973 was the formation of an Interagency Grizzly Bear Study Team, consisting of research biologists from the Park Service, the Forest Service, the U.S. Fish and Wildlife Service, and representatives of the states of Wyoming, Montana, and Idaho. The purpose was simple: to learn about this "new" grizzly bear population that was now more or less dispersed from the dumps. Two objectives were to learn more about:

1. The status and trend of the grizzly bear population.
2. The use of habitats by bears and the relationship of land management to the welfare of the bear population.

Here at last was an agency-crossing effort that the Craigheads had espoused since at least 1967 (though they were concerned more with management than research, and weren't sure this study was all that necessary considering all the data they had already gathered), and it got off to a rocky start. Anderson, burned by his last encounter with grizzly bear research, placed severe restrictions on the team of researchers, disallowing even radiocollaring. But by 1974 the team was at work, and was quickly establishing not only the need for additional research but their ability to do it.

Richard Knight, head of the team, had his work cut out for him; the entire conservation community was waiting to see what the team would find, and was probably also waiting for the slightest opportunity to criticize those findings. Knight eventually proved to be as durable as the Craigheads, and, as we'll see later, he produced a far more exhaustive study, but it was a slow start.

It was a start that got a considerable boost in 1974 from the National Academy of Sciences. In 1973, the Secretary of the Interior, responding to the towering national controversy over grizzly management, asked the Academy to "study and evaluate data on the population of the grizzly bears in Yellowstone National Park and to make recommendations concerning the scientific and technical implications of that data." The chosen committee was chaired by a distinguished ecological scholar, Ian McTaggart Cowan.

The Committee on the Yellowstone Grizzlies, whose report appeared in 1974, reviewed a small mountain of reports and publications form the Craigheads and the Park Service. Among the most important new ones was a computer analysis of the bear population made by the Craigheads using data gathered during their study. It projected possible future bear populations depending upon management actions, and it predicted a dire future for the grizzly if the number of bears killed annually did not stay low.[6]

It's worth interrupting the narrative here to mention that at the moment this new computer report appeared, the entire controversy took on a new complexion, though I don't think many people realized it at the time. Perhaps because of continued criticisms from Glen Cole, the Craigheads had become more tolerant of the idea that perhaps they had not counted all the grizzly bears. According to this new report, they estimated that their dump censuses counted about 77% of the grizzly bears in the Yellowstone area. This is significant because up to this time there was at least one participant in the debate—the Craighead team—who was working only from "real" information, that is, from the actual number of bears they had seen in the field. The day they moved into the computer modelling arena, where their expertise was no greater than (in fact less impressive than) the expertise of many other scientists, the whole discussion moved to a new, more conjectural plane.

The Craigheads postulated the 177-bear average of their counts from 1959 to 1970 was 77.3% of the total population, which, during that period, would have been 229 animals. Cole, on the other hand, estimated that the Craighead census efficiency was only about 50%, and that there were between 319 and 364 bears in and near the park. From here on out, debates centered over how to best estimate the number of hypothetical bears, an exercise at which the Craigheads proved no more convincing than anyone else.

The committee found fault with much of the Park Service's program.[7] They stated that Cole's research program was "inadequate to provide the data essential for devising sound management policies for the grizzly bears of the Yellowstone ecosystem." They objected to restrictions placed on the Interagency Study Team, saying that "it is not possible to determine new biological parameters without re-establishing a recognizably marked element of known size in the population." This was an important step because it recognized that there was, indeed, a "new" population that could not be relied upon to behave, in terms of reproduction or distribution, as had the dump-influenced population, and that was going to have to be studied, from scratch, all over again.

They agreed, in general, with the Craigheads that "it is most probable that the grizzly population was substantially reduced" from 1968 to 1973, but they also said that "there is no convincing evidence that the grizzly bears in Yellowstone are in immediate danger of extinction."

Their reaction to Craighead work was almost as interesting as their criticism of the Park Service. Though they essentially agreed with the new Craighead population estimate (the committee used 234 as a best estimate), they criticized the Craighead computer model as too rigid. They were inclined to agree with Cole that some "compensatory processes," such as increased cub survival once the population was dispersed, had to be figured into new population projections. On the other hand, the committee admitted that they had no way of knowing yet if such processes had occurred. And yet on the other hand they were inclined to believe that the processes were going to permit the population to recover. Something for everyone, though not in every sentence.

Their recommendations for the Interagency Study Team were especially timely, and included, as already mentioned, the right to mark bears, as well as increased involvement by independent researchers and a clearer separation of the team, physically and fiscally, from Yellowstone research offices. They further recommended that the team not be headed up by an employee of the National Park Service, but by "a neutral individual acceptable to all cooperating agencies."

For the bears, the committee emphasized reducing all known bear deaths in what was now being called the Yellowstone Ecosystem to ten or less a year. There was special concern about the number of bears killed outside the park as "nuisances," bears that caused stock or other property damage. One of the strongest messages the committee sent to all participants through this report was that it was imperative to keep the number of bears killed each year as low as possible.

The response by the various parties to the committee's report was probably predictable. The press, and various supporters of the Craigheads, went right to the many specific criticisms of the Park Service and made them into headlines. The Park Service went right to the line about the bear population being in no immediate danger of extinction and felt vindicated. Being an agency with formal responsibilities in a matter of this sort, the Park Service responded specifically to the report. Cole, in a memorandum to the research files, analyzed various committee calculations, showing to his own satisfaction that their population estimates did not hold up as well as his.[8] The Park Service refused to consider having a "neutral individual" head up the Interagency Study Team on the grounds that it would "pre-empt agency management responsibilities," and further pointed out that Knight was recruited directly from the academic community to head the team.[9]

The suggestion that a Park Service head of the team would somehow be tainted must seem especially annoying to the Park Service now that Knight has frequently proven himself to be an independent, tough scientist, and now that push has come to shove and most of the meaningful funding for the Interagency Study Team comes from the Park Service. In those first years many agencies were willing to chip in, but in the long haul the Park Service is paying the bills.

There is an extraordinary footnote to the committee's work. In 1975, Cole and Cowan communicated further, comparing notes on the committee's population calculations, and Cowan reversed his earlier position, agreeing with Cole that the Craigheads seriously underestimated the uncensused portion of the population. Cowan concluded that "we will now be estimating that the total population averaged 301 grizzlies over the 1959-70 period."[10] This, though it amounted to a more or less complete vindication of Cole's earlier estimates, and though it gave the Park Service additional reason to believe their management program was on the right track, didn't get much publicity. In fact, most later writers, especially in the popular press, were unaware of it.

The Interagency Study Team responded to the committee's report in many ways. Team budgeting was separated from park budgeting, and the team's headquarters were removed from the park offices to Bozeman, Montana. The team got into the radiotracking business, at first with bears that were trapped outside the park but eventually with bears throughout the Yellowstone Ecosystem.

I have often wondered if, when the committee recommended increased involvement by "independent researchers" they actually thought the Craigheads would be invited back in just then. If so, they were to be disappointed. But if "independent researchers" meant an influx of personnel from the academic community, then the Interagency Study Team was just what the committee was after. About a dozen graduate projects, resulting in theses or dissertations, have resulted from the team's cooperation with nearby universities (the Craighead project resulted in one such thesis).

The report of the Committee on the Yellowstone Grizzlies is something of a milestone in the story of the controversy. Obviously, the report settled very little. It may have, for at least a short time anyway, reduced the level of hysteria about the condition of the grizzly population. After 1971 the number of bears killed in the Yellowstone ecosystem dropped quickly. In 1972 the total was twenty-four, with nine killed by the Park Service control program. In 1973 the total was eighteen, and in 1974 it was sixteen. In 1975 it was three, and there was talk in the Park Service of a problem solved and a bear population that had now adjusted to its new wild lifestyle. There was a lot of truth to that, but the problem was only evolving. It may never be fully solved as long as people and bears want to use Yellowstone. Since 1975 we've learned a lot about what will be required to at least keep the problem under control.

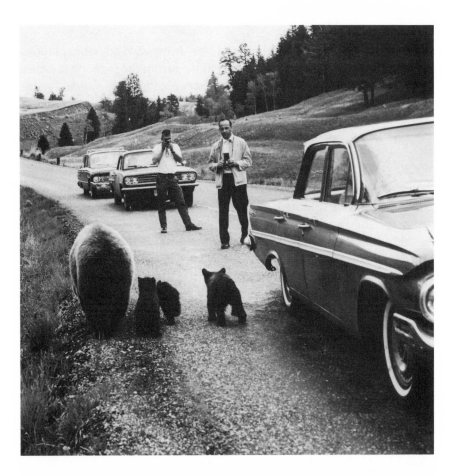

A "bear-jam" a few miles east of Mammoth Hot Springs in the 1960s, in this case with photogenic triplets. N.P.S. photo.

Before turning to that, though, we must catch up on the black bear. For most Yellowstone visitors in the 1970s, the only evidence of the bear management program was the disappearance of black bears from the roadsides. The black bear story was rarely an issue in the controversy, though since the early 1980s blacks are getting a little more attention as the debate goes on. Their divorce from roadside feeding proceeded swiftly. All campgrounds were equipped with bear-proof garbage cans by 1970, and by 1971 all but two of the cabin complexes were also "sanitized." This meant that every day the Park

Service was emptying 2,000 bear-proof garbage cans. Roadside beggar bears were chased from the road, or trapped and transplanted. Incorrigible ones were destroyed or removed from the park. At the same time, the ancient regulations against bear-feeding were suddenly, and strictly, enforced. Visitors who for decades had enjoyed a holiday at the Yellowstone zoo suddenly faced fines for their efforts. By 1975 it was possible to spend two or three days driving the park roads and not see a single beggar bear.[11]

Many visitors were disappointed, just as some had been when the last public feeding ground had been closed in 1941. Most people, when the situation is explained to them, will grudgingly admit that it is better for the bears. For some, a trip to the park was not worth the trouble without bears to feed. For others, it seemed the Park Service was somehow failing them because it could not make bears easier to see. Very few people are old enough to recall the days before roadside begging became common, when Yellowstone's bears were rarely seen except at a few dumps. Even the oldest "old-timers" know of nothing in Yellowstone but beggar bears. The change in black bear distribution was accomplished much more easily than a corresponding change in visitor attitudes about bear feeding. Park visitors may never stop asking rangers "where are the bears?" though I understand that by the late 1980s the question was being asked less.

Yellowstone's bear controversies are a marvel. To those not involved it must seem incredible that professional scientists and managers, all of whom were commited to protecting the natural resource, could make such a mess of their communications and reduce normal administrative process to such confusion. To those who were involved, the mess is old news. If they could have figured out a way to avoid it, they probably would have. The controversies were ugly; they degenerated into quarrels. The controversies were destructive; they enabled people who don't care about bears, and who wanted to develop some grizzly bear habitat outside the park, to point out that the researchers couldn't even agree on the status of the animal, so why should they worry? The controversies may have had one small benefit though, one that surely could have been achieved in a less painful way. They did at least alert many people to the problems faced by the bears of Yellowstone. As we will see, the bears, especially the grizzlies, will need all the friends they can get.

Chapter 18

The Greater Yellowstone Grizzly Bear

*T*he controversy over grizzly bear management did not end in 1975, but, following the report of the National Academy of Sciences committee, management did enter a new phase. The committee, by formally delineating the full scope of the problem of protecting the bear, helped to focus attention on the future. Though there was certainly plenty of reason to debate the events of the early 1970s, there was something more important to be done, and that was to concentrate on making sure that the grizzly bear, whatever its exact status in 1975, had the necessary help to survive. To provide that help, scientists, managers, and a broad assortment of conservationists would have to spend less and less time reevaluating statistics from the past and more and more time learning about the needs of the bear in the present. What changed, then, was a divided management structure that left each agency more or less independent in managing the grizzlies that were at any given time under its jurisdiction. Piecemeal, as I'll show in a moment, the necessary bureaucratic equipment was developed to do what a few foresightful people had been urging for years: manage the bear's domain in and around Yellowstone on an ecosystem basis, not on a fragmented, boundary-segmented basis.

What changed at the same time was that the park's various critics and supporters, both individuals and organizations, devoted more and more energy to seeing to it that this boundary-crossing effort was taken seriously. It became widely apparent by 1975 that the future of the bear depended largely on giving it room not only in the park but in the rest of its remaining territory near the park. Though bureaucratic boundaries will never completely disappear, after 1975 there was less talk among thoughtful people of individual bears as "Gallatin Forest bears" or "Yellowstone Park bears." They were all bears of the Greater Yellowstone Ecosystem, and they needed the whole place to survive.

The Park Service provided an important piece of the machinery in 1973 when it initiated its bear monitoring program. The monitoring system provided a coordinated, centralized clearinghouse for all bear sightings, black, grizzly, and unknown, in the park. With this system it has been much easier to know what bears (and people) are up to at any time in the park. For example, the system allows managers to alert a ranger that a series of sightings over the past few days seems to suggest that a grizzly bear sow with cubs may be heading for certain meadows (or trails) in his area, and that he might want to keep hikers in that area alerted. This is not a scientific program, mind you; its goal is management. But it has yielded considerable information that complements what the scientists are learning, and it has given managers a much better grip on potential problems than they had before. But it was only a small part of what was needed and what eventually would be created in an attempt to have what is almost universally called a "recovered" population of grizzly bears.

Recovery became the appropriate term for the management process in 1975 when the grizzly bear in the Yellowstone Ecosystem was officially classified as "threatened" under the terms of the Endangered Species Act. Once an animal has been formally classified as "threatened," which is not as grave a classification as "endangered," its future gets a new look by a whole lot of people.

This classification came at a time when there were still people convinced that the grizzly bear population was in no danger, and when there were others who were expecting the last grizzly bear to vanish any minute. Like anything else the government might have done right then (or any other time, come to think of it), the classification was criticized from many quarters.

The advantage it gave the grizzly bear was that once so classified, an animal has certain legal rights. Perhaps most important of these is that the animal's habitat needs will be clearly defined, and a "recovery plan" will be developed. The classification as "threatened" compelled agency managers in and around Yellowstone to determine the critical habitat necessary to the recovery and support of a healthy grizzly bear population, and then implement policies that will protect that habitat.

Black bears trapped in developed areas are usually hauled by truck to an isolated portion of the park; only grizzlies get flown to distant backcountry sites because of costs and the grizzly's greater determination to find its way back to a good source of food. N.P.S. photo.

For the most part, this seemed of little concern inside Yellowstone Park, at least as far as formal development goes. After all, practically all of the park was wilderness, with less than 2% actually developed. However, thanks to the research of the Interagency Study Team, we know that even the park is not measuring up as it should as habitat. There are a couple especially illuminating examples.

First, there are the troubling developments called Fishing Bridge and Grant Village. In 1975, Fishing Bridge was a complex of stores, two campgrounds, and other services just east of the outlet of Yellowstone Lake. It has been one of Yellowstone's most popular developments, built early in this century.

Grant Village is a modern sort of resort-type development along the west shore of the Lake, built mostly in the 1970s and 1980s. It is enormously unpopular with the conservation community, who see it as a monstrous anachronism from an age when national parks were more concerned with hospitality than with preserving ecosystem values. I have yet to find anybody in the National Park Service who actually likes it; during the fires of 1988, local gallows humor observed that they'd built the fire line on the wrong side of Grant Village.

The park's master plan, in its 1973 form, said that when the Grant Village complex was complete it could serve to replace Fishing Bridge, the latter known to be in a glorious natural setting that deserved better than a trailer park on it. In the early 1980s, as the Grant Village complex neared completion, the Park Service began to show real interest in actually removing the Fishing Bridge development. They phased out the cabins over the course of a few years, but ran into intense public and political opposition to doing any more.

At the request of the director of the National Park Service, in 1984 Yellowstone's staff put together a detailed report on the ecological effects of the Fishing Bridge development. The development, which included a 308-site Park Service campground and a 353-site concessioner operated trailer park, sits astride the peninsula between the Yellowstone River and Pelican Creek. The report described this area as "a crossroads of energy forms and life forms that is unique in Yellowstone Park."[1] This has many implications, but for grizzly bears the results are plain. Grizzlies have few better habitats in Yellowstone than the Fishing Bridge area, and even when there are no human food sources there, the bears want to live there. As a result of human presence and the bears' natural interest, the report estimated that since 1966 Fishing Bridge has cost the bear population at least nine adult females, with an additional loss of at least nine female cubs that those females were prevented from producing. The report also demonstrated that Fishing Bridge has experienced a strongly disproportionate number of human injuries by grizzly bears; between 1968 and 1983, 62.5% of all injuries that occurred either in a

0   40
km

● Highest Density
▨ High Density
⌒ Common Sightings
– – Occasional Sightings

Densities of grizzly bears in the Yellowstone Ecosystem, 1973–1984. The solid innermost line is the park boundary, and the outer dotted line is a general boundary of what most managers consider grizzly bear range. Most of the highest density areas—those in black—in the park coincide with areas of preferred grizzly bear vegetation, high concentrations of elk and bison, or both. Courtesy of Interagency Grizzly Bear Study Team.

development or within one mile of a development occurred at Fishing Bridge.

Working for the Park Service as a consulting researcher, I helped write that report. As the information came in from various researchers and technicians, we could see again and again that back in 1973 the park planners had been right; this was a singular place, with exceptional value to grizzly bears. The final report made it quite clear that, had the Fishing Bridge development never been built back in the early days, it would certainly never be allowed now. It has been a frightening grizzly population sink.

But, as the Craigheads learned long ago in a different sort of controversy, just having a great deal of scientific information doesn't necessarily prove you'll get your way. Citizens' groups, including a national recreational vehicle group called the Good Sam Club (Fishing Bridge was and is the only campground in the park with full-service hookups for campers) and business groups in Cody, Wyoming, applied pressure through Wyoming Senator Alan Simpson, preventing the Park Service from entirely removing Fishing Bridge.

As of 1991, the Park Service had managed to remove its campground and reduce some of the other facilities, but that has not satisfied conservationists. Defenders of the grizzly bear point out that, back when Grant Village was being built, the U.S. Fish and Wildlife Service only agreed that it would not have adverse effects on the grizzly bear because the Park Service promised to remove the Fishing Bridge development. Now both developments are there, and both are having their effects. The last sentence of the 1984 report sums it up:

> If Fishing Bridge alone were able to seriously affect the grizzly bear in Yellowstone, Fishing Bridge operating in concert with Grant Village has a potential cumulative effect that is disastrous.

The problem is bigger than a misplaced development. The problem is increased pressure on grizzly bear habitat throughout the park. As the Interagency Study Team gathered data on the movements of the free-ranging bears of Yellowstone it gradually became clear that those movements, even miles from any development, were significantly affected by human presence. By the early 1980s, for example, it was apparent that the entire lower Pelican Valley, one of the richest bear habitats in the park, was largely deserted by the bears once summer came and hikers and fishermen moved in.[2] Scientists use polite terms like "avoidance behavior," but practically speaking we are just squeezing bears off their range.

Again the Park Service took steps to mitigate the damage, and again the public outcry was great. Continuing research, as well as the bear monitoring program, yielded the sort of solid information that allows managers to fine tune management. In 1983, a group of "Grizzly Bear Management Areas" was established in Yellowstone's backcountry. They totalled about 20% of the park, and each was designed to protect the bear. Some, such as those around trout spawning streams, were closed to visitors for a few weeks a year. Some were restricted so that hikers could not travel except on established trails, or in groups of four or more. And some were essentially closed to the public. In each case the Park Service, basing the decisions on what they knew about bear use of the area, limited human use only as much, and as long, as seemed absolutely necessary, and it was made clear that the closures were experimental, with an eye toward seeing how the bears responded to these sanctuaries. No major visitor attractions were affected during the tourist season. Less than one percent of park visitors would even be potentially affected by the closures.[3]

But all that was lost by the time it got to the public. *Newsweek*, for example, ran an incredibly inaccurate article under the title, "Whose Park Is It, Anyway?" in which a variety of outfitters and local businessmen were quoted on grizzly bear ecology.[4] They brought in the Craigheads' opinions (misrepresenting at least one of them), though the brothers had not studied Yellowstone's bears for fifteen years. They even misquoted me (one knows one has become fully part of the problem when one is misquoted in *Newsweek*). But not a word did we hear from the Interagency Study Team, the only current scientific authorities on Yellowstone's grizzlies. The *Newsweek* article hopelessly confused the proposed Fishing Bridge closure with the backcountry closures, treating them like part of one simple plan. The average *Newsweek* reader must have been indignant that these Park Service people were being so dumb and keeping him out of the park.

But the *Newsweek* article was only typical of the sort of journalism that has occurred in these complex environmental issues. It took a comfortingly simple view: the government is doing it, the government does lots of things wrong, therefore this must be wrong. As has so often happened, ecological realities were simply overrun in the popular press by colorful quotes, with no regard for the actual knowledge or bias of the person quoted.

This story does have a fairly happy ending, though. The Park Service did not fold under this pressure, and the management area system is alive and well in 1991. More, it has proven itself perhaps even beyond the ambitions of its orginators. In 1990 and 1991, I took my Yellowstone Institute Grizzly Bear Ecology and Management class to the north slopes of Mount Washburn and, from the road, watched grizzly bears for hours. Prior to the closure of this large roadside area to hikers, grizzly bears were rarely seen here; now it is perhaps the foremost grizzly bear observation area in the lower forty eight.

The rhetoric of these debates is worth consideration here. The first refuge of those who oppose any restriction or new management of human use in the park is to point to the founding legislation of Yellowstone where it says that the park is "for the benefit and enjoyment of the people." It doesn't, they proudly announce, say anything about bears! It surely doesn't, but a century of subsequent legislation, the laws that really defined the park after the founding legislation created it, have a great deal to say about bears. Most specifically, the National Park Service Act of 1916 required the Park Service to conserve the wildlife and to allow people to enjoy it "in such a manner and by such means as will leave them unimpaired for the enjoyment of future generations." That's pretty clear; our enjoyment of the bears depends upon the bears being protected from impairment. As important, the Endangered Species Act leaves no room for hesitation; the federal government is supposed to protect the bear's habitat.

National parks are, by legal definition, different from most other places of public recreation. Because of the dual mandate that also requires the Park Service to keep the park unimpaired, public use of the parks must be more gentle. Otherwise the most piggish definition of "benefit and enjoyment" would probably prevail. Obviously, neither the public enjoyment nor the preservation of the natural setting will be perfect; visitors cannot eat park elk, and park elk cannot graze where there are hotels. Those kinds of compromises are implicit and explicit throughout park legislation. But we aren't talking about compromise this time. We're talking about a bear population that is threatened, and that may go down the tubes if we don't strike some new balances between human use and natural protection.

But park resource management problems are nothing compared to what the grizzly faces in the lands beyond park boundaries. Out there, there isn't even a National Park Service Act to lean on. There is instead the far more complicated legislation, and infinitely more political arena, of the national forests.

Yellowstone Park is almost completely surrounded by national forests, those marvelous "lands of many uses" where no one user is ever satisfied that he has truly gotten his fair share. The problem is that half of the Yellowstone grizzly bear's habitat is out here too, and grizzly bears long ago proved that they are not adept at sharing their range with humans. To a great degree, since the fireworks of the early 1970s, when the park was constantly at the center of attention, people concerned about the bear have shifted more and more of their attention to these surrounding wildlands, because it is on forest and private lands, rather than in the park, that the most habitat is in immediate danger.

The national forests are managed by a "multiple use" system, whereby a balance is sought between recreation, logging, mining, wildlife protection, and so on. Because of the extraordinary character of the region around Yellowstone, much of which is no less scenically grand and ecologically diverse than the park, a lot of it has already received substantial legislative protection. Much of the Shoshone National Forest, east of Yellowstone, is already classified as wilderness or is proposed for wilderness. A large portion of the Gallatin National Forest, which is both north and west of Yellowstone, is also wilderness. So is some of the Bridger-Teton National Forest to the south of the park. But in all cases there are perilous gaps, and sometimes huge regions, where the grizzly must compete with a wide variety of human uses.

The U.S. Forest Service has the same legislative obligations as the Park Service when it comes to grizzly bears. Though they may welcome many uses on their land, the Endangered Species Act requires them to protect the bear's habitat. That process is not going uniformly well. Rick Reese has summarized the many threats posed by developments in his book *Greater Yellowstone: The National Park and Adjacent Wildlands*:

Courtesy of the Greater Yellowstone Coordinating Committee

The Greater Yellowstone Area

The impacts of these threats taken one at a time could be mitigated, but taken collectively, and in the absence of some immediate protective measures, their cumulative effect threatens to disrupt this system of wild lands to such a degree that an irreversible degradation of the biological and geological communities of the Greater Yellowstone Ecosystem and Yellowstone National Park seems inescapable.[5]

That is the gloom that hangs over the grizzly bear. If I had a hundred pages to spare I could list all the threats specifically (as Rick has, in his book, which takes the pressure off of me to do it again). They run the full range of national forest and private land uses: oil and mineral development with their accompanying disruptions for roadbuilding and exploration; increased recreational pressure, including ski resorts, second home building, hiking, hunting, backpacking, snowmobiling, and the like (we are all part of the problem, however holy we may feel about our environmental awareness); logging; geothermal energy development (this one, geologists suspect, could end up killing the park's geysers as well as the bears, because no one knows if the subterranean "plumbing" of the geothermal areas near the park is hooked up with the geyser basins); and, if I may generalize even more, the creeping chamber of commercism that infects all beautiful land.

In the past, and to far too great an extent now, each little intrusion on grizzly bear habitat has been justified through narrow vision. ("The bears can get along without these four acres along this stream where I built my summer cabin—heck, there's five million acres out there for them.") By piecework, nickel and dime, we have been whittling away the grizzly bear's habitat for a century in the Yellowstone area. We are still at it. The message we're getting from the bear, through the Interagency Study Team, is that we must stop. Not soon, but now. To their credit, the national forests around the park are responding with some sympathy to the needs of the bear, and not only because they are legally required to; some of the new appointments in management in these forests are themselves known grizzly bear defenders (Steve Mealey, whose study of Yellowstone grizzly bear feeding habits in 1974 and 1975 was the first M.S. thesis to come out of the Interagency Study Team work, was appointed supervisor of the Shoshone National Forest in 1983). But the bureaucratic momentum to try to do everything with the same resource is tremendous, and conservationists and scientists frequently complain that the forests (to say nothing of the private lands near the park) are still not living up to the bargain.

And, at times even more troubling, the private lands of greater Yellowstone are largely without control, and each landowner is welcome and legally entitled to go his or her own way. Some are conservation minded, and some aren't. Some love condominiums, some love wilderness. All of them are entitled to make a living.

What has emerged in the past decade, and what the national forests and a host of special interests are trying to come to terms with, is a very old idea, really, but one that has never before been presented with the vigor and force it now has: that the entire Yellowstone region, perhaps fifteen million, perhaps eighteen million acres, needs some unified, long-range management direction that will keep preservation of the area's unique natural characteristics foremost at all times. There is now an organization, The Greater Yellowstone Coalition, in Bozeman, Montana, working to promote that goal.

In 1985 there were congressional hearings in Washington on the future of the area; the various land managers involved more or less defended their part in the system, with most disapproving of any sort of umbrella administration, while various conservationists urged just such oversight. It was clear, however, that the two agencies were not doing nearly enough, and that they should do a lot more.

The National Park Service is in a peculiar and relatively unfamiliar position in this issue. Traditionally, national park and national forest managers had very little to say about how neighboring lands were managed. That was seen as none of their business. But now that it has become clear that none of the parks are ecologically complete, and that the parks cannot truly fulfill their legislative responsibilities without the cooperation of neighboring land managers, isolationism is on its way out.

No land manager in Greater Yellowstone, for example, can afford to pretend that grizzly bear management and preservation is going to be achieved without a great deal of cooperation with other land managers. More important, no land manager in Greater Yellowstone can afford to pretend that the unique values of Greater Yellowstone can be preserved if we continue to treat the national forests around the park like just any national forests. In 1985, Yellowstone Superintendent

Robert Barbee pretty much summed up the current hopes of bear defenders:

> We are not the first, however, to suggest that merely because multiple use is the guiding principle of the national forests does not mean that it must be applied uniformly throughout the national forest system. Some forests may be best managed for timber harvest, or grazing, or recreation, even to the exclusion of some other types of use. That possibility, or option, seems perfectly applicable to forests in the greater Yellowstone ecosystem. Considering the area's extraordinary values, we believe that the entire Yellowstone area may be best managed, not by trying to do many things satisfactorily, but by concentrating on doing one thing especially well. That one thing is protecting the integrity of the natural systems which are the area's single most important resource.[6]

I can't say that things are going very well in protecting Greater Yellowstone. There has been enormous progress in the past twenty years; the two agencies have overcome a lot of the historical rivalry that kept them from even communicating in the past. But the political pressures against long-range planning and protection of ecosystem values are intense.

The findings of the 1985 congressional hearings took hold among Greater Yellowstone managers. Communication improved, and so did coordination, to the point that the Greater Yellowstone Coordinating Committee, comprised of the Supervisors of Yellowstone and Grand Teton National Parks and the six national forests, as well as four regional Park and Forest Service administrators, began to act like a real coordinating committee. In August of 1990, the National Park Service and the U.S. Forest Service published a draft document, *Vision for the Future, A Framework for Coordination in the Greater Yellowstone Area*. Speaking as a historian, I have to say this 72-page report (which I helped write) was a milestone in the history of the two agencies. Representatives of the national parks and national forests of Greater Yellowstone sat down together and wrote up what could be done, working within the legal constraints of existing legislation, to ensure that "the extraordinary values of this region" would be protected into the distant future.[7]

The *Vision* was not a document of legal force or record, only a general statement of principles. It did not go nearly far enough to satisfy conservationists. It did not attempt to specifically define, for example, how much timber could be cut on a given national forest, or how bears might be managed in a given park. It only attempted to describe the sort of condition in which the federal lands in the ecosystem should stay, and how the those lands might still be used for many things without overly reducing the value of the whole. It was vague, and it was polite.

The response was not. Commodity extraction groups combined forces in a devastating campaign to destroy the document, and they succeeded. A year later, a final draft was released. It was a tenth the length of the first, and contained virtually no details and very little value. The Vision's concept, that the federal lands in Greater Yellowstone could be managed to best protect what is widely being called the last intact ecosystem in the planet's temperate zones, had been overwhelmed by regional and local political forces.

This was only the most recent round in a very long battle, and the future promises to be entertaining, if not necessarily good. The politics have already become very nasty. Within weeks of the release of the final draft, two of the region's lead resource management officials— one Park Service and one Forest Service—were given forced transfers to other regions. A Congressional inquiry in the summer of 1991 prompted the Park Service official, Rocky Mountain Regional Director Lorraine Mintzmyer, to reveal that the order to destroy the substance of the Vision document came all the way from White House Chief of Staff John Sununu. Regional congressional delegations were accused of engineering the transfers because the two officials were too sympathetic to environmentalist's concerns. Claims and counterclaims were everywhere.

If Greater Yellowstone gets lucky, perhaps all this attention will help somehow. For the moment, however, interagency cooperation has been dealt a serious blow, one that will only harm the chances to save the grizzly bear in Greater Yellowstone.

Greater Yellowstone has an intriguing political atmosphere. Most (but not all) of the congressional delegations representing the people of Greater Yellowstone are not thought well of by conservationists; most of those senators and congressmen consistently get the worst ratings in the nation from the League of Conservation Voters.

But keep in mind that the conservation community, including the defenders of bears, are asking more of the citizens of Greater Yellowstone than is asked of most Americans. Greater Yellowstone is in a lot better shape, ecologically, than is most of the United States. Nobody is launching a crusade to save the Greater Long Island Ecosystem, or the Greater San Francisco Bay Ecosystem. Greater Yellowstone, by virtue of its surviving ecological integrity (including its grizzly bears) attracts a great deal more attention from people who want to save whole natural systems; it is a lot easier to save one than reconstruct it later.

Thus, we are asking more of the people who visit and inhabit Greater Yellowstone. We are asking them to take it easier here, to use the land differently than it is used in most other places. We are asking this, in some cases, of people whose families have lived here, using and loving the land for several generations. We are also asking it of people whose livelihoods either are, or are perceived to be, at stake. The political campaign that gutted the *Vision* document wrongly convinced many people that protecting the Greater Yellowstone Ecosystem necessarily means the destruction of the area's traditional ways of life and the ruination of the regional economy. The emotions stirred by the Greater Yellowstone debates are as deep as they are heated.

It has too often happened that reasonable traditional uses of this area, such as logging, mining, and ranching, are perceived by some conservationists as somehow inherently evil. Many people working in those industries have an abiding love for the land, and are serious and aggressive in their stewardship of it. Logging, mining, and ranching can and sometimes do have damaging effects on grizzly bear habitat, and the conservation community is justifiably alarmed about some of those effects (a large new mine being planned for near Cooke City, just outside the northeast corner of the park, is particularly frightening to them). But many of the recreational activities favored by hard-core environmentalists also put bear habitat at risk; practically anything humans do in Greater Yellowstone has an impact on the bear. The goal is to understand and control those impacts, not remove humans from the system.

Economic conditions generated far beyond the boundaries of the ecosystem have brought hard times to some local industries, and the new movements to protect ecological process, or save grizzly bears, or restore wolves, seem only to add to the hard times. I suspect that most reasonable people believe that Greater Yellowstone can and should support a variety of industries as part of the complex regional culture and economy. Exactly at what level those industries will operate remains unclear, and will depend on many things other than grizzly bear preservation.

On the other hand, the people who point out that Greater Yellowstone is composed of *national* parks and *national* forests are right. There is implicit in the statements of all too many local and regional people the conviction that only people living in Greater Yellowstone know what's best for it. These are public lands of national significance. Greater Yellowstone's bears belong to, and are the responsibility of, all Americans. Part of the price of making all or part of your living from public lands is that other people, many of them far away, must have a say in how those lands are managed, too. This has become a central, and sometimes disquieting, fact of life for all of us who make Greater Yellowstone our home.

This little rumination could too easily lead to a nice bland statement about how we all have to get together and work out a compromise—let us sit down and work out our differences. In fact, that is probably what will happen. In citizens' groups, interagency teams, and a variety of other forums including courtrooms, Greater Yellowstone's fate will be decided. Perhaps it will even happen that some greater good will be served by the process; it works out that way sometimes.

But a vast amount of scientific information tells us that the grizzly bear cannot afford any more compromises. It has already lost too much. The science we have at hand, whatever its other limitations, plainly tells us that we have already made all the compromises—all the things that have eaten up prehistoric habitat—that the grizzly bear population can afford. Some say we've already taken too much of what the bear needs, and that the only hope is to give some back, somehow.

And so, as has often happened before, Greater Yellowstone has become a kind of testing ground, a place where we as a nation must decide just what is most important to us. Yellowstone Superintendent Robert Barbee, in speaking of the need to save Greater Yellowstone, has said that there is no question what future generations would want us to do. It is certain that Americans a hundred, or two hundred, or more years from now will not forgive us if we set the Greater Yellowstone grizzly bear on a course to extinction. But, as Bob said, people in the future don't get to vote in this process. We must vote for them, as well as for ourselves. So far, the bear is losing the election.

Chapter 19

How Many Bears Are Enough?

A moratorium was placed on all grizzly bear hunting in the areas around Yellowstone in 1974. As mentioned earlier, on July 28, 1975, the grizzly bear in the lower forty-eight states was declared threatened under the terms of the Endangered Species Act, and the wheels were slowly set in motion for the preparation of a recovery plan for all six identified areas still occupied by grizzly bears. All six were in Montana, Wyoming, and/or Idaho, though in 1979 a hunter surprised himself and the world by killing a female grizzly bear in southwestern Colorado; if more bears are discovered there (and the chances are slim), that area will be added to the recovery plan as well.

The formalization of modern bear management and the development of the recovery plan is a complicated bureaucratic process that has involved numerous state and federal agencies. Starting in 1974, the Park Service in Yellowstone prepared a draft Environmental Impact Statement for their ongoing management plan, to cover not only research and park management, but cooperation between various involved agencies in efforts to keep bear mortality down. The document moved slowly through writing, public review (with ample criticism), extensive revision (thanks to the ample criticism), and, finally, publication of the completed statement in 1982.

In 1979, work began on the actual Grizzly Bear Recovery Plan, the primary guiding document that was the responsibility of the U.S. Fish and Wildlife Service. The Fish and Wildlife Service has responsibility for monitoring other agencies' management of endangered

The modern bear-proof garbage can defeats the efforts of practically all bears. N.P.S. photo.

species. The first draft of the plan was completed in 1981, and the final draft was approved in 1982. The plan said it provided "a biologically sound program that will result in the recovery of the species and its habitat to a level that will not longer require protection under the Endangered Species Act." As science taught us more about the nature of the grizzly bear population, the need arose to revise the plan, and as of late 1991, the new version, which I'll say more about later, was out for public comment.

Since 1983, all grizzly bear recovery efforts in the lower forty-eight have been coordinated by the Interagency Grizzly Bear Committee. The committee was established as part of an agreement between the Departments of Interior and Agriculture and the governors of Montana, Idaho, Washington, and Wyoming. It is composed of representatives from the various agencies, both state and federal, for whom grizzlies are a concern. Their goals include not only oversight of research projects like the Interagency Study Team but also a variety of law enforcement and public education efforts.

In 1979 the Forest Service published its "Guidelines for Management involving Grizzly Bears in the Greater Yellowstone Area," a careful and thorough document prepared by Steve Mealey, who at that point was a wildlife biologist for the Shoshone National Forest. This document dovetails in function with the general recovery plan and the park's Environmental Impact Statement. It is the "Guidelines" that provides the specifics of bear management in and around Yellowstone. It established five different "management situations," that is, five ways that land in the Yellowstone area could be defined:

> Management Situation 1: areas containing grizzly bear population centers, key to the survival of the species, with seasonal or year-long grizzly activity, under natural, free-ranging conditions.
>
> Management Situation 2: areas lacking in grizzly population centers, with some useful habitat and occasional presence of grizzlies possible. Such areas are considered unnecessary for grizzly bear recovery, but may be included in Management Situation 1 as information is gained on the population.
>
> Management Situation 3: areas where grizzlies are present infrequently but are possible.
>
> Management Situation 4: areas of great potential suitability that do not have grizzlies but are needed for the recovery of the species.
>
> Management Situation 5: areas without grizzlies, or only rarely with grizzlies, that are thought unsuitable for bears and are unnecessary for recovery.

Of the five, only Management Situation 1 currently holds an unqualified welcome sign to grizzly bears. In Management Situation 2, bear use is to be taken into account when decisions are made, but bears do not get preference over all other uses. In Situation 3, bears get no breaks, and will be "discouraged" from staying around. Situation 4 areas are not lost to the bears, and, depending upon what research reveals, may become grizzly areas. Situation 5 is probably so inhospitable that grizzlies won't be an issue.

The park itself is designated Situation 1, as are large portions of the surrounding wilderness. In some areas near the park, already-established uses have eliminated what was once obviously Situation 1-quality habitat, so that, for instance, a Situation 1 boundary line may abruptly swerve around a small community. The assumption there, apparently, is that a good many of the developments already existing in the Yellowstone area—practically all of them, in fact—can stay without endangering the grizzly as long as we're careful about what's left. But many pro-grizzly people have never been comfortable with such arbitrary designations, and it's easy to understand why. Bears don't know these situation boundaries any better than they know park boundaries or county lines.

The question comes back, again and again, to this: How many bears are we hoping to maintain in the Greater Yellowstone Ecosystem? Though it is conceivable, if unlikely, that grizzly bears from other populations might find their way here, or that bears from Greater Yellowstone could reach other populations, what we have in Greater. Yellowstone is an island population, dependent upon its own ecological and genetic resources to keep itself going. So we need to know if there are enough bears to do that.

In the past twenty-five years, many scientists have taken a shot at estimating the number of bears in the park. We've already seen the large difference between the Craighead estimates and those reached by Cole and the National Academy of Sciences.

Those estimates, though, were mostly for the population prior to the great disruptions of the dump closures. When the Craigheads, in 1974, published their estimate that there had been an average of 229 bears during their study, they also estimated how many had survived the increased control kills of the dump-closing years. Their conclusion was that by 1974 there couldn't be more than about 136 grizzlies left in the Yellowstone ecosystem, and that the number was declining. The National Academy of Sciences, of course, using Craighead data but incorporating Cole's suggested portion of bears missed by the

Craighead count, estimated that the pre–dump-closure population was 301 but did not make an estimate on what it might be in 1974, only that it was depressed but probably recovering.

Cole was more confident than that, and in 1975, based on the first findings of the Interagency Study Team (which did not make so bold as to agree with him) and additional observations by park staff, estimated that the population might be recovered from whatever depression in numbers was caused by the high number of removals in 1970–1972. He estimated the population at 250–320, an estimate he stuck with in subsequent years.[1]

The Interagency Study Team was understandably reluctant to jump in with any attempt to reinterpret other people's data and somehow combine it with what they had gathered to that point, so their first try was merely a careful generalization about possibilities: in 1975 Knight and his team allowed that there were probably somewhere between 237 and 540 grizzly bears in the Yellowstone ecosystem.[2] In 1980 Knight and his associates were willing to suggest that there were probably 300–350 grizzly bears.[3] In 1981, stressing that they were making a "point estimate" and not a final calculation, Knight and his team used their accumulated data to estimate 247 bears in the population.[4] This estimate, like the next one, was based on only that portion of the population that they had observed and handled, which made it difficult to know how accurate it was because their "sample size" was relatively small. Though in the years up to 1980, they typically observed or handled 100 to 130 grizzly bears in a summer's study, they had no way of being certain exactly what proportion of the population those bears represented.

Population estimation was and is an exercise in extrapolating from a known element of the population to the rest of it. For example, in 1981, when the team estimated 247 bears as a minimum population size, they did it as follows. They knew from observations that they had at least 30 adult females. They knew that at that time the observed ratio of adult males to adult females was 62 to 38, which meant there were about 49 adult males, giving them a total of 79 adult bears. They knew that the ratio of subadults to adults was 68 to 32, so there were about 168 subadults, for a total population of 247.[5]

Repeated calculations of this sort, year after year, tend to even out the discrepancies of years when observation conditions are not good or when the sows have a smaller than average or larger than average

Interagency Study Team leader Richard Knight and Team member Bonnie Blanchard prepare a grizzly for radio-collaring and release. N.P.S. photo.

"crop" of cubs. But the accuracy of the calculations always depends on the success at determining just how many sows with cubs there are in a given year. It is not a perfect method, but with a dispersed and hard-to-observe population of animals, it is often all you have. Knight and his team did not overstate its reliability, but they used it as they could for general "ballpark" estimates.

Then, in 1982, in the team's annual report for the 1981 field season, came a new estimate that stirred up a great deal of excitement: 197. As usual, the team did not want this taken too literally:

> We wish to emphasize that this is a point estimate based on some small sample sizes, and we are unable to assess its accuracy at this time.[6]

It was also more of a minimum estimate than a mean estimate, so that it probably reflected what the population was at least, rather than at most. But after all the optimistic high numbers it was a shock, and it started a whole new round of uproar, some of which we'll get to in a moment.

By 1984, the team had ten years of information on the new population that was divorced from the big dumps. They were in a position to make some comparisons, and those comparisons reveal many things about the early stages of the controversy.

The biggest news, to most people's minds, was that this population of approximately 200 bears (a minimum estimate) was gradually declining, largely because the number of female grizzlies being killed was too large. Again, the scientists counseled caution in reading these calculations. In a report in *Ecology* in 1985, Knight and L. L. Eberhardt summarized their calculations this way:

> Clearly the population will decline into the future if our estimates of certain essential parameters are correct. The simulations suggest that extirpation is not likely over a 30-year period, but there is, of course, no way to be sure that present conditions will persist for 30 years. Most likely they will not, in view of the virtual certainty of greatly increased human use of essential parts of the Yellowstone Ecosystem. Nor do we have any way to predict the impact of reduced population size on its viability.[7]

I want to come back to population viability at reduced size in a little while, but it's possible to do some scorekeeping here that many controversy-watchers might find useful.

First, as soon as the figure of 197 bears was made public, and then again when the projected decline of the population was announced, the first reaction of many people was that the Craigheads had been right all along. The bears were in trouble, just as they'd said years earlier. Let's look at what they might have been right about.

In 1974, the Craigheads estimated there were about 136 grizzlies left in the ecosystem. This was not a minimum estimate. Now, in 1982, Interagency Study Team reported a minimum population of about 197. If the Craigheads were right that the population was declining in 1974, how did it "decline" from 136 to 197? If indeed the population had been declining since the early 1970s, then it must have been considerably larger than 197 back then. If that was the case, then Cole may have been right about its size but utterly wrong about the direction it was going in. It was apparently going down, though it still had a long way to go to reach 136. Knight and his colleagues suspected that there were indeed a lot more than 136 bears in 1974, though they were as usual reluctant to push any one number too hard. Stephen Herrero, a Canadian scientist, has suggested that the population may actually have recovered in the mid-1970s and then gone into a decline not directly related to the high management kills of 1970-1973.[8]

It isn't always fruitful in a situation like this to look back and try to figure out who "won" each argument, partly because as the science progresses it often makes earlier hypotheses irrelevant by introducing new variables. There are some new variables in this story, but there is also some point in looking back. The Craigheads and Cole were both quite confident about their projections and calculations. It would serve us to see how they hold up.

As far as the population's size, it appears that the Craighead estimate of 1974 was much too low. Knight's 1982 estimate of 197 was a minimum estimate, meaning there were at least that many bears then. We can't tell how many more there may be in the total population, but at this point it's at least clear that some of Cole's assurance that the population was all right in 1974 was justified. Of course he was estimating 319-364 bears in the population then; for those numbers to be proven right, it would have to be established either that 1) Knight has missed a lot of bears in his estimates or 2) the population has declined since 1974.

On the other hand, it's always hard to fault a conservative estimate like the Craigheads made. Their estimate may have been too low, and perhaps it generated unnecessary alarms, but with an animal as slow to reproduce as the grizzly bear, it's hard to play it too safe, and it's almost impossible to get federal agencies too alarmed about an endangered species.

The Craigheads were worried that the closing of the dumps would reduce the nutritional budget of the bears, which could have serious consequences for the grizzly population in terms of average litter size and the health of individual bears. Cole was confident that though litter size would perhaps drop it would be because more younger sows would give birth to smaller average litters.

The average litter size during the Craighead study was 2.24. The average litter size from 1973 to 1980 was 1.91. The average litter size from 1981 to 1990 was 2.4, something neither Cole nor the Craigheads predicted. During the first ten years after the dumps were closed, grizzly sows had their first litter almost a year later than had the dump bears. But in the 1980s that changed, and a few grizzly sows began successfully mating even earlier in their lives than had sows during the Craighead study.

Since the Craighead study ended, there have been several studies of bears influenced by dumps, and they generally indicate that dump bears are in better physical condition than non-dump bears because of all that easy food. Even in Yellowstone Knight was able to study some bears that fed in the smaller outlying dumps the first few years of his study and then reverted to natural foods after those dumps were closed; those bears got smaller when they lost the dump foods.

If the only goal was to make the biggest possible bears, maybe dumps would be a good idea. But that isn't the real goal, and as time passes and more information accumulates, it becomes clear that we are still learning just how much the bear population can change.

Yellowstone doesn't give us a constant laboratory to work with, and in the 1970s, a formidable variable was introduced that to some unknown extent makes the obvious differences in the bears since the dump closures less impressive. Yellowstone experienced a drying trend in the 1970s; Professor Harold Picton of Montana State University published a paper in *Nature* in 1978 that offered an alternative hypotheses for the decline in litter size, at least:

> The decrease in litter sizes observed since the closure of garbage dumps seems to be largely a consequence of unfavourable weather during the periods of the final fattening of the mother, winter sleep, birth, lactation, and early spring foraging.[9]

Picton's paper was based only on the first five years of the post-dump period, but it added a note of caution to conversations about litter size that has never gone away, and was reinforced by two more, published in 1986. These, with several more years of population data, reinforced the other one, observing that climate conditions were favorable for grizzly reproduction in the 1960s (during the Craighead study), but less so in the 1970s.[10]

Further complications of the theoretical exercises involved in figuring out how the bears are doing were suggested by Dale McCullough, a populations specialist at the University of California, in 1983. McCullough, in a paper presented at a bear biology symposium that year, pointed out that the average litter size since the dumps closed does not necessarily mean much:

The percent of adult females with litters, a more reliable predictor, has proven impossible to obtain in recent research. Thus the conclusion that reproductive rates have declined (Knight 1983 based on low mean litter sizes may be misleading because it might be offset by a higher percent of females with litters.[11]

McCullough's point was that, unlike the dump days, when the Craigheads could easily determine average litter size because so many bears were visible at dumps, Knight was working with a much less visible population, and his sample may not be complete enough to accurately portray average numbers of females with young. As we will see in a moment, the "completeness" of current counts (or, more precisely, the degree of incompleteness) could have a greater effect on estimates of population trend.

McCullough offered a second, even more intriguing thought. He pointed out that a higher average litter size is not necessarily a sign of a healthy population. Indeed, many animal populations exhibit what is called a "density dependent response" to population numbers, so that when a range approaches its ecological carrying capacity the average litter size will decrease. The sizeable hunting mortality of the 1960s, when total grizzly mortality was more than nineteen per year, may have kept that grizzly population at a level where there was sufficient "room" for consistently large litters. Now, or since the early 1970s anyway, with a great deal more concern about bear mortality, it is difficult to be sure exactly what the lower average litter size means. As McCullough put it:

> A recent concern is an apparently high adult mortality in the ecosystem. If in fact adult mortality is high, the reduced adult density should be reflected in high mean litter sizes. Therefore, an increase in mean litter size, rather than being cause for optimism, may be cause for concern, and decline cause for optimism. . . . In conclusion, litter sizes can be interpreted as a good, bad, or indifferent sign about the status of the population. In the face of uncertainty we are forced to be prudent, and interpret low mean litter size as a bad sign.[12]

But there is more to current uncertainty than these ruminations on varying litter size. A smaller average grizzly bear may just be a logical

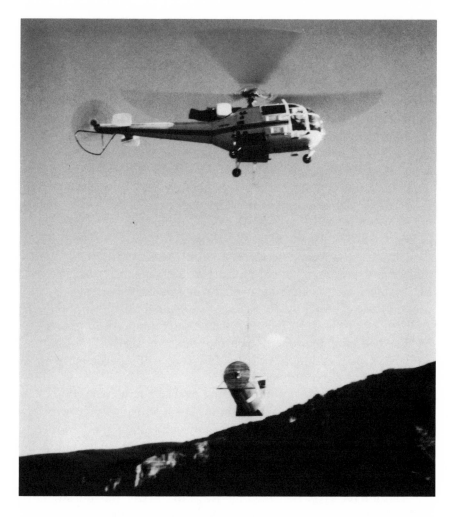

A grizzly in transfer trap being airlifted to a backcountry release site in the early 1980s. N.P.S. photo.

consequence of changing that bear's habits. Not only does it not get as much free food, it has to do different things than it used to in order to get food at all. Look at the pictures of those bears at the dumps; they were lovely big butterballs, perfectly adapted to preying on leftover Salisbury steaks and stale boysenberry pie. A bear in Yellowstone today spends more of its time chasing down less passive types of food. Whatever the available nutrients, the resulting bear is likely to be

175

leaner and lighter than a bear that does not have to do as much chasing.

The last year before the second edition of this book was published, 1985, was regarded as a poor one for new cubs. Only nine sows were seen with new cubs. As this book went to press, all I knew was that things weren't looking good, and that some unknown number of sows had just given birth in their dens. But by the summer of 1986, Yellowstone was crawling with new cubs. A record 25 sows were observed with cubs at heel, and a lot of people breathed a little easier, knowing the population was still capable of such a boom, even if it was just one year.

But it wasn't just one year. Cub crops have continued to average much higher than in the 1970s: 13 in 1987, 19 in 1988, 16 in 1989, and 24 in 1990 (with 57 cubs, the most ever counted in Greater Yellowstone).

Climate changes, uncertainty about census efficiency, density dependent responses, alterations in bear behavioral needs. These are the sorts of factors that have made most scientists cautious about pronouncing confidently about the exact status of the bear population. As time has passed, in fact, the scientific community in general has become less confident about such pronouncements. Things don't look anywhere near as simple now as they did to the participants in the early stages of the controversy.

In a sense, though, all this arguing over just how many bears there are, or just how quickly they reproduce, or how big they grow or how long they live, is missing the important point. If, as the Park Service tells us, the goal of management in Yellowstone is to have a population in balance with its setting, then the question remains, "How many bears are enough?"

There have been two popular ways to answer this question. The first was the approach taken in the 1982 Recovery Plan, where, based upon Cowan's 1975 reevaluation of the Craighead computer analysis, we were told that a "recovered" population in the Yellowstone ecosystem would be about 301 bears. The planners immediately acknowledged that, if it should prove true that the garbage was sustaining the population at an unnaturally high number before 1970, then it might become necessary to redefine a recovered population at some lower number. But until we know more, they assumed we should stick with those early estimates just to be safe.

But then there is another approach that has addressed the issue of grizzly bear recovery from its gloomier end. Several population specialists have, in the past few years, attempted to calculate just how small the population dare get before it cannot recover and will be extirpated. They define a "minimum viable population" as one that has at least a 95 percent chance of lasting for 100 years. Like the computer projections of population and population future, these calculations do not agree. They do not even approximately agree. They range from 50 to 125.[13] But even at that great a variation, they give us some general range that we can at least know we had better stay above.

When I last revised this book, it was already clear that many people were uncomfortable with such a flat and ecologically insensitive recovery goal as existed. To say that Greater Yellowstone must have 301 bears, a number with nothing more behind it than arithmetic based on a dump-fed population, seemed to say far too little, and to show no sympathy for the inherent flexibility of the population. The 1960s, 1970s, and 1980s, all showed us different bear populations: different reproductive rates, different food habits, different behavior, and so on.

That's what Knight and Eberhardt were referring to when I quoted them earlier about being unsure of "the impact of reduced population size on its viability." They were wondering, tentatively, if the decline is headed somewhere besides total disappearance. They assumed it was:

> In the absence of the supplemental food supply provided by the garbage dumps, it seems quite likely that the Yellowstone grizzly population will, if man-caused losses can be reduced sufficiently, stabilize at a new population level.[14]

What that level might be, and whether it would be high enough to assure the bear's survival, they could not say. Bears are so mobile that if their numbers shrank so that Yellowstone Park alone, without the surrounding country, could contain their ranges, even then they would not be safe because they are so inclined to move long distances, and because subadults would always be wandering out looking for a range of their own.

The word from the Interagency Study Team on population trends has not been as simple as saying that the population was probably on a decline. The discussions of climatic influences on grizzly bear numbers are not mere asides; they are central to the issue because they are what determine habitat conditions. Knight and Picton, in their evaluation of climatic effects on the bear population, went one step further than saying the climate is affecting the bears. They suggested that, whatever the current population size, it may be the best the bear can do under present climatic conditions:

> Climate correlations such as presented here are indicative of high environmental resistance due to climate. This suggests that the population is near its ecological carrying capacity.[15]

What was being suggested by Knight and Picton is that, no matter what the carrying capacity may have been in the 1960s—229, 301, or whatever—it probably isn't that now. However many bears the Yellowstone ecosystem may have been able to support back then, it can't support as many now. In fact, they suggested, it may be supporting all it can. If, as they estimated, it is now supporting at least 200 bears, then the population is well above most people's "danger point" of how many bears the population must have to survive.

Bears, like most other animals, do not have flat, constant population sizes; they fluctuate with environmental conditions. As Knight and Picton were suggesting, Yellowstone's grizzlies do just that, responding to a drying trend in the climate (and doing so at the same time that they have adjusted to a loss of dump foods). If their suggestion that the population is at or near its carrying capacity turns out to be right, then 200 bears may be all we get. Perhaps 180 is all Yellowstone can support sometimes, perhaps even fewer. Perhaps Knight and his team, who are properly cautious about saying they've got the population just right, have missed several females in their census work, and the population right now is 250 and stable; Knight has assiduously avoided falling into the trap of announcing he's sure he knows how many bears there are. What seems most important is keeping track of the population's trend, and knowing that the number hasn't dropped below some minimum safe figure.

With all of this becoming more and more obvious, the Interagency Grizzly Bear Committee produced and released a new draft of the Recovery Plan that now, in late 1991, is out for public comment. The new plan is more responsive to a variety of factors relating to the bear population. It no longer relies on some magic number, but on a series of conditions:

Young grizzly bear being fitted with expandable radio collar that it can "grow into" over more than one season of radiotracking. N.P.S. photo.

1) Adult females with cubs of the year must appear in 15 of 18 delineated bear management units in Greater Yellowstone, and must maintain a certain distribution over a three-year period.

2) Average annual man-caused mortality cannot exceed 11 bears, no more than two of which can be adult females, over a six-year period.

3) There must be a six-year average of 15 females with cubs.

4) The management agencies must establish adequate regulations and policies to protect both the animals and their habitat.[16]

In some ways, this new definition is already being met. The six-year running average of sows with cubs, for example, is well above fifteen. In other ways, especially regarding adequacy of regulation and ongoing protection of bears and habitat, I hope I've already made it clear that things don't look so good.

I have not yet encountered any scientist or bureaucrat in the National Park Service or outside of the government who is optimistic for the long-term survival of the grizzly bear. As the bear population approaches the point where it could fully satisfy the numerical requirements of this new plan—assuming the new plan is approved— there is more and more talk about "delisting" the bear, taking it off the Endangered Species List. That talk may appeal to the people who have ambitions to increase development in Greater Yellowstone, but it has little or no appeal with the agencies in charge of managing the bear. That is extremely significant, I think; when the managers themselves, faced with an opportunity to declare victory and get out from under a tremendous political and financial burden, still don't jump to delist the bear, the bear is obviously not ready for delisting.

Nor is there much agreement over the adequacy of the new recovery plan itself. It has been criticized for many things, including the following: for simply using old population boundaries when the bears have apparently occupied a lot of new territory; for never adequately developing a "cumulative impact" computer model that will allow for ecosystem-wide analysis of any new impact on grizzly bear habitat; for relying on the arbitrarily drawn management boundaries that ignored the realities of grizzly bear ecology to suit the needs of economic development; for not clearly defining how land managers within the recovery zone must behave, relying instead on vague language that encourages landowners and managers to do good; and for not recognizing the true long-term needs of a population.[17]

This last one is interesting, and gets back to the numbers game. One scientist has now estimated that in order to protect genetic viability for centuries (he does not think one century is a long enough requirement), the Greater Yellowstone grizzly bear population must number "on the order of 2,000 animals."[18] The Recovery Plan draft proposes only the periodic introduction of an animal from another grizzly bear population to protect genetic well-being. If the idea of somehow packing 2,000 grizzly bears into Greater Yellowstone seems preposterous, the idea of successfully bringing a new bear in every so often is at least problematic. There is a great deal that is not known about how this population functions genetically: how many males control the breeding, how big a risk inbreeding poses in grizzly bears, and so on.

What realistic conservationists seem to be hoping for is that adequate migration corridors can be maintained between Yellowstone and other grizzly bear populations to preserve genetic health. Judging from what has already happened to practically all grizzly bear habitat in the lower forty eight, this is a great thing to hope for, but not a great thing to count on.

What might happen to the population in the long run, say in hundreds of years, is hard to concentrate on, what with the problems of today. The immediate problem continues to be man-caused mortality. Consider the mortality rate of adult females, which the new Recovery Plan proposes to keep to two or less a year. Between 1973 and 1990 it averaged 2.5, and between 1985 and 1990 it averaged 2.0. With intense vigilance, education, and public education, Greater Yellowstone is still barely meeting the goal. In 1990, the Park Service removed one adult female (sent to a research facility), another was hit by a car, and two more were killed outside the park by hunters or poachers. Three males were also killed.

A recent conference on Greater Yellowstone grizzly bears was titled "Forever Threatened?" It appears that we may never be ready for delisting. It appears that, no matter how well the bear population is doing at any time—and it is doing very well these days—we may never be able to afford to let ourselves off the hook that the Endangered Species Act has put us on. It is a truism in government that money dries up as soon as the emergency is over, and the greatest fear I encounter among my associates in the National Park Service is that, once off the list, the grizzly bear will lose its dearest friends and its critically important financial support.

At a Park Service resource management training session in January of 1991, Yellowstone Superintendent Bob Barbee summed up the grizzly bear's situation very well when he said, "There's nothing that brings about apathy so quickly as the appearance of success." Recent population figures do prove a kind of success. They prove that the alarms of the early 1980s took effect. They prove that the federal agencies, when compelled by their legislative mandates, their constituencies, and the hearts and consciences of their employees, can do the job. They prove that the bears are very good at making new bears when we give them half a chance. But they do not prove the kind of success the grizzly bear will need to survive well into the next century.

Chapter 20

Don't Feed the Bears, Again

*T*he concept of minimum viable population is one with many ramifications. It depends not only on the bear's biology, but upon our effects on the bear's behavior. There is a population of brown bears, less than 100 of them, that have been living in a few hundred square miles in and around Italy's Abruzzo National Park for centuries. They are surrounded by populated country, and they are extremely shy. As Steve Herrero, one of the scientists who has studied them, has put it, "Thousands of years of coexistence between Europeans and brown bears have left behind a race of bears that excel at avoiding people."[1]

We have been doing the same thing, subtly, with the grizzly bears in our national parks. Yes, they are safe from hunting in the park, but for generations the most aggressive ones, the ones most likely to attack humans or go after human food, have been the ones most likely to be removed from the population and given no opportunity to contribute to the gene pool. The tendency to remove aggressive bears is probably increasing as human pressures around Yellowstone increase; aggressive bears are the ones most likely to be shot by sheepherders near the park, or hit by cars near developments, to say nothing of being killed by managers for attacks on humans.

On the other hand, grizzlies in Yellowstone have had two kinds of opportunities to become accustomed to humans and thus to increase the likelihood of someone getting hurt. The first opportunity was food, which bears learned to associate with humans, and for which bears would endure a great many discomforts and overcome many obstacles. In most of the Greater Yellowstone Ecosystem now, bears don't get the chances to get food that they used to. There is still the occasional fool who intentionally baits in bears, but they usually don't get away with it long.

The second opportunity is simply human presence. Bears, after seeing so many humans nearby, become used to them. They may become less likely to run away. Biologist Dale McCullough, writing in the Wildlife Society *Bulletin* in 1982, pointed out that getting rid of human food does not automatically solve all bear problems:

> Availability of food and positive conditioning are only part of the problem. Even elimination of human-related foods (assuming this is practical) may not solve the problem of habituation. Restricting negative condition and favoring habituation by frequent, innocuous contacts between people and bears (typical of park situations) can create problem bears without any reinforcement by food per se.[2]

What McCullough was suggesting is that not long ago, in fact when the Park Service began to clean up its act and divorce bears from human foods, it was widely assumed (even if it wasn't consciously thought) that once the garbage was gone, all problems would be gone. But it doesn't work that way. The bears, once divorced from garbage and made "wild" in some ecological sense, still encounter people. There is no portion of Yellowstone so isolated that a bear living there is unlikely to encounter humans. One difference between the grizzly bears of the dump days and the grizzly bears of today is that the modern bear is much more likely to encounter people, not only because the bear is free-ranging but because there are a lot more people. Backpacking increased several hundred percent in Yellowstone in the 1970s.

What all this means for bear-human encounters is difficult to say for sure. I know that some hunters and some game managers think they've got a sure-fire answer, one they're quick to offer in Yellowstone every few years. They announce, smugly, that a hunting season in the Yellowstone area would teach those bears who's boss around here. The idea that hunting will make animals wary of people is an old one, and it is often true. But the reasons it works are more complicated than most hunters suspect. There seems to be an assumption that if you shoot a few bears now and then the rest will somehow learn (whether they heard any of the shots, or saw any of the dead bears) to avoid humans. The process by which bears become wary from hunting is a "selecting process"; that is, a process whereby over the course of many generations of bears the most aggressive individuals are regularly culled from the population. An open hunting season offers no assurance that the aggressive bears will be the ones killed. If shooting bears was to be adopted as a way of making bears more cautious, it would have to be applied discretely to individual bears that are judged to show signs of being too aggressive. It would also have to be applied only outside the park, because a host of laws and conservation groups would hardly allow hunting inside the park.

But even at that there is a great deal of looseness in the principles of shooting as a way of conditioning bears to avoid humans. For one thing, as I have already suggested, it could be argued that for many years now managers, poachers, sheepherders, and other people who legally or illegally kill grizzlies in and around Yellowstone have been selecting out the most aggressive animals. Do we have any way of knowing that hunting would operate in a more efficient manner? No, we don't. More important, the mortality level that already exists is too high; until it drops dramatically, the possibility for sport hunting is a theoretical one anyway. But most important of all, the confidence of hunters aside, there is still a great deal we don't know about how grizzly bears react to human presence or human aggression.

A study in Glacier Park indicated that bears with no connection to human foods who regularly encountered humans became habituated to them in an interesting way. After seeing enough people on the trails, these grizzlies became much less apt to charge people than were bears who only encountered an occasional person. More charges occurred on lightly used trails than on heavily used ones.[3] What does this tell the manager who thinks that bears who are used to seeing humans are more dangerous because they've "lost their fear?"

As always, the issue is complex, and quite often it will come down to the imponderable and irreducible single element of temperament: both the individual bear's and the individual human's. Several research projects are currently underway to help us better understand how bears react to humans. A research project under the Interagency Study Team has actually gone out and created "encounters" with bears in order to radiotrack disturbed bears (fainthearted researchers need not apply) to see the extent of disruption of their routine.[4] Other researchers are experimenting with rubber bullets to see if bears can be conditioned by some combination of pain and human voice noise to avoid humans (this is a tough one, considering how much pain grizzly bears have shown they are willing to endure in order to get what they want).[5]

Steve Herrero, mentioned earlier, has written a simply superb book called *Bear Attacks, Their Causes and Avoidance* (1985). In it he considers not only the science of these habituation problems, but the philosophical implications:

> If we want to have both grizzly bears that regularly flee from people and also have high levels of human recreational use but no hunting, then we might try to mimic some of the effects of hunting. Repellents might be applied to bears when they first experience people. The question is, do we want to condition grizzly bears to avoid people? Is this to be the grizzly's fate in its last sanctuaries in the contiguous United States? If we were successful we might drive grizzlies away from important habitat, causing possible population decline. Since the grizzly is classified as a threatened species in the lower forty-eight states under the terms of the Endangered Species Act, it is questionable whether using deterrents that decreased grizzly populations would be legal. A combination of research to tell us what is possible and a lot of soul-searching to help us decide what is desirable will be needed to resolve these issues.[6]

We have a lot to learn yet about bears and people. Never before have we been trying so hard to learn it, but then never before has it mattered so much. If we decide we are going to do something to the Yellowstone grizzlies to change their behavior, we're going to have to do it very carefully.

Keeping bears and people from hurting each other is a subject that seems, even more than most bear-related subjects, to bring the easy-answer experts out of the woodwork. All ya gotta do is open up the dumps again, that'll take care of it. All ya gotta do is shoot a few of them now and then, that'll keep 'em in line; heck, back in the sixties we hunted grizzlies in all the states next to the park, and everything was okay. As I've said before, easy answers ignore complicated realities. Maybe hunting did make the bears more cautious back in the 1960s. Indeed, maybe the dumps had less to do with it than hunting; maybe those bears were hunted often enough when they left the park that they were less likely to bother people even when they were in the park. But then, of course, there were hardly any people using the backcountry back then, and there are several times as many now; we have no way of knowing that it wasn't simply a lack of people to attack that accounted for the low number of backcountry attacks in the 1960s.

Or consider the arguments of the more articulate proponents of dumpfeeding, such as Frank Craighead. He said that the dumps segregated humans from bears, and he also said that grizzlies did not associate the food they got in dumps with humans. Park Service managers and biologists had a lot of trouble with that statement, and one of the reasons was that as soon as the dumps were closed, at least by Craighead accounts, the bears immediately went looking for other sources of human food; that suggests that the bears were associating the dumps with humans.

This easy answer syndrome is one of the most puzzling—or perhaps comforting—elements of the bear controversy. The hunting magazines run editorials pronouncing upon the efficacy of hunting the grizzlies. The protectionist magazines run editorials against such "slaughter" of wildlife. Everyone has a pet theory. It is probably just as well they're all out there, each making its respective racket, because the resulting din is at least democratic and kind of balances itself out, leaving

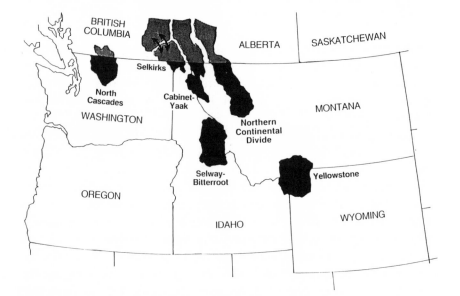

Remaining grizzly bear habitat in the lower forty-eight.

186

managers and scientists securely in the middle and inclined to take a middle course. What it comes down to is that several agencies are in the business of trying to manage the grizzly bear at the same time that they are trying to learn just what kind of management the grizzly bear most needs.

Just how much we have to learn has been tragically demonstrated a few times in recent years. In late June of 1983 a young man named Roger William May was dragged from his tent at Rainbow Point Campground near Hebgen Lake (west of Yellowstone Park) and killed by a grizzly bear. It happened in the middle of the night; the campground is a short distance west of the park boundary. The bear that did it, #15 on the Interagency Study Team's roster of study subjects, was captured near the site shortly after and destroyed. Though there were some garbage problems nearby, there was no really obvious reason why May was singled out. Bear #15 had been livetrapped by the team a total of nineteen times over the previous ten years, but that did not make him an extraordinary bear. C.B.S. News hopped on a suggestion that Sernylan, the drug used to tranquilize trapped bears, could have caused hallucinations or somehow made the bear go crazy, but biologists doubted there was anything to the idea.[7] Wyoming biologist Larry Roop said "it has as much credibility as saying people who take nitroglycerine for heart disease are going to fall dead in the streets when their chests explode."[8] But it was good for some exciting headlines.

Then, in July of 1984, a young Swiss woman, Brigitta Fredenhagen, was killed while camped along on upper Astringent Creek some miles east of Canyon Village in the park. She was dragged from her tent, apparently after going to sleep, and was killed and partially eaten. The board of inquiry could find no significant shortcomings in her way of keeping camp; she had "apparently received and followed all safety recommendations."[9] This bear was never located and as far as could be known never showed aggression of this sort again. It was judged to be a subadult grizzly bear, two or three years old judging from various measurements taken at the site.

These two incidents would once have been called "unprovoked attacks" but are now seen as evidence of something we still don't fully understand (the old "unprovoked attack" phrase seemed to imply that the attack was the bear's fault). They added a profound urgency to the ruminations I've just reviewed about bear behavior. They also added some sensational flavor to a renewed interest in bear feeding.

The excitement in the early 1980s over the new population estimates and the projected population decline brought about a resurgence in interest in somehow bolstering the bears with some additional food, either in the form of reopened dumps or some other nutrition. Alarm spread once it was known that the Interagency Study Team had reported a smaller-than-expected bear population, and the result was a whole new round of bear-feeding debates. It was covered in the popular press, though it wasn't reported with any especial accuracy; there was just this overwhelming feeling among concerned people that, well, we have to do something, don't we, rather than just watch these bears disappear?

Supporters of supplemental feeding were diverse. They included Frank Craighead, now standing alone among grizzly bear biologists as an advocate of reestablishing bear-feeding, the Wyoming Outfitters Association, the Murie Chapter of the Audubon Society, and Wyoming Senator Alan Simpson. They were not only loud, they were influential.

Early in 1983 a special task force appointed by the Interagency Grizzly Bear Committee met to consider the possibilities and consequences of supplemental feeding. It was a momentous meeting, because the task force included not only representatives of the National Park Service, the U.S. Fish and Wildlife Service, and the Wyoming Game and Fish Department, but right there in the middle of the list, representing the Wildlife-Wildlands Institute of Missoula, Montana, was John Craighead. This made for a rare and promising combination of perspectives, and the report the committee produced made for good reading.

The task force recommended unanimously against supplemental feeding, pointing out that if human mortalities were kept low enough the bears could get along in the Yellowstone area just as they had done for thousands of years. They did not rule out the possibility of applying supplemental feeding some time in the future, but they said that supplemental feeding is "not a cure-all and should not become a substitute for proper management of habitat and human activities inside and outside of Yellowstone Park."[10] This same sentiment was expressed independently, by the way, at about the same time, by Dr. Charles Jonkel, another leading grizzly bear authority who has concentrated on studying the bears of northern Montana. He wrote that supplemental feeding is "a quick fix approach, not worthy of serious consideration."[11]

Their main concern here was that, even if supplemental feeding worked, and somehow reconcentrated the park's bears at feeding stations, and actually did boost their nutrition enough to help (and none of those things were assured of happening), it missed the point of having a grizzly bear recovery plan. It shortcircuited the process by which the various government agencies were being compelled to give the bear sufficient habitat to care for itself.

The task force found it difficult to envision a supplemental feeding program that would have a good chance of working. Simply reopening the dumps would be of questionable worth, even if it was legal, because the dumps would not provide food in the fall, after the visitors leave; without food in the park in the fall, the bears would certainly wander out to feed on gut-piles and get shot accidentally or on purpose by hunters. Moreover, the elk population was now very large, at least three times as large as during the dump days, and the bears had just spent fifteen years getting used to the new possibilities for nutrition from elk meat; there was serious question if dumps or feeding stations could entice the grizzlies away from all those good gut-piles and other fall opportunities outside the park.

The report had little use for the idea of using "surplus" elk, pointing out that in order to provide sufficient elk to feed the bears the park's northern herd—the largest and most visible—would have to be massively manipulated and reduced by half, something that, even if it made ecological sense would be a political nightmare. The task force then pointed out that the northern herd, if reduced, would provide virtually no springtime carcasses, critical protein for newly emerged bears. Again, these grizzlies had just spent fifteen years getting used to this newly enlarged food source, and many were now denning near areas of known springtime carcass concentrations. Noting all of this, the task force concluded that feeding bears on elk "could create biological problems as acute as those currently under consideration." They didn't mention the political problems, but considering their audience I suppose they didn't have to.

The task force also feared that establishing feeding sites would necessitate closing large portions of the backcountry to protect the bears and the visitors from each other. Indeed, Yellowstone Park Research Administrator John Varley, who was not on the task force, commented to me that it would be virtually impossible to keep people from getting to the bears once the feeding sites were known. That, of course, would make things just that much more convenient for poachers, who were getting up to $10,000 for the various parts of a prime grizzly at the time.

On a more mundane note, the task force also pointed out that the supplemental feeding project, wherever the food came from, would be enormously expensive, and the bill would have to be paid every year.

The task force had some hopeful things to say, too. They observed that the increased number of elk was gradually taking up some of the slack left by the dump closures, as were the increased number of bison. They did not mention the greatly increased trout population of Yellowstone Lake, but could have. They also suggested that managers investigate ways to use food as a short-term tool to control bears. If, for example, a known sheep-killer is radiotracked on his way to a sheep herd near the park, managers could drop a road-killed elk or a dead horse in his path and slow him down while the sheep are moved.

Of course the task force didn't need to say most of that. As soon as they'd recommended against supplemental feeding as unnecessary at this stage, they had said all that was really critical.

It was terribly nice, I thought, to see the Park Service and at least one of the Craigheads in formal agreement on something, and it must have been some kind of milestone in the controversy, too.

Supplemental feeding of the bears is an illuminating aspect of the controversy. Here is an animal population that we as a nation desperately want to save. Our first reaction, a perfectly under-standable and laudable one, is to get out there and do something conclusive. Feeding wildlife has been popular in this country for more than a century. Though many biologists now recommend against it under almost any circumstance, it still has a good sound to the public, and still is quick to surface when some animal is perceived to be in trouble. All of the complexities of what happens to an animal population under artificial feeding can be lost in the heat of the need to do something, to act. I wouldn't be surprised if some day the bears of Yellowstone have to be fed to be kept around, but we seem a long way from that day. In the meantime it will occasionally be difficult for us to distinguish between our need to do something we can feel good about and our need to do something that will actually help the bear.

Chapter 21

Keeping the Bears

*I*n all the excitement over the status of the grizzly bear population there is risk of missing another kind of excitement, over the huge amounts of information we have gained from the Interagency Study Team project. This happened before, at the conclusion of the Craighead study. That study ended in such bitterness and controversy that hardly anyone took the time (or felt like taking the time) to celebrate a major scientific achievement. I'd like to avoid letting that happen again.

By 1991, the Interagency Study Team had put in eighteen years of intensive research in what is probably the longest and most productive grizzly bear research project ever. More than 100 papers, theses, reports, and publications had been produced, and enough data is in hand to complete many other projected reports. My natural history discussions in Part One of this book at least suggest the vast extent of what this study has taught us. A second and equally exciting study began in 1983, and has captured the attention and imagination of many grizzly bear enthusiasts and researchers. Steve and Marilynn French, founders of the Yellowstone Grizzly Foundation, have concentrated on behavioral studies. Working closely with Dick Knight and with Park Service bear managers, they have spent thousands of hours observing bears, and have in many ways improved our understanding of the Yellowstone grizzly bear. Their findings have also informed this book in many ways. Independently funded, the Yellowstone Grizzly Foundation is also able to campaign aggressively on behalf of grizzly bear conservation, and has developed some of the most impressive educational programs ever mounted on behalf of bears.

Marilynn and Steve French of the Yellowstone Grizzly Foundation. Photo by the author.

In various capacities—as a consulting researcher, as an independent writer, as an instructor at the Yellowstone Institute, and as a friend—it has been an honor and a pleasure for me to work with members of both these research teams. In the long history of bear-human interactions, I can think of no grizzly bear population blessed with so many able students and so many effective friends.

The attention that is now routinely given the grizzly bear has moved the black bear almost entirely off the political stage, but not out of the public mind. The black bear has not been studied in Yellowstone since the 1960s, and there is great hesitation about doing so now because any such study might disrupt some grizzly bear activities; it would be very hard to trap just black bears, for instance. But the Park Service is interested in such a study, and it is probably coming, because scientists are growing curious about the smaller bear.

Estimates of black bears in Yellowstone usually ran to several hundred. Cole made an informal estimate of 650 in the early 1970s, and that is the last real attempt to figure out how many there are. There may be fewer than that, though, and a few Park Service critics, including Frank Craighead, have found time to suggest that here, too, the park has a problem.

Tentative hypotheses are offered by several biologists. The redistribution of grizzly bears and their return to something more like a natural set of feeding habits may have somehow influenced the black bears. Perhaps the blacks had occupied some niches which the grizzlies are now taking over. Perhaps the dry spell in the 1970s took its toll on them as it did on the grizzlies.

When grizzlies and blacks coexist, blacks become specialists in avoiding grizzlies. Maybe the blacks have stabilized at some new, lower population level. Maybe there never were as many black bears as the casual early estimates suggested. Maybe, critics suggest, the Park Service killed more blacks than were reported and the population has (for some reason not provided by the critics) not recovered. There is a severe shortage of information here. Some people will look to science to fill it, others will happily fill it with conjecture or rumor. What puzzled me when I was working in the park was that people could complain that there were no bears in the park, but as soon as someone left out an ice chest, or a couple of half-eaten hot dogs, a bear would materialize like ants at a picnic. It happened again and again. You couldn't have gotten a bear into that campground any quicker if you'd hired one. That suggested to me that, at the very least, there were enough black bears in Yellowstone to keep a few noses aimed at every campground.

In the late 1970s and early 1980s, I lived for five years in Vermont, on the edge of Green Mountain National Forest. It was some of New England's better bear country, with black bears taken by hunters in all directions from my little village. I spent a lot of time out at odd hours, returning from a variety of fishing and social expeditions, down along the creeks just at those gloaming hours when bears are supposed to be active, and I never saw one. They were there; the hunters proved it every fall, and the beekeepers occasionally regretted it. They were just remarkably secretive. Finally, just shortly before I moved from Vermont, a bear ran across the road in broad daylight a couple hundred yards from my house, just as I happened to be driving that way. That bit of personal experience only reinforces the historical lesson

Yellowstone offered me: just because you can't see them doesn't mean they aren't there.

But to many people it doesn't even matter if they're there. I gather from my readings and conversations that to some people the loss of bears, especially the loss of the grizzly, from Yellowstone would not matter. What, they would say, was really lost? We couldn't see it, and it surely wasn't good for anything in today's world. I wouldn't have written this book if I had any sympathy for an attitude like that. It smacks of the common human arrogance that asks only "What's in it for me?" as if everything can be measured in terms of some abstract market value.

But in a sense they're right, because the loss would be hard to quantify. The loss of a scientific specimen, a priceless one, would matter only to scientists and naturalists and a few of us who can't get enough information about bears. The vacating of the bear's ecological niche in Yellowstone would be felt subtly throughout the system, but the system would go on without disastrous changes; there do not seem to have been many changes when the grizzly was wiped out of the rest of its range. The disappearance of an animal so seldom seen by the public would not matter that much to the average visitor. It would certainly be felt by anyone who loves to be in grizzly country, but such people are still in a minority.

The loss, at last, would be cultural. Some of the best bear biologists have reflected at length on this subject, which at first appears rather airy. It is not. Every person in the country would lose something if the grizzly disappeared. A superbly restrained expression of this is found, of all places, in the findings of a court case that had nothing directly to do with bears. In the 1974 case Minnesota Public Interest Research Group v. Butz, in which the U.S. Forest Service was challenged for not preparing an environmental impact statement before cutting timber in northern Minnesota, a very useful phrase was coined: "existence value." The suit had been brought under the terms of the National Environmental Policy Act (1970), one objective of which was to make the federal government responsible for preparing an E.I.S. for any "proposals for legislation and other major Federal actions significantly affecting the quality of the human environment." In the Minnesota case, the court described such effects in broad terms, so that one does not necessarily have to personally experience something to need and appreciate it:

> Existence value refers to that feeling some people have just knowing there remains a true wilderness untouched by human hands, such as the feeling of loss people might feel upon the extinction of the whooping crane even though they had never seen one. . . .[1]

On these terms, the existence value of the Yellowstone bears is immeasurable. Unfortunately, our society is not comfortable with quantities it cannot measure, and so is apt to disregard them.

To most Americans, bears and other wildlife are a distant and minor concern. Not one in 10,000 will ever see a grizzly, much less have a chance to learn to appreciate it. As one observer put it, "a reverence for the bear was common among North American Indians . . . . In our culture, by way of contrast, we seem not to reverence any animal unless it be the golden calf or the Wall Street bull."[2]

But I don't think that's the last word, especially as far as public concern for the grizzly bear goes. Recent national surveys have shown that when the average American is asked, he or she shows a clear preference for preservation of grizzly bears even if it costs a lot or requires people to give up some land. Bears have more friends now than they ever have, and those friends have slowly learned how to make a difference. They can play a crucial role in the future, taking up the slack when the agencies lack the initiative, and jumping on the agencies when a program shows signs of slipping.

Just when we think we begin to understand the threats to the bear, new ones show up. There is a proposal in the works for a major new bear zoo along the west boundary of Yellowstone Park, a thing that has conservationists alarmed not only for its confused message to the public—come look at captive bears in the middle of superb wild bear habitat—but for its possible damage to the wild bear populations through spread of disease, attraction of wild bears into a development, and so on.[3] There is the ever more ominous prospect of global climate change, which could have disastrous effects on grizzly bear habitat in Greater Yellowstone.[4] There is dramatically increasing visitation to Greater Yellowstone; it is undeniably our property, all of us Americans, but we are in danger of destroying it with our desire to enjoy it. I often wonder if the bear has a chance—if Greater Yellowstone itself has a chance.

But we can do it. That may be the best lesson I've learned from studying the bear management controversy of the past 25 years, and from watching how we've struggled to come to terms with our responsibilities in Greater Yellowstone. Nothing is predestined here. We can save this place. We can have the bears and enjoy and use their country. We have the scientific knowledge, the bureaucratic machinery, and the wisdom to keep it all in the kind of shape our descendants will be grateful for.

Part Three

The Bears of Yellowstone
An American Romance

Chapter 22

The Bear as Person

O utside of the primates, it is unlikely there is another animal that can match the bear in complexity of image. Most others, in fact, are quite simple in their popular stereotypes: dogs are faithful, cats are fickle, owls are wise, rats are dirty, and mules are stubborn. In literature the portrayals of bears have been diverse. As a member of Frank Baum's terrifying trio of "lions and tigers and bears," as a ranger-hatted friend of forest children ("Only YOU . . . "), as a mythic spectre in Faulkner's "The Bear," as a kindly *Jungle Book* giant, as a stitched and clumsy little fellow named Pooh, and as a host of animated hucksters, the bear has done it all. Bears are silly and magnificent, untouchably wild and hopelessly tame, shameful cowards and bold heroes. The bear is the most confusing of our animal ideas, and that may be its biggest problem. It has the unfortunate capacity to seem human. Bears stand comfortably (one scientists noted "the bipedal habit which . . . seems to be behind much of the anthropomorphic adoration, respect, and fear—"). They work hard, but not if they can avoid it. They play, loaf, and give all the outward signs of humanity, including theft, malice, and humor (they are called "the clowns of the forest," and "the happy hooligans"). Moreover, they have attractive qualities as animals—they are roly-poly, loveable, easy to please, and rare enough to be novel.[1]

To the average Yellowstone visitor they represent some combination of the above characters, and probably others. All of this seems a lot to expect of an animal, even one so charming as a bear, but the sight of one never fails to make the day successful. I have often been confronted by families who "haven't seen a thing here in the

199

N.P.S. photo.

park." Usually I find that they have seen deer, elk, moose, bison, and so on, "but we haven't seen any *bears!*"

It is not hard to understand the preference. The bear's ability to interest people has been amply demonstrated by authors who have found its flexible character so useful. The visitor watching a magnificent bull elk graze in a mountain meadow, even if that visitor has never seen an elk before, will get restless quickly. He's seen horses do the same thing, back home, for hours. The bear is a different matter; it turns over rocks, climbs trees, eats candy wrappers (and elk), hibernates, mauls people . . . now there's an animal a man can appreciate! It may do none of those things while he watches it, but his knowing that it might makes the difference.

It might have been better to entitle this final part of the book "Bear Appreciation," for that is the subject. We have examined the ecology of bears, and we've seen where they fit in the park's management program, but we have not faced the personal side of the story—What is in it for me, as a park visitor, when I want to enjoy the bears? The assortment of lore, legend, and advise that follows will not provide a simple answer to that question, but it will shed some light on the possibilities.

There is one element in bear lore that is almost universal, and that is humor. Practically every bear story told around a campfire has comic relief. The bear manages to be funny by its very appearance. Its activities with men are so rarely harmful that they approach slapstick, but under many circumstances, even unpleasant ones, laughter is a nervous release. Losing lunch to a bear is funny. Being treed by a bear is funny. Being chased, as in a cartoon, with whirring legs and melodramatic music, is even funnier. But being caught by a bear is not funny at all. We can laugh at the situations as long as we respect the realities.

For years a popular yarn on the campfire circuit has involved the way to tell a grizzly bear from a black bear: sneak up behind it and kick it, then climb a tree. If it climbs up after you, it's a black. If it knocks the tree down, it's a grizzly. A more recent variation is to kick it and then simply stand there. If, two seconds later, you are still alive, it wasn't a grizzly. A popular joke a few years ago concerned a hiker who was treed by a grizzly. The bear fumed, roared, and clawed at the tree, but the hiker was safely out of reach. After a few minutes the bear left, but just as the hiker was about to climb down he saw the bear returning with a second bear. Together, the two bears shook the tree, but were unable to loosen the hiker's hold. They gave up and left, and again he started to climb down. This time he saw *three* bears coming down the trail, and they shook the tree so that it waved and swayed, but the hiker held fast. When they finally left, he was sure he would be safe, because he could not imagine there was yet a fourth bear nearby to help them. Just as he began to climb down, he looked down the trail and saw the bears returning, carrying a beaver.

In that story, when you read of the bears coming down the trail, odds are that your mind saw upright, pot-bellied, short-legged Yogi-type bears. They were probably grinning. We carry many images with us, and apply them subconsciously to fit what we hear. The bears of Yellowstone, as described in Parts I and II, deserve the best, most honest image we can give them. They are even more enjoyable and stimulating in real life than they are in caricature.

Chapter 23

Famous Yellowstone Bears

*I*ndividual bears rarely become famous as characters or individuals. They may become well known anonymously, by mauling a hiker or being photographed by hundreds of visitors, but only once in a while does a singular, identifiable character emerge. Often, as we will see later, an individual bear gets well known locally. Countless Yellowstone bears have been named and admired by park personnel and visitors. Before begging was stopped, black bears often returned to the same roadside area each year ("Lucy's back at her station"), and others made themselves reputations in campgrounds. It doesn't take long, and names are convenient and quickly applied.

I recall a small black bear that frequented the Mammoth Hot Springs area in the mid-1970s. Because this bear had a long patch of blonde hair on its back, it became known as "Streaker" (an unusual public performer then in fashion had something to do with the inspiration). The name became more appropriate when Streaker learned to recognize ranger patrol cars. At some point in his life Streaker must have been driven from the road by an impatient ranger, for he "streaked" for cover at the sight of the car.

In the 1960s and later, when many bears were trapped and transplanted, they were often known by their numbers, referring to the identification number they were given for radiotracking purposes. In 1977 one ranger in my acquaintance expressed concern when he was assigned to a backcountry patrol in an area where Number Nine had just been released. Number Nine was a boar grizzly of more than 700 pounds.

Naming seems unavoidable. Some criticized the part for using numbers, as if this somehow depersonalized the process of dealing with bears. In view of the bears that had both numbers (official) and names (unofficial), the criticism seems silly. Further, rangers and biologists long ago proved how relative all words are. Fifty-four quickly becomes "Ol' Fifty-four," which can have all the sentimental weight of "Mergatroyde."

But a few bears, real or fictitious, have made the big time. Ernest Thompson Seton produced two storybook characters based on Yellowstone originals. The first was Wahb, a minor but lasting contribution to children's literature. Wahb's story, *The Biography of a Grizzly*, first appeared in 1899.[1] In the book, Wahb was born in the mountains east of the park and grew into an enormous and dreaded giant who fought a lifelong battle with ranchers. He died peacefully in Death Gulch near Wahb Springs. *The Biography* has gone though countless printings, and Walt Disney based a feature movie on the story, altering only the ending so that it was adequately happily-ever-after. For half a century Wahb reigned as Yellowstone's most famous bear. Seton, who was criticized for anthropomorphism, would have been amazed at Wahb's successor, for where is there a more manlike bear than Yogi?

Seton also produced Johnny Bear, an insecure little black bear who appeared in *Lives of the Hunted* and *Wild Animals at Home*.[2] Johnny was a fairly wimpy little character, and lacked the quality to endure.

Perhaps the first *real* Yellowstone bear to become famous was Jesse James, the famous begging bear of the late 1910s. His exploits appeared in national publications, and were even featured in the 1919 Report of the Director of the National Park Service. Jesse was a fleeting celebrity, however, as his identity was lost as more and more bears (and Jesse was by no means the first) joined him along park roads. In 1925, an identical character, "Spud," was written up in *American Forests* magazine.[3] Once beggars were common, it was impossible for one to be more famous than the rest.

In 1931 Naturalist Dorr Yeager captured a newly born black bear by taking it from a den under a building at Old Faithful. His story of raising "Barney" at Park Headquarters was published, but Barney was not destined to have lasting fame.[4]

It was not until the late 1950s, in fact, that Yellowstone inspired another nationally-known bear character. At that time Hanna Barbera produced a refreshing new television cartoon series, "The Huckleberry Hound Show." The fame of one of the featured characters

"'AIN'T HE AN AWFUL SIZE, THOUGH?'"

"Wahb," the hero of Seton's epic animal story Biography of a Grizzly.

"Barney," the black bear cub raised by park naturalist Dorr Yeager, in 1931. N.P.S. photo.

on that show eventually eclipsed not only Huck's but also that of the New York Yankee catcher for whom Yogi was named.

Yogi Bear was stereotypical. He embodied known habits of black bears, especially their fondness for human food ("Pickanic baskets") and their seeming clownishness. He was a roaring success (soon given his own program), the most famous bear ever, and all right there in Jellystone Park.

Yogi has made life miserable for countless rangers. "Hey Mr. Ranger sir, where can we see Yogi?" He has also caused consternation among all who wished to have Yellowstone's bears treated as wild animals. Yogi was weekly reinforcement of the worst misconceptions visitors had about Yellowstone's bears. Rangers are paid to answer the same question again and again ("What times does Old Faithful go off?" "Does it always rain here?" "Where's the bathroom?"), so their burden would not have been reduced had Yogi not been created. But solving the beggar problem was a little different. The cartoon generated immense sympathy for the hero, who was, after all, just guilty of a little good-natured tomfoolery. The ranger in the cartoon was not quite mean, but he was not rally a nice man, either. Rangers have frequently encountered hostility from visitors who insisted on seeing and feeding bears.

It is not fair, however, to blame Yogi's creators for this problem. Yogi is now as valid a part of our culture as Mother Goose or Aesop. There is nothing wrong with talking animals in fiction, and Yogi is good wholesome entertainment. It is not Yogi's fault that some people are unable to distinguish between an animated creation and a wild animal.

If Yogi is blameless, some other recent portrayals of bears are not. Fictionalized accounts of wild animals, using live bears, have been popular in movies and television for years, and many do great damage to the image of wild animals. Some turn bears into gigantic buffoons, with all the aggressive tendencies of any easy chair. Others are nothing less than monster movies. The more savage the monster, of course, the bigger the box-office success of the film. None of these films have involved Yellowstone, or any other national park, because Park Service officials would not allow it. The impression made by one film monster with almost supernatural ferocity is a deep one, especially on young minds. In some people it may never be erased.

Chapter 24

Hunting Yellowstone's Bears

I enjoy a good hunting story, and have devoted an entire book to telling the stories of some of America's most remarkable bear hunters. But I confess I have an aversion to the blood-and-gore tales so popular in bear literature—"The enraged drooling beast, eyes red with pain and fury, roared as it stood over the helpless hunter." It is well established that bears are peaceable enough if we let them alone. But bear hunting stories are revealing, not only of bear natural history but also of human values. The stories are sometimes shocking, sometimes exciting, and often a little funny, too, and they add yet another dimension to our understanding of the bears of Yellowstone.

Hunting was a legal and even popular form of recreation in Yellowstone prior to 1883. In the past century, most popular writing about bears has been done by hunters or ex-hunters. Before the many research projects of the last twenty years were undertaken, we owed practically everything we knew about bears to hunters. They produced some sensitive and lasting natural history, and some very good writing.

I am surprised at how many people assume that because hunting is illegal in national parks, park personnel must disapprove of hunting elsewhere. Many, if not most, of the people I've worked most closely with in Yellowstone over the past twenty years have been avid sportsmen, and so am I. As I've perhaps suggested already in this book, sport hunting was early on perceived to be incompatible with the park's goals, and that perception continues to prevail; I agree with it, and think there is ample evidence to support it.

In fact, the movement in the 1880s to ban hunting in Yellowstone was led in good part by sportsmen, who saw the park as a sort of reservoir for game, a place from which the wild country near the park could be perpetually restocked. The park's relationship with its neighboring lands, as I discussed it in Part Two of this book, will always be complicated, because the animals move as nature, not political boundaries, dictate. Likewise, the park's relationship with sport hunting will always be complicated; as animal rights and anti-hunting activists increase their attacks on sport hunting, wildlife managers, even those in national parks, will be confronted with difficult issues. But most of the hunters I'm about to consider came from a simpler age, when a great many things we now struggle with seemed quite clear.

Not all of the accounts that follow are truly hunting tales. One concerns the destruction, by odd but practical means, of a dangerous grizzly, and another tells of a hunting trip that strained all definitions of good sportsmanship.

It is the opinion of some authorities that the well-armed bear hunter is the least safe person in bear country; that hikers, bird-watchers, fishermen, and ranchers will sustain far fewer injuries per encounter than hunters. One well-known naturalist is convinced that the bear can sense an aggressive attitude.[1] Scientists won't necessarily go that far, but it is clear that the non-hunter usually enters the wilderness in greater humility, with more willingness to fit into the picture without disturbance. Perhaps therein is part of the justification for hunting stories. There is something to be said for a little sensational drama of this kind. Violence between man and bear, as it occurs in a few wild parts of the country, is the closest most of us will ever come to the realization that humans, like all other animals, can be a prey species.

In 1870, two years before the park was established, A. Bart Henderson was one of several prospectors working in and around what is now the northeast corner of Yellowstone. He differed from the others in that he kept a diary, full of references to game. Most daily entries were only a few lines long, but bear encounters were frequently mentioned. On July 4 he noted "I killed several deer and three bear." On the sixth he "killed a large bear near camp." On the ninth, in an unusual burst of verbosity, he came close to telling a story.

> Dad & myself left camp to prospect. Met an old she bear & three cubs. After a severe fight killed the whole outfit, while a short distance further on we was attacked by an old boar bear. We soon killed him.

He proved to be the largest ever killed in the mountains, weighing 960 pounds.

We returned to camp, after killing five bear & doing no prospecting. Home and James returned from Rock Mountain—rough country, no gold.[2]

Such perfunctory calm about what must have been an enormous animal is admirable (we are not told how the bear was weighed), but leaves all too much to the imagination. On the next day he reported killing six more. On the eleventh his entry, which today would be worth a cover story in a major outdoor magazine, was brief:

Clear and beautiful. All hands out prospecting. Found 3 cents to the pan today. I was chased by an old she bear today. Clime a tree & killed her under the tree.

The important news, "3 cents to the pan," came first. Henderson's understatement is magnificent. On July 28, it was

Clear and warm. Remained in camp to prospect—no gold. Killed several elk, buffalo and deer. Buffalo bull run thru camp while all hands were in bed. Home had wounded him. Located trail & killed a bear.

One wonders if Home wounded him earlier, or while he was running through camp. Another question remains; some have read accounts like these as proof that Yellowstone's bears (and, indeed, all grizzlies) were initially very aggressive with humans. Quite a few of Henderson's encounters were obviously had while hunting—at least two involved "she bears," who may have felt cubs were threatened—so it is difficult to generalize. We can only regret he did not elaborate.

The same year, in September, other Yellowstone adventurers encountered a grizzly with more lighthearted results. Walter Trumbull, a member of the Washburn-Langford-Doane expedition, reported on the hunt that took place south of Yellowstone Lake.

Some of the party who had gone a short distance ahead to find out the best course to take the next day, soon returned and reported a grizzly and her two cubs about a quarter mile from camp. Six of the party decorated themselves as walking armories, and at once started in pursuit. Each individual was sandwiched between two revolvers and a knife, was supported around the middle by a belt of cartridges, and carried in his hand a needle carbine. Each one was particularly anxious to be the first to catch the bear, and an exciting foot race ensued until the party got within 300 yards of the place where the bear was supposed to be concealed. The foremost man then suddenly got out of breath, and, in fact, they all got out of breath. It was an epidemic. A halt was made, and the brute loudly dared to come out and show itself, while a spirited discussion took place as to what was best to do with the cubs. The location was a mountain side, thickly timbered with tall straight pines having no limbs within thirty feet of the ground. It was decided to advance more cautiously to avoid frightening the animal, and every tree which there was any chance of climbing was watched with religious care, in order to intercept her should she attempt to take refuge in its branches. An hour was passed in search for the sneaking beast, which had evidently taken to flight. Then this formidable war party returned to camp, having a big disgust at the cowardly conduct of the bear, but, as the darkie said, "not having it bad." Just before getting in sight of camp, the six invincibles discharged their firearms simultaneously, in order to show those remaining behind just how they would have slaughtered the bear, but more particularly how they did not. This was called the "Bear Camp."[3]

Nathaniel Langford mentioned the incident in his diary, explaining that "we traced her into a dense thicket, which, owing to the darkness, we did not care to penetrate, for not one of us felt we had lost that particular bear."[4]

An incident of the sort that gave the grizzly its great reputation for strength was reported by Superintendent Norris in 1879.

A fine young horse, somewhat lamed by scalding in the fire holes, having been left near Obsidian Canyon, was killed by a grizzly that in devouring the carcass and fragments of game killed in the vicinity, continued to haunt the place. In trailing him in the snow nearly knee deep some weeks afterwards, I killed two large antlered elks, but a few yards apart, and, it being nearly night, I only removed their entrails and camped along near them, confident that bruin would visit them before morning. I then found that he had dragged the elk so near together as to leave only a space for a lair of boughs and grass between them, which he was intently finishing, when I, at a distance of 100 yards, opened fire with a Winchester rifle with fourteen ordinary bullets in the chamber and a dynamite shell—being all that I dared to use at once in the barrel. This I first gave him high in the shoulder, the shell there exploding and severing the main artery beneath the backbone. He fell, but instantly arose with a fearful snort or howl of pain and rage, but got four additional ordinary .44 caliber bullets in the shoulder, and nearly as many falls before discovering me, and then charged. Hastily inserting another dynamite shell, I, at a distance of about 50 yards, as he came in, sent it through his throat into his chest, where it exploded and nearly obliterated his lungs, again felling him; and as he arose, broke his back with the seventh shot. Either one of these would have stiffened any other animal, and surely have proved fatal to him; but deeming delays then dangerous, I peppered him lively. Finding Stephens across Beaver Lake, we returned with our saddle and pack animals, and after killing a pair of wood martens that were preying upon the carcasses, we dressed the animals, packing all possible of them 26 miles to our blockhouse at the Mammoth Hot Springs. We there found the hide of the bear just as spread out, without stretching, to be 8 3/4 feet long from tip of snout to roots of tail, and 6 feet 7 inches at its widest place; and from his blubber brought in, Stephens tried out 35 gallons of grease or oil. Its extraordinary size is the only reason for at all mentioning the animal in this report.[5]

He later reported about the grizzly's temperament:

Although, save in defense of . . . carcasses or of its young, this bear seldom provokes attack upon man, it invariably resists one, and if wounded usually charges furiously, either to its own death or that of its foe, and not infrequently both. Indeed, it may be truly said to be the mountaineers most dreaded foe.

Early hunters differed on this matter of ferocity, some saying the animal usually fled when shot, others saying it attacked. Overall it must have been unpredictable, as it is now.

Bears were rarely removed from the park by administrators until after 1900, and then only as ordered by the acting superintendent. Once a bear was labelled a troublemaker, shooting was the customary means of destroying it. Occasionally the circumstances called for different tactics (A. Bart Henderson likely would have called them more "severe").

The enormous grizzly that killed Frank Welch in 1916 was finally destroyed by order of the acting superintendent with a little help from Major Fries of the Army Corps of Engineers. (The Corps was in charge of park road work at that time, and had work camps along the roads. Welch worked in one of these.) Major Fries provided a nearby camp, which had also been visited by that bear, with "fifteen sticks of 40 percent dynamite." A generous bait of garbage drew the great bear over the dynamite, and according to one observer the explosion "raised that bear up maybe four or five feet . . . broke every bone in his body."[6]

One last hunting episode should be included here, though it is a disappointing tale. In 1920 Saxton Pope and Arthur Young received permission from the Department of the Interior to kill four Yellowstone grizzlies for the San Francisco Museum of the California Academy of Sciences. In the agreement they made it clear they were going to use bow and arrow (the sportsmanship of hunting grizzly with bow is still debated—most bowhunters who go after grizzly or brown bear are backed up by a rifleman—but clearly Pope and Young were incapable of consistent clean kills). Their avowed purpose, aside from collecting the specimens, was to see if it could be done. They found a group of four (sow with three young—probably two-year-olds) and commenced firing. Their first arrows hit the sow and a cub. The two bears immediately attacked one another, perhaps assuming their nearest neighbor was the cause of their pain. Pope's second arrow missed them, then both put arrows in the sow, who finally saw the hunters and charged. The bowhunter's guide, Ned Frost, then shot her with a rifle, which stopped her long enough for the hunters to put two more arrows in her and kill her. The cubs, one wounded, escaped. Pope described this, and killing of several other bears, in page after embarrassing and gruesome page, in his book *Hunting with the Bow and Arrow*. The superintendent's report on the whole affair was outspoken, and not concerning poor sportsmanship:

> The party proceeded to the Grand Canyon, where they established their headquarters. Soon three grizzlies were killed, and the party was notified that only one more bear could be killed.
>
> As there were difficulties in finding another suitable specimen, permission was requested to kill a large grizzly seen near the Canyon garbage dump. This permission I refused on the ground I felt that this would spoil the amusement the tourists were then taking in seeing the bears.

Nevertheless, the party stationed themselves on the trail used by the grizzlies in going to the garbage, and there killed four more bears. After this killing, no bears, black or grizzly, appeared for nearly ten days, thus causing disappointment to thousands of tourists. Not only were seven bears killed, but four cubs were left motherless and one other was believed to have been wounded.[6]

Pope's account is triumphant, even gloating. They had, indeed, killed grizzlies with the bow and arrow, but had they not been backed by a rifleman the very first bear they shot probably would have done them in. The episode, whatever good it did their fame, was very sloppy hunting, and if the superintendent was right, a violation of their agreement. Hunting might not be so unpopular today if fewer hunters behaved like that.

Chapter 25

Making Themselves at Home

*Y*ellowstone Park, in spite of its vast wilderness, is in some respects not typical bear habitat. Bears are very adaptable animals, and they have made some surprising adjustments to living in the park.

Black bears were long willing to enter developed areas, such as campgrounds and residential areas, but some time, probably around 1900, they discovered the convenience and comfort to be had by denning under buildings. Bears reportedly burrowed under or broke through walls of buildings (hotels and stores, most often) in what had become a well-established habit by 1920. In 1925, Ranger Joseph Douglas reported:

> On or about December 18 an old black bear and brown cub holed up for the winter under the Lake Hotel. For several days previously the old bear had been seen taking quantities of green willow branches into the prospective den. Later she was seen scraping into the den quantities of snow. Since the date mentioned the winter keeper has been feeding the bears about twice weekly, the animals showing their heads at the den entrance in quest of the table scraps. This is thought to be the first time a bear has thus "registered for the winter" at the Yellowstone Lake Hotel.[1]

At least some of the chosen buildings were vacant in the winter, and food was usually not an incentive. A dry and ready-made den was probably a welcome change for a bear.

A few years later it occurred to the rangers to take advantage of

214

what was actually an excellent opportunity to learn about bears. The case of Barney, mentioned earlier, was such an effort, but produced little of value. During the winter of 1931–1932 Ranger Curtis Skinner managed to devote some time to studying one family at Old Faithful. In October, Skinner arranged a den-site under the "old government mess house" by digging a hole through the foundation wall and preparing a den-shaped enclosure inside. He kept it baited, and though several bears fed at the bait none chose to den there. Skinner knew of bears under at least four other buildings in the Old Faithful area, so he had no trouble finding other subjects. He chose an apparent family group (cubs could be heard crying from rooms above the den) under the Haynes store. In February a hole was cut through the floor and he was able to observe the family. He twice succeeded in removing the cubs and weighing them. It turned out that there was also a second adult under the floor (it was a spacious area). This lone bear "appeared to be causing the mother some trouble and during the observation the two older bears engaged in noisy combat."

Skinner's findings were in some ways at variance with traditional bear lore. he learned, for example, that bears do not sink into a deep coma-like sleep. His account is instructive, even with all the additional information we now have:

> At various times during the winter, I had the opportunity to look in upon four different dens containing adult black bear. I found none of them asleep, although they were decidedly lethargic and reluctant to move even when molested.[2]

For all its shortcomings (Skinner was absent in early winter, so he did not make observations then), this was one of the earliest attempts to seriously and systematically study any aspect of Yellowstone bear life.

As building standards improved, and as bears were no longer drawn into developed areas by food, basement-denning disappeared. There were other unusual accommodations available to bears, though, and not just for sleeping.

Bears make use of Yellowstone's thermal areas in all seasons. Like many animals, they are probably drawn to the heat during cold spells. The snow is less deep in the geyser basins in the winter, and often there are patches of bare ground and even green plants. Also like other animals, bears occasionally are victims of thermal accidents. The carcass of one black bear was found in Prismatic Lake (now Grand Prismatic Spring) in 1908, apparently the result of such an accident.[3] Large animals, like bears, bison, and men, do break through the thin crust around large hot springs once in a while. Another bear, reported on in 1940, had a more pleasant experience:

> On the afternoon of August 29th, we were stalking a Black Bear on the Mammoth Terraces in order to get a picture. Bruin was very accommodating and suddenly decided to take a bath. He ambled over to the base of Angel Terrace, looked around for a moment, and then climbed up the terraces to one of the pools. After testing it for temperature, Bruin crawled in, carefully dipped up the water with his paws, and went about his bath.
>
> The pool is about four feet long, three feet wide, and eighteen inches deep. The temperature of the water was about 90°F. Judging by the bear's action in locating the pool and by his activity afterward taking a bath in the warm water of the Hot Springs was evidently not a new experience for him.[4]

Equally common has been the practice of sleeping in naturally heated dens. Bears sleeping in extinct hot springs openings, or thermally heated dens of other kinds, have been discovered at Mammoth Hot Springs, Norris, and in the Old Faithful area. The ones in Mammoth have been both at the Hot Springs themselves and down along the Gardner River, about a mile away. Runoff from the Hot Springs disappears back into the ground nearby and reappears down along the river. Its temperature by the time it reaches the river (it may be reheated in transit) is about 140°F, quite enough to warm a number of den-size crevices.

Near Norris four caves were discovered in 1951 that had very similar shapes and were apparently intentionally dug (presumably by grizzlies, since black bears dig much less) in the thermally heated ground. None had active springs in them, but all were warmed a few degrees by heat transferred from warmer ground below. The investigator, Merrill Beal, reported:

> I would hesitate to call these caves steam heated, for such a condition would probably make for a very uncomfortable winter hibernating spot. However, since the ground temperatures are

Dead grizzlies in Death Gulch, 1897.

considerably higher than normal and remain quite constant, hibernation in one of these dens might be likened to sleeping in an electric blanket, and it is likely that the bears using the caves derive a certain amount of additional comfort as a result of this influence by hydrothermal activity.[5]

One of Yellowstone's most bizarre bear stories involves the peculiar little thermal area named Death Gulch. The gulch is actually a shallow basin in a small draw on the upper Cache Creek drainage. Because of the location of the thermal activity, the basin is occasionally filled with unbreathable gases from a hot spring. The area of heaviest concentration of the gas is rarely more than 15 feet deep and 100 feet across, but early investigators found that this was a large enough area to kill wildlife, including grizzly bears. Death apparently occurred by asphyxiation rather than by poisoning. It was this spring which inspired Seton to end his tale of Wahb by having the aging bear voluntarily enter the gulch and peacefully fall asleep.[6] Dr. T. A. Jaggar reported on an 1897 visit to the gulch:

> Climbing through this trough, a frightfully wierd and dismal place, utterly without life, and occupied only by a tiny streamlet and an appalling odor, we at length discovered some brown furry masses lying scattered about the floor of the ravine about a quarter of a mile from the point where we had left Cache Creek. Approaching cautiously, it became quickly evident that we had before us a large group of recumbent bears; the one nearest to us was lying with his nose between his paws, facing us, and so exactly like a huge dog asleep that it did not seem possible that it was the sleep of death . . . One huge grizzly was so recent a victim that his tracks were still visible in the white earthly slopes, leading down to the spot where he had met his death. In no case were any marks of violence seen, and there can be no question that death was occasioned by the gas.[7]

The scientists were discrete about the duration of their visits. It appeared to them that the gas trap was only truly potent on certain windless days, and that a predominance of bears was probably the result of the circumstances; there was no vegetation to interest many other animals, and once one had succumbed its rotting would invariably attract other bears. Dr. Jaggar, whose camp was on Cache Creek just a short distance below where the streamlet entered it, noted unhappily that the streamlet "has its source far above the animals; indeed it trickles directly through the worm-eaten carcass of the cinnamon bear—a thought by no means comforting when we realized that the water supply for our camp was drawn from the Creek only a short distance down the valley."

Chapter 26

Bears, Tourists, and Rangers:
The Eternal Triangle

In 1953 a survey was conducted of Yellowstone's visitors. When asked "were you aware while you were in Yellowstone that bear feeding is prohibited?" 95% answered yes.[1] Feeding by visitors was quite common at this time, common enough to keep dozens of black bears along the roads. There were probably two big reasons for the easy lawbreaking. First, feeding was being allowed because rangers were only occasionally enforcing the law. People have an astounding capacity for doing things for no better reason than that they can get away with it. The second reason was (and is, for people still do it at every opportunity) that they could not see what was wrong with feeding a "poor hungry bear." Most visitors apparently had no great sympathy for park ideals—if they even understood them—so they did not appreciate any distinction between a Yellowstone bear and a zoo bear.

Rangers have tried reasoning with visitors in many ways, but one of the most effective approaches to talking people out of bear-feeding (rather than fining them out of it) has been to make them realize that it hurts the bear. Pointing out to people that begging degrades the character (a wonderfully loaded expression) of a wild animal has worked. A report prepared for the United States National Park Service and the National Parks of Canada in 1969 summed up the power of this viewpoint:

> The public generally is opposed to pollution. The roadside bear, no less than the urban rat, is a direct result of environmental pollution. Once the public becomes aware of this fact, we anticipate the demand to see demoralized beggar bears will

219

be replaced by a demand to clean up the park environment and restore the bear to its natural habitat and behavior patterns.[2]

The comparison with the rat is the clincher. It is completely appropriate, and, once heard, is seldom forgotten. Bears, of course, have no "morals." The demoralization is actually our own, brought about by abuse of a valuable ethic.

Other more practical points can be made in the bear's behalf. Black bears managed to survive on their garbage-enchanced diets, except those that were hit by cars, pestered by people until they injured somebody and then were destroyed as "dangerous," or ingested too much harmful material. Bears feed by smell. If something smells interesting, or sweet, it will probably get eaten. Candy wrappers, broken pop bottles, and aluminum foil qualified, and were consumed in quantity. Glass, foil, cigarette butts, and film wrappers are not digestible, but they are all too common wherever people travel. Even feeding the bear "something good" was wrong, because it kept the bear there until it could be further abused. Worse things than accidental mistreatment occurred. A black bear can be in a pretty mean mood if he's just been fed a firecracker.

Making people aware of the danger to the bear seems to be more useful than telling them bear feeding is dangerous to people. Even the parents of young children are willing to take horrible risks. Recounting a few injuries to them will make them cringe at the campfire program, and the family will walk very close together back to their tent afterwards, but in the brave morning light many will succumb. Visitors with children were responsible for some of the most outrageous behavior in the beggar-bear days. In the interests of photography children were told to go stand by the bear. Smaller children were placed on the bear's back, and even smeared with jelly so that the bear could be photographed licking it off.

There is no getting around the horror of such behavior, the hundreds of injuries, and the callous treatment of very vulnerable wild animals, but if the point has not been made by now there is no hope, for the readers or the bears. The story has a lighter side, and that side is the reason for this chapter.

Down in The Dumps

Running into a bear in Yellowstone has always been a most-remembered part of the visit. Many scratched fingers, fenders, and ice chests were proudly displayed back home. Paw-prints in the dust near a tent were photographed, and trees were examined for claw marks. Everybody wants a bear story.

The public feeding grounds were an endless source of yarns. Owen Wister, the author of *The Virginian* and other western novels, was a regular visitor to Yellowstone in the 1890s:

> I walked out once in the early evening at the Lake hotel and counted twenty-one bears feasting. I saw a bear march up to a tourist and accept candy from his hand, while his wife stood at a safe distance, protesting vainly, but I think rightly. I saw the twenty-one bears suddenly cease feasting and withdraw to a short distance. Out of the trees came a true grizzly, long-snouted and ugly; and while he selected his dinner with ostentatious care and began to enjoy it, a cinnamon bear stole discreetly, as if on tip-toe, toward the meal he had left behind him. He got pretty near it, when the grizzly paused in eating and merely swung his head at him—no more than that; in a flash the cinnamon had galloped humptily-dumptily off and sat down watching. He came back presently; and the scene was reenacted three times before I had enough of it and left; each time when the cinnamon had reached a certain point the grizzly swung his head, and his invariably sufficed. It is my notion that the cinnamon was a bit of a wag.[3]

The proximity of the dumps, and therefore a lot of grizzlies, made life exciting for many people who were not even interested in the bears. Shortly after the turn of the century a stableman was searching for some stray horses not far from the Canyon hotel.

> As he entered a little glade, a big bull elk dashed through closely pursued by a grizzly. The stableman yelled, the grizzly stopped for a moment, and then started after him. As he put it, "I just natchully faded away. I reckon that atmosphere is all het up yet with the way I come through it."[4]

It became apparent in the 1890s that a guard was needed at the dumps, so a soldier was stationed, rifle in hand. Later, after soldiers

221

were replaced by rangers, it became tradition for the ranger, if asked about the danger of the bears, to exclaim that he wasn't there to protect the *people*; he was there to protect the *bears*.

Once formal educational programs were started by the Park Service, another feature was added, the mounted ranger who gave a talk on bears while the crowd watched the feast. One of the most famous of these rangers was Philip Martindale, who spoke of the coolness of his horse under considerable stress:

> The bear feeding grounds lecture stadium at Old Faithful seats now almost 2700 people and is usually crowded at the 7 o'clock lecture on wild animals. Most always certain loud noises, laughter, hand clapping etc. prevails during the lecture.
>
> It is only about 125 feet from the crowd behind the (cable) to the lunch counter or platform where the food is placed to attract the bears, and the horse (as a lecture platform) is backed up to within 30 feet of the platform which is in turn only about 50 feet from the woods.
>
> Training and confidence are responsible for the fact that the horse will not even turn when a grizzly comes in behind him, but this has taken time and patience.

Philip Martindale, astride an amazingly calm horse, giving his "bear-talk" at Old Faithful in the 1920s. N.P.S. photo.

222

> On a certain night early in August a grizzly came around the pit by mistake and came directly toward my horse, within 15 feet in fact. I waited for him to turn but finally decided and quickly that he did not see me. I made a noise and sudden motion which caused him to stand up on his hind legs and then he turned. Their eyesight is so unquestionably dull living as they do in deep timber.[5]

The dumps were a grand show. Spectacular and bloody fights occurred between grizzlies over food, and once in a while an exceptionally bold black bear would join in. There is no denying the initial thrill of seeing several—to say nothing of several dozen—adult grizzlies ponderously sorting through the piles of trash. First sight of a grizzly is a thrill under any conditions. But quickly one comes to realize that the scene is actually an ugly one, and wishes, with some selfish regret, that the bears were a little harder to see.

The Panhandlers

Most encounters, however, did not occur at the dumps. They took place between black bears and visitors along the roads and in the camps. Owen Wister described a campground scene of 1891 that remained part of the Yellowstone adventure for over half a century:

> One night in 1891 our sleep was murdered by sudden loud rattling and clashing of our tin plates and other hardware. We rushed out of the tent into silence and darkness. In the morning our sugar sack lay wounded but still with us. MacBeth while dragging at it had tumbled the hardware about him. He was not educated enough to stand that and had taken to the woods. Another bear took to a tree that week. As dusk was descending, campers found him in suspicious proximity to their provender and raised a shout. The shouting brought us and others not to the rescue, but to the highly entertaining spectacle of a tree surrounded by fascinated people waving their arms, and a bear sitting philosophically above their din. Night came on, the campers went to bed, and the bear went away.[6]

Tourists and bears were constantly interested in each other: "'Do you mean to tell me those cute creatures will harm anyone?' says a lady, 'Why they smile and wiggle their tails in the most cunning

On the steps of Roosevelt Lodge in the 1920s. N.P.S. photo.

manner!' 'Yes lady,' replies the ranger, 'but you must not trust either end of a bear.'"[7]

The "hold-up" bears that became famous gathered huge crowds. As the traffic backed up there was created, in ranger-parlance, a "bear-jam," as in "There's a goodawful bear jam at Diamond Lil's station." Some store employees still remember visitors who, having overheard the term somewhere, asked where they could buy a jar of bear jam.

Sometimes the best performance was to the biggest crowd. One was reported by Horace Albright in the 1940s:

> I remember only one very sad case of a woman and a bear where mental torture and burning humiliation were doubtless a thousand times more terrible than the pain and the sting from a bear's tooth. In this case, the lady had a big bear on his hind legs up on the landing platform at the Canyon Lodge. She had the bear reaching for food as dozens of shutters clicked, for some 500 tourists were being seated in

open buses for the day's journey to Mammoth Hot Springs. Someone yelled at the "bear expert" doing the feeding and she turned around. The bear thinking the show was over and the food gone dropped to all-fours and in so doing caught his claw in the lady's shoulder straps and took off all her clothes except part of her girdle and her stockings, yet did not even give her a scratch. She wanted the bear killed, but after a full investigation we found the bear not guilty of any wrong-doing.[8]

A more private embarrassment took place in a story less well substantiated but equally well known in the park. A couple was honeymooning in their tent in a park campground when a bear began to tear through the tent's doorway. According to oral tradition (the most colorful kind), the young husband whipped out a knife—at which point the wife can be imagined, hands clasped on breast, eyes full of pride, thinking "My hero!"—and cut a hole in the other end of the tent, making a swift getaway into the night. The tent collapsed on bear and spouse, who were extricated without harm by neighbors. On the subsequent success of the marriage, oral tradition has remained silent.

Another equally well circulated (and undocumented) incident involved a family asleep in their motor home. During the night they were awakened by a racket, and looked out to see a large bear annihilating their ice chest. The wife exclaimed, "Look, that bear has our ice chest!" The husband answered with knowing wisdom, "No, that's *his* ice chest. . . ."

In earlier days, when cars were more often open or cloth-topped, bears found them easy pickings, ruining many a roadster. One incident, which was anything but amusing at the time but which now has a Keystone Kops air about it, took place in the vicinity of an Oldsmobile rumble seat about 1930:

Mr. Anderson and his family were driving toward the Cooke entrance of the park and were beyond the Buffalo Ranch. In rounding a curve near the Devils Well, a female grizzly and her two cubs were seen feeding on a carcass near the road. There were two cars preceding the Anderson car and the road was muddy with considerable slush snow in it. As the cars approached, the mother grizzly charged and jumped down into the cut made by the snowplow in recently clearing the road, but for some reason, just before the cars reached her, she sprang back up on the snow bank at the side of the

225

road. While she was in the cut, her cubs disappeared over the hill into Soda Butte Creek. When the mother regained the bank and failed to see her cubs, she immediately gave chase to the cars which were then about fifty yards ahead of her. A brother of Mr. Anderson, who was riding in the rumble seat of the six cylinder Oldsmobile, became alarmed and warned the Ranger by rapping on the rear window. Vigorously blowing the horn, the Ranger tried to get the cars ahead to speed up all that they could, but due to the condition of the road, much speed was impossible. The grizzly quickly overtook the cars, and then jumping up on the snow bank, lunged out and down at the car. Several attempts were made in this manner to catch the car, but the grizzly missed each try as she lost time in jumping up on the snow before leaping for the car. Needless to say, the Ranger's brother had crawled down into the back of the car and had closed the rumble cover! They were chased from Devils Well to Hoppe's Prairie, a distance of approximately two miles, and the

TEDDY BIDS THEM ALL GOOD BYE THIS MORNING.

Local newspaper cartoon at the close of Roosevelt's 1903 visit to Yellowstone.

226

maximum speed (remembering road conditions) was 28 miles per hour. The bear had just come out of hibernation, which must also be considered.[9]

Presidents and Bears

A surprising number of chief executives have been interested and involved in the Yellowstone bear story. The most famous was Theodore Roosevelt, who, in fact, inspired the American toy, the "Teddy Bear," in 1902 when the cartoonist Clifford Berryman portrayed the sportsman-president with a small black bear in Mississippi. Roosevelt was unwilling to shoot that particular bear because the circumstances were unsporting, and the cub quickly became one of his symbols.[10]

In 1903 Roosevelt visited Yellowstone on a two-week vacation jaunt. He expressed great interest in seeing the bears, which had already become famous because of their dump-feeding. It was early spring, with the snow still several feet deep over most of the park, so a call was made to the Lake Hotel to learn if any bears had yet appeared in that area. The winterkeeper at Lake said they were not out, but it was later learned the he simply did not want to be bothered with the presidential party. Roosevelt, an experienced bear hunter, found the park bears fascinating:

> It is curious to think that the descendants of the great grizzlies which were the dread of the early explorers and hunters should now be semidomesticated creatures, boldly hanging around crowded hotels for the sake of what they can pick up, and quite harmless so long as any reasonable precaution is exercised.[11]

Both Presidents Harding and Coolidge saw and fed the beggar bears along park roads on their visits to the park in the 1920s (Harding had heard of Jesse James). After seeing the familiarity of all the park wildlife, Harding was moved to comment, "As I watched the wildlife of the Park today, unconcerned and unmindful of the human beings about them, manifesting their confidence in the security of the situation, I thought how helpful it would be to humankind if we could have a like confidence in one another in all the relations of life."[12]

Another president had close and extended contact with the bears of Yellowstone. In 1936, a clean-cut (weren't they all?) young ranger at Canyon found himself assigned to ride shotgun at the bear-feeding

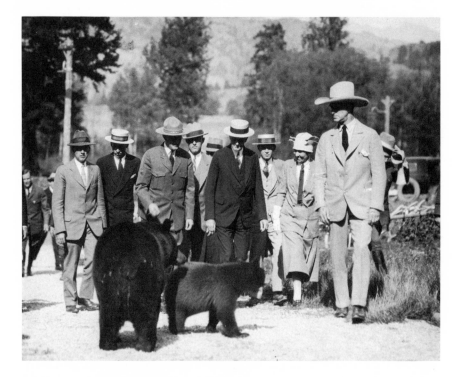

Park superintendent Horace Albright, President Coolidge, and Mrs. Coolidge all seem much less concerned about the bears at Tower than do the President's bodyguards during this 1927 visit. N.P.S. photo.

grounds. He could not have known that on his next visit to the park, in 1976, he would be president. Gerald Ford has fond memories of Yellowstone (during his years as president there was an oil-painting of Old Faithful in his office), and recalls with some relief that he never had to use the shotgun. Years after his Yellowstone summer, he was so fond of telling his children about his bear adventures that they asked him, "PLEASE, don't tell us the story about the bears again, Daddy!"

"Who's in Charge of this Bear?"

Park managers have faced some extravagant demands in their efforts to keep both bears and people happy in Yellowstone. In 1913 the secretary of the interior received a letter from the president of the American Humane Association, the latter having heard that

Yellowstone's bears were not being properly cared for. He understood that they were fed well from the dumps during the summer, but that during the winter no food was provided them and that they became so hungry by spring that they "sometimes eat the flesh from their paws." Acting Superintendent Brett answered for the secretary, explaining about hibernation, and assuring the president that the bears were "thoroughly competent to look after themselves."[13] One cannot help but wonder if Col. Brett, while he wrote this letter, was plagued by visions of his troopers, wading through the snow with sacks of food on their backs, searching for bear dens so they could waken the animals to feed them.

Soldiers and rangers have been expected to handle almost equally difficult situations over the years; "Get that bear out of my car! He's eating all the marshmallows I bought to feed him." "I chased the bear that tore my tent up this tree and kept him there until you got here. He's yours now." The following is taken from a report filed by Ranger Elbert Robinson in 1960. Hearing of a seriously injured bear near Firehole Cascades, he got his rifle and drove out to put the bear out of its misery. On the way he was stopped by another car:

> A young man about 20 to 24 years old approached with a tissue in his hand and carefully unfolded it and showed me a rusty nail about 2 1/2 inches long. He proudly stated that he had removed the nail from a bear's foot, and acted as if he expected a compliment for his brave act . . . I told the boy that he did not realize how fortunate he was that he had not been bitten, beaten, or clawed to pieces. He stated that the bear had his head in a garbage can and his foot was sticking out with the nail plainly visible and all he had done was reach over and pull the nail out.
>
> This report has been prepared because of the unusual circumstances and to prove that the Good Lord still provides and watches over a certain class of people that need someone else to do their thinking for them.[14]

The bear, whether black or grizzly, has an endless capacity for destruction. This, much more often than injury, has brought officers "to the rescue," looking for ways to move the bear away from the people with a little risk as possible.

Bear traps in Yellowstone are simple devices. The bait hangs on a cable far enough inside the culvert trap so that the entire bear is in it before he can reach the bait. When the bear pulls on the bait, a lever releases the heavy cage door behind him. Numerous bait recipes have been tried, incidentally. Peanut butter, honey, ham, bacon, and many others work. Often the ranger takes whatever leftovers are available at the local hotel. One troublesome young grizzly that was raiding some rabbit pens just north of the park was baited with a saucer of milk. The owners of the rabbits had noticed that their cat's milk bowl was always emptied when the bear visited, so milk was used to bait the trap.

Bears often become trap-wise, and so before drug-firing guns were developed rangers faced a ticklish problem: how to get the bear into the trap/trailer for transportation to a remote area. Some bears could be lured in with different foods than they were accustomed to, and small ones could be netted (with a long-handled affair known as a "butterfly net"). Many smooth captures were made, but sometimes things went wrong, and this happened with depressing regularity in front of large crowds.

Dale Nuss, one of Yellowstone's most experienced bear-handlers, tells of a small yearling that was causing trouble in the early 1960s at Old Faithful. After repeated attempts by rangers to catch him, Nuss and one of his men set out with trap, cookies, butterfly net, and iron resolve, to get the bear. Locating him was easy—at the center of the "damndest bear jam you ever saw." They started with the net:

> One of us was throwing the cookies, the other was standing with the net. Of course all the people were watching. This little bear would sneak up, eyeball us, eyeball those cookies, and finally he'd make a pass at them and we'd make a pass at him with the net; we'd miss and of course everybody would cheer. This went on about 45 minutes, until the bear decided he was smarter than we were and left.

They followed him to an empty picnic area, where he climbed a tree. Quickly setting up a cookie-baited rope snare at the foot of the tree, they took the other end of the rope and retreated to a nearby picnic table to wait. It was approaching noon, and soon a crowd had gathered, unaware of the bear, at the other picnic tables. At last the bear climbed down, and just as planned he stuck his head in the snare.

I forget which one of us had the rope. Our plan was for him to go *that* way and we'd go *this* way; well, it didn't work that way. The bear came right after us . . . Whichever one of us was runnin' with the end of the rope, well, the *other* one finally got smart and grabbed the middle of the rope and took a dally around a tree. Then the other guy dropped the end of the rope and went over and grabbed the net, and we had him. Then after we had him, we didn't know what to *do* with him. He had arms and legs and heads and everything through that net. We couldn't get him out to get him in the trap, so finally we just shoved the whole damn thing in the trap and away we went.[15]

As awkward as roping was, it had long been a staple of management technique. Roosevelt had mentioned that, as early as 1902, the bears "sometimes get tin cans stuck on their paws, and the result is painful . . . scouts in extreme cases rope the bear, tie him up, cut the tin can off his paw, and let him go again. It is not an easy feat, but the astonishing thing is that it should be done at all."

Capturing bears with drugs, though now developed to a fine sophistication, still involves many risks. Determining proper dosage is very difficult, since it can depend on the bear's age, sex, weight, degree of excitement, and general physical condition. Those are not things easy to judge from a distance. An overdose can be fatal (more than one ranger or researcher has administered mouth-to-mouth resuscitation to a bear that was having trouble breathing), but underdose can be dangerous to the trappers if the bear revives too quickly. More flexible drugs have been developed recently that give the trapper more leeway in estimating the proper dosage.

Most drugs are not instantaneous. The bear usually flees after being hit by the drug syringe (it has a long hypodermic point that is designed to penetrate the coat and the skin), and, as one ranger put it, "the bear always seems to run down a hill and across a muddy stream before it conks out, so that you've got to drag it back through the mud and up the hill to the trap." Never dress up for a bear trapping.

Trapping is only one part of the acquaintance park residents have with bears. Having the bears of Yellowstone for neighbors, and even houseguests, is a story in itself.

Chapter 27

Living With Bears

*I*t is difficult for the visitor, and for the new employee, to realize just how much a part of daily life bears once were in Yellowstone. Before modern management got the bears out of the developments, one simply expected to see them, every day. Now, with strict regulation and sanitation, most bears are kept wild and free-roaming. A bear in a campground causes real concern. Then, with food available everywhere, bears were a regular thing—a matter of routine.

There are still residents who remember chasing bears from kitchens, or teaching their children to look around before going outside. Interestingly, as they look back on it, some comment that it did not seem at all unusual at the time: "You often carried an axe handle if you went out at night around the camp. Nobody thought anything of it."[1] Park personnel have rarely been injured, perhaps because they quickly became conditioned to be more careful.

Bears often damaged buildings in the park. In 1891, Elwood Hofer, who was trapping park animals for the National Zoo, wrote from Yancy's Hotel near Tower Junction about his bear problems:

> I had a splendid Grizzly or Roachback cub and was going to send him into the Springs (Park Headquarters) next morning the team was here, I heard a racket outside went out and found him dead an old bear that made a 9 1/2 inch track had killed and partly eaten him. Last night another one came, one that broke Yancy up in the milk business. You know how the cabins stand here. There is a hitching post between the saloon and the old house, the little bear was killed there. In a creek close by was a milk house, last night another bear

came there and smashed the whole thing up, leaving nothing but a few flattened buckets and pans and boards . . . I don't care about the milk but the damn cuss dug up the remains of the cub I had buried . . . Bear are very thick in this part of the Park, and are getting very fresh.[2]

In 1932 the superintendent reported "the interiors of three snowshoe cabins were wrecked by grizzly bears." These small backcountry cabins, used by ranger patrols, were especially vulnerable. Some were very sturdy, but they were no match for a bear. One destroyed in 1924 was described:

> The door had been opened by main force. The bedding, including the mattress, had been all taken outside and strewn on the snow for distances varying up to 100 feet. The bed itself (a large heavily built affair) had ben moved two feet out from the wall; the stove had been moved from its place, the zinc-covered cupboard had been turned over, broken into and contents emptied, provisions all eaten or (such as pepper and cinnamon) at least bitten into, excepting one small specially resistant tin. Every frying pay, dish pan and kettle had been knocked from the walls. A sack of oats had been torn from its nail on the ceiling, and contents eaten.[3]

One patrol cabin was so badly damaged in the 1960s that a new one was built to replace it. A large grizzly that wants to get into a small building may enter from almost anywhere. This particular bear, a sow with two cubs, had further distinguished herself by biting holes through a *cast iron* skillet.

Milton Skinner reported that at one of the small backcountry cabins in 1915 a solitary man spent most of a night keeping four grizzlies from digging through the roof. His only weapon was a pitchfork:

> The roof was of clay and sod and was still frozen, for there had been no fire under it, although the sun had melted the winter snow from the top. Still more fortunately the split poles supporting the earth were heavy and stronger than usual and overlaid with thin sheet iron, so that the bears had much more trouble than they would have had ordinarily. It was a difficult job but in time they got through the clay, bent back the sheet iron and began to spring the poles apart. Then began a long, hard fight. Whenever a crack showed, the

pitchfork was jabbed up through, and whenever it struck a paw or the bear's underparts it brought snarls and "woofs." The paws were so tough, very little damage was done to them, but once in a while a fortunate jab brought blood from nose, breast, or belly. Occasionally a nose or paw came down through a crack, but a steady clubbing on them caused their withdrawal and more howls. The bears would not give up the contest, but now that the strong odor of the ham, bacon and fresh meat came direct to their nostrils they redoubled their efforts. The poles were strong and the sheet iron protected the roof, but still it is likely they would have succeeded if they could have held out long enough, for George's violent efforts . . . were fast tiring him. There were many times during the long night when it seemed as if he must give up, but finally dawn began to break. At first the bears hardly noticed it, but after a time they became less active and shortly after sunrise they jumped down and retired, growling, to the woods, But the roof was a wreck.[4]

Before modern maintenance equipment was available, many of the park's road crews were located at small camps along the roads. These camps, each with a small crew of men, had kitchens and storehouses, and were frequently under siege. Each seemed to have its resident bear(s). Some camps had specially built meathouses (there was no electrical refrigeration at the time, and this was in the early 1950s!), made of 3-inch planks with 3-inch steel bands circling them, and *spikes* in the door, but at night, as one worker recalls, "the grizzles would come in and take that meathouse apart like a matchbox."[5]

The problem was worst at the close of the season, as in 1927, when the following report was filed:

> After the close of the tourist season, the abundant supply of table scraps from the hotels being at an end, the bears usually become more bold and look to the road camps and woodcutter's camps for a larger part of their rations . . . Two of the woodcutter's camps at the Canyon were so infested with bears, especially grizzlies, that regular night guards were kept busy warding away the prowlers by means of Roman candles and other devices . . . As many as fourteen bears, together with an undetermined number of cubs, have been seen at one time about a given camp.[6]

Many a bear has been made a "pet" by park personnel. This occasionally happened at the road camps. William Hape, a park maintenance supervisor for many years, remembers a small black bear cub that was accustomed to sleeping in the bunkhouse during the day and being sent out at night. It has been more common, and infinitely more dangerous, near the hotels. Hotel employees, many of whom are new to the park, have baited bears in (in no sense taming them) until the visitation was a nightly event. Much like the camper who leaves food out to attract a bear "so I can get a picture," they are playing a very dangerous game. The greatest risk is to the chance passer-by, who is not in on the plan, and who stumbles onto a bear where a bear ought not to have been.

Living with bears is easy if everybody cooperates. Living in a place like Yellowstone is a special experience in many ways, but knowing that one is surrounded by bear country is one of the finest rewards of all.

Chapter 28

Camping With Bears

The most important thing about camping in bear country like Yellowstone, whether in a roadside campground or in the backcountry, is to take the park regulations seriously. The rules about how to prevent bear problems are based on many years of experience. Too many times people don't pay enough attention to them, especially now that bears are harder to see along the roads than they once were. Don't be fooled; the bears are there.

At the same time, everybody involved must admit that no guideline is foolproof. Bears are individuals. No two will behave the same, therefore no precaution is foolproof. Vigilance and common sense, as represented by park regulations, are the best bet for a trouble-free camp, but there is no guarantee they will work every time.

In the Campground

Be careful with food. Do not leave any food or food container (full or empty, brand new or very old) out any longer than you need to. There is no such thing as a bear-proof ice chest. Lock all food and food containers in the trunk of your car rather than taking them into your tent. If possible, avoid cooking strong-smelling foods. If you are sleeping in a tent or other soft-sided shelter, it is best not to sleep in the clothes you cooked in. If a bear passes through the campground and is not drawn to odors, it will move on.

Do not be afraid to be a little nosy to see that your neighbor is being careful too. If he gets a bear into the area, it could be some member of your party that ends up being hurt. Because you cannot be sure that everyone else has been careful, and because bears travel a lot at night, carry a flashlight and make a little noise as you walk around at night. Two or three people walking together make more noise than one.

These precautions are easy, and they only take a few minutes. If you have a family, explain to the children why they must be careful. They will probably help more if they know.

On the Trail

While hiking, stay alert by watching for bears and bear signs and listening for sounds of movement nearby. It is good to make noise as you travel, either by talking or wearing a bell or by carrying a can with a pebble in it.

But again, nobody's making you any promises. There's a new joke in bear country about the way to tell black bear and grizzly bear droppings from each other: grizzly bear droppings are the ones with little bells in them. Actually, a study done in Glacier showed the hikers wearing bear bells were charged by bears far less often.[1] But a recent study with captive grizzlies had a different result: the bear being tested twice slept through the noise. The scientist making the test was Gary Miller, a biologist at the University of Montana in Missoula, and his conclusions were discouraging for bell-wearers:

> The bells were of the type sold to hikers in Glacier and Yellowstone National Parks to warn bears of the approaching hiker and thereby prevent an encounter. In these tests, the assistant, less than 6m from the bear, failed to arouse it. Warning bears before getting too close is a good strategy for preventing encounters, but the bells currently sold to hikers are inadequate.[2]

"Bear repellents" are a hot topic in outdoor magazines these days, and you will see some advertised. Many have now been tested, and others are being considered. Charles Jonkel of the University of Montana has been a leader in experiments in aversive conditioning. The goal is to find some way of either making bears fear people or give people some way to ward off bears.[3] A host of traditional and modern aversives has been studied by Jonkel and others over the past few years, everything from recordings of bigger bears broadcast to keep bears away from developments, to a wide assortment of sprays.

Some of these sprays—recently those on, almost on, or on and then off the market have included "Counter Assault," "Halt," "Bear Skunker," and "Animal Alert"—have been shown to work, some of the time, under laboratory conditions or even in the field. Some of them are quite promising (to say nothing of the fascination they hold for anyone interested in the study of animal behavior), but no scientist is even close to saying that you can count on them. You may get a bear that happens to like the taste of skunks, or who just last week walked through an electrical fence and isn't going to mind having his eyes burn for a while, or who got sprayed twice last month and has figured out how to dodge it.

I do have one very important piece of advice if you decide to carry one of these sprays. Buy at least two cans, even though the good ones are expensive. Take one out and (very carefully) use it up, just to see how far it goes. Until you've done that, you have very little idea of how close a bear must be to you before you can have any hope of affecting his behavior. With even a little breeze, you probably can't count on hitting the bear with much density of spray beyond 20 feet. Until you've seen the spray, you stand a good chance of overestimating how far away 20 feet is.

Once you've sprayed a can, then think about a rapidly moving bear, or rapidly moving self. Picture the real situation: unreliable light, perhaps a windy day, the spray can attached to your belt. This isn't going to be easy.

I don't want to underplay the instances where people are sure their lives were saved by using the sprays. But I do want you to know what you're facing. The two grizzly bear behaviorists I know and admire agree that the sprays are possibly as great a risk to you as they are an advantage. They tell me that by the time you let the bear get close enough to spray it, you've already waited too long to play dead should you miss or should the spray be ineffective (and I personally doubt that there's anything you could spray into the face of a really large grizzly bear—one of the population's dominant big males—that would guarantee he would go away).

One of these experts, Steve French of the Yellowstone Grizzly Foundation, refers to the sprays as "brains in a can," meaning that people tend to assume that as long as they have their can of Bear-Raid or whatever with them, they don't even have to think about bears until one comes along.

There does seem to be some sympathy among the experts, however, for keeping the can with you in your tent. The reasoning is something like this. If the bear decides to come into the tent after you, it's already decided to eat something in the tent, possibly you, so you have nothing to lose by spraying it. Consider buying three cans, then, so that you can also test one after it has been lying in a very cold tent all night; I'm not sure what effect that will have on its power.

In a moment I will look at some of the more traditionally touted bear repellents, but there is something more important for the new hiker to learn first, and that is that it's much better to avoid the bear in the first place than to be put in the position of trying to repel it.

As I said, making noise helps. A group of hikers is statistically safer than an individual partly because they make more noise as they go down the trail. Be especially careful in situations of limited visibility, or where a noisy stream or high winds might drown out your own noises.

Avoiding an encounter—surprising a bear at close quarters—is the big goal. If you hike wisely you will not surprise an animal. Once you have surprised a bear at close range, whatever happens to you as a human being, you are a failure as a hiker.

When you see a bear at a distance, say at 100 yards or more, keep that distance. There are options at this point that depend on your own judgment:

1. You can try to detour around the bear. This may not be possible, but if you try it keep upwind of the bear and at a good distance from it, so that it can scent you without feeling surprised. If you are not familiar with the country, or the trail does not allow you to circle,

2. You can wait, and enjoy the rare view, hoping that the bear might move off. Do not assume that just because it has moved out of sight that it is far away. It might have bedded down five feet from the trail.

3. You can go back the way you came until the bear is well out of sight, and then approach again making lots of noise. The warning noises might cause the bear to move off. Most hikers in Yellowstone who have logged many miles are familiar with the sound of something running off somewhere ahead of them. If you proceed at this point, do it loudly and alertly.

4. You can call your trip off. Never be afraid to do this for fear of ridicule. Though it is rarely necessary to call a trip off because of

bears, the person who makes fun of someone who has been "bear-spooked" will be secretly wondering what he or she would have done under the same circumstances.

Now to the most often asked question—"What should I do if I do surprise a bear?" There is no easy answer to it. Each bear reacts according to its feelings at that moment, and black bears and grizzly bears are considered to react differently from each other in general, but experience has shown that some actions are better than others.

1. Do not run, because it may cause the bear to chase you. In some circles running or otherwise displaying great fear is known as "acting like dinner." If the bear rears up on its hind legs, you will feel like fainting, but remember that this is an investigative position. It often means the bear has not decided what to do yet either. Avoid looking the bear in the eyes; that sort of direct confrontation, eye-to-eye, apparently signals assertiveness on your part.

2. Immediately, but without sudden motion, look for a tree that can get you at least 20 feet from the ground. Do not overestimate your ability to beat the bear to the tree. If you decide to go for the tree, drop something interesting, like your pack, to distract the bear for a moment. If you climb the tree, wait at least thirty minutes after the bear has left before climbing down. Bears can be surprisingly cagey and patient.

3. If there is tree, and the bear seems uninterested, you might be able to quietly back away out of sight. Some authorities have recommended talking softly, or shouting at the bear or making other loud noises (take your pick, right?)

4. If there is no tree, and if the bear continues to show interest or approach even as you back away, you may have to try the hardest alternative of all. Play dead. Roll up in a ball with your hands covering the back of your neck, and act like you are invisible. The bear may come over and sniff at you, or even paw you around a little. If you yell or struggle the chances are greater that you will be injured.

Trees are an interesting subject. It used to be that most authorities recommended climbing a tree, but these days some are saying don't. The problem is that the time it takes you to get twenty feet up a tree is the time it takes a bear to travel a really long distance, and quite a few people get pulled out of the tree and perhaps injured more severely than they would have been if they had immediately played dead.

Playing dead seems to equate, in the bear's mind, at least, with ceasing to be a threat.

I think it unfortunate, though, that opinion among popular writers seems to be swinging so far against climbing trees at all. There are no end of accounts of people who were by all the evidence saved or protected from a bear by climbing a tree. So I suggest that you keep the tree as an option, remembering this: if you've never seen a grizzly bear run, you will have a very hard time imagining how fast it is, and how quickly it can eat up the yardage between you and it.

As you hike, try a little experiment. Every now and then, without looking around first, suddenly pretend that you have confronted a bear. Imagine it at some spot you can see. Then look around, and inventory all your options. What do the trees look like? Are they like so many Yellowstone lodgepole pines, straight as telephone poles with no branches you can even reach? If there are trees you can climb, how long would it take you to get to them, and then to get 20 feet or so up them? A little mental exercise like that now and then might help put you in the proper frame of mind, if anything can, for a real encounter.

Playing dead is also an interesting subject. It used to be that the recommended position was rolled up in a ball, with your fingers interlaced behind your neck, elbows together in front of your face, to protect your head and your face with your hands and forearms. In 1990, at my grizzly bear course at the Yellowstone Institute, Steve Herrero, who I mention now and then in this book, said he was reconsidering that position. He was thinking that it might be better to lie on your stomach, fingers laced behind your neck, and your legs spread apart and rigid. That way, it would be harder for the bear to roll you over and do any harm to the front of your head and body.

All advice about bear encounters (except perhaps, "Stay home") is hopeful generalization. Hikers have also avoided injury by charging back at bears, which seems to work especially often with younger inexperienced bears. I've even seen this recommended, but I don't, just because most people who encounter a grizzly bear these days aren't going to have the foggiest idea whether or not it's a subadult.

There are also tales of people pulling out their axes and fighting off a grizzly bear. More power to them. It isn't recommended by anybody, but it does bring up an interesting point.

The most careful advice these days does not treat all bears the same. For example, grizzly bears are generally more assertive, and fighting back if you are attacked by one is generally seen as a bad idea because it will probably make your injuries more severe, especially if the bear is just trying to neutralize a perceived threat (that is why you are supposed to lie still for a very long time if you play dead, until the bear is far away; if it has already hit you once, and it sees you move much, it may decide it needs to come back and hit you harder). Black bears, on the other hand, are most often encountered at close quarters near roads and developments, where all they really want is your food. If you back away from a black bear who is threatening or approaching, you stand a good chance of satisfying it. But if you are attacked by one in the backcountry, especially where black bears don't routinely get hikers' food, you might be best off to fight back. If you are attacked by a sow black bear with cubs, she's almost certainly acting in defense of the cubs, and so fighting might be inappropriate.

All of this assumes that you can tell a black bear from a grizzly bear, that you really do have the time and the circumstances to make choices in the first place, and that the bear reacts in accordance with statistical tendencies that it has no loyalty to. As I said earlier, the best course is to avoid the encounter.

In Camp

While camping, your biggest risk is attracting a bear with odors. Why do some hikers insist on cooking foods like bacon and fish? Freeze-dried foods are much more convenient, and a lot less smelly. Portable cookstoves are better than campfires, though many people do not want to give up that traditional wood fire. The small stoves also do you less harm; when you cook over a big blazing wood fire your clothes and hair will smell of whatever you cooked. For the staunch of constitution, cold junk food bypasses the whole cooking dilemma. Keep backpacks and other gear away from the smoke, too. Remember that when you get home, too—try not to hang your backpack next to the refrigerator.

Some parks with grizzlies warn menstruating women to stay out of the backcountry. There is very little reason, in terms of scientific data collected so far, to suggest that menstrual odors have made any difference in bear attacks.[4] Bears are interested in all kinds of odors; it's how they make their living. Any sexual odor may attract or at least interest a bear, but then so might a twinkie. Just try to keep odors to a minimum. Cosmetics and deodorants may also be strange and interesting odors to a bear.

Food storage should be systematic, as should all good packing. Keep all of your food in plastic bags, all bags in one container, and keep that container from contaminating anything else you carry with odors. At night suspend your pack (or at least that container) 20 or more feet from the ground, in a tree at least 100 yards from your camp. Flatten all empty food containers and keep them with the food. Do not use the fire pit as a garbage can. Carry out everything you brought in.

Sleep a good distance from the fire, because the fire pit will have lingering odors of food. Studies of bear-injured hikers have shown that hikers in tents are statistically less likely to be hurt by a bear than hikers sleeping only in a sleeping bag on the ground. You might locate your sleeping bag so that your head is pointed toward a tree.

These are basic guidelines, such as you will be presented with at a ranger station. As more research teaches us about bear behavior, some of them may become outdated. They are only the barest outline, in any case.

My best single advice is to read Steve Herrero's book, *Bear Attacks: Their Causes and Avoidance* (1985). Steve, one of the leading bear researchers, is also a great teacher, and has done a splendid job of gathering together all the useful information on past attacks, all the relevant natural history that affects how bears behave, and all the good advice one could hope for.

The Yellowstone Backcountry Permit System

In the early 1970s, because of increasing backcountry use, Yellowstone Park initiated a backcountry permit system. It works, at no charge, entirely to the advantage of the hiker. All overnight hikers are required by law to obtain the permit. As they receive it, they are made familiar with trail conditions, hiking opportunities, bear activity, and many other useful things.

Day hikers, incidentally, are welcome to seek the same advice. The ranger station is the best place to find out about bears. If an unusual amount of bear activity has been reported for some area, it may be closed to hikers. For that same reason, you are not permitted to make your trip reservations weeks in advance; in the meantime a bear could move into your chosen area. Don't ever get smug about bears—"I'm an experienced hiker, and I don't need help." I have often encountered hikers, especially eastern hikers, who think they know "all about bears." Grizzly country is a whole new world to them. Nobody knows all about bears.

Some Dangerous Misconceptions About Bears

It is often said that you can outrun a bear by running downhill. This is not true.

It is said, though less and less often these days, that bears, even when they kill people, do not eat them. This is academic to the person, but bears, though they do not normally regard humans as a food source in the way they see berries or gophers, are meateaters. It may simply be that they have never learned to eat humans. In any case at least a few grizzlies have, undoubtedly, consumed human flesh.

It is generally said that adult grizzlies cannot climb trees, but even this rule has exceptions. Some have been known to haul themselves fifteen or more feet up a tree, climbing more or less like a black bear does. There are records, in Yellowstone and elsewhere, of large adult grizzlies climbing trees. If a tree has many ladder-like branches it will be easier for the bear to move up into it. A bear estimated at 500 pounds was observed to climb 21 feet into a large apple tree (a very good climbing-tree, as many children know) near Yellowstone's north boundary.[5] Also, a scrambling leap can carry a grizzly some feet beyond its normal reach. If you choose to climb a tree, climb fast and climb high.

It is often said that dogs scare bears (in some states dog-packs are used to hunt bears). Dogs are illegal in Yellowstone on any trail, and must be leashed at all times even in developed areas. Indeed, during the army administration, it was illegal to bring one into the park. Your dog has probably never seen a bear, and you have no way of knowing what it will do. Dogs excite and frighten or anger bears, and may greatly increase the chance of attack. In some black bear country, a few hunters recommend always having a dog, but they are hunting, not hiking.

It is said that black bears, truly wild ones, are harmless to hikers; that they are terrified of people and always run away when approached. Any large wild animal is dangerous. In 1978 a black bear stalked and killed three boys in a park in eastern Canada.

It is said that grizzlies do not attack sleeping people. This is not true, though, as mentioned earlier, sleeping in a tent seems to be safer.

Back to bear repellents for a moment. Here are some of the popular ones that have been recommended for years. All but one of them involve very close-range action with the bear. They require the hiker to perform some last-minute maneuver with a bear that has been encountered at very close range, and, perhaps, is even charging. Keep in mind that hundreds of pounds of singleminded power is charging toward the hiker as he/she whips out (and it had better be handy—no burying it in the pack) the Wonder Weapon.

1. Tear gas. At least two types were tested against Yellowstone black bears years ago, and neither was found effective. Assume that the grizzlies are stronger and better able to take such abuse. And what is the range of commercially available tear-gas weapons?[6]

2. Airhorns. These are the obnoxious little cannisters used by the drunken alumnus sitting behind you at football games. They are advertised as being effective against dogs and wild animals, and have been recommended in major outdoor magazines as a good way to scare off bears. Loud noises were often used to drive bears out of campgrounds in the old days in the park—pots and pans were banged together, for example.

I once participated in an informal test of such an airhorn on a sow grizzly with one yearling. The bears, feeding at a dump, were within thirty feet of the front of the patrol car, and, though facing away from the car when the airhorn was sounded, the bears were not frightened. They gave a bit of a start, as anyone would who was feeding quietly in the middle of the night if one of those things was blasted. They looked around for the source of the noise, and then resumed eating. A second, much longer blast on the airhorn produced a second little jump, and shortly after that the bears wandered away. If they experienced any emotion it was annoyance rather than fear.

3. Firearms. Firearms are illegal in the Yellowstone backcountry. Even park personnel, some of whom live back there, rarely carry them except for law enforcement purposes. Practically no hiker of the 1970s has the combination of skill, discretion, and coolness to know when to use one. If you are of a mind to break that law, you will have to do it by concealing the weapon, and that will make it useless to you if you need it fast. More than any other device, firearms breed a false sense of security.

245

4. Mothballs. Here is an interesting one. It has been claimed that a few bags of mothballs (paradichlorobenzene) around camp will keep bears away. One article even said that they had been tested in Yellowstone, at the dumps. Former Yellowstone Resource Management Specialist Ted Bucknall agrees that there was such a test, but that the bears ate the paradichlorobenzene. Not very convincing proof of effectiveness, I'd say . . . .One hiker, according to the above-mentioned article, carried mothballs with him during four years of hiking and had no trouble with bears, "which proved," according to the writer, "that grizzlies have a definite aversion to paradichlorobenzene." No, that is very muddy logic. All it proves is that the hiker, like countless others, hiked for four years without having any bear problems. For all we know it was pink shoelaces that kept the bears away. Mothballs, like many other chemical compounds, may be unpleasant to some animals, but scientific research has not yet shown them to be an effective repellent.

Science is pretty amazing. Perhaps someday there will be something you wear, spray, eat, or sing that will guarantee your safety. In a way it would be a shame, because an important and humbling part of the grizzly country experience is that sharpening of senses—the tuning-in on one's surroundings—that it brings out. This point was most vividly brought home to me one rainy day in Glacier National Park. A party of hikers travelling the opposite direction on the trail had been fishing, and one of them was carrying a small trout. For at least 100 yards after passing them, the air was heavy with the smell of that one little fish. If my jaded senses could do that well with one trout, imagine what a grizzly can do.

In more a century, five people have been killed by bears in Yellowstone Park, and only one of those was in an area that could be defined as backcountry. It is all very well to tell an apprehensive hiker that the odds are very slim he will be hurt, but it rarely allays fears. It shouldn't, really, as long as the presence of grizzlies does not stop him from hiking. The bear is part of the experience, a very exciting dimension of wilderness hiking that few other places can provide. Many hikers prefer grizzly country for that reason.

We, as protectors of the bears, are the ones who must make the sacrifices if we are to coexist with them. They will only behave as they know how. This means there must be restrictions on people, and, in the future, the restrictions may become even greater. If restrictions on hiking in Yellowstone seem to limit your freedom too much (and hiking has a lot to do with freedom), try to think of it as cooperation. The bear's freedom is important, too. If that is not good enough for you, then you probably should not hike in Yellowstone.

Chapter 29

Looking for Bears

*I*f your primary interest is in just getting a really good look at a bear, go to a zoo. There you will have a fine opportunity to study the animal, get an idea of its movements and its shape and its way of occupying space. At the zoo, you might even earn a head start on other observers if you go looking for wild bears, because you'll already have developed something of a "search image" that might help you pick a bear out of its surroundings. But, just as bird watchers don't count birds they've seen in captivity on their "life lists" of birds seen, bear watchers don't consider watching zoo bears any sort of accomplishment. Real bear watching is a lot more involved, and exciting, and satisfying, than that.

Wildlife watching might best be compared to a lot of other outdoor sports, because success is not a sure thing. Just as when you go fishing you have no guarantee you will catch anything, when you go looking for wild animals you are hoping for the best.

Modern nature programs on television tend to distort things. In order to show you the whole life or ecology of some animal, they compress years of events into half an hour. In order to give you a good look at the animal, they use huge lenses that close in on the animal and often give you very little visual image of how it fits in the vast habitat of which it is only a tiny part. And, my friends in the film business tell me, in order to make a nice film without spending a ridiculous amount of time, many film-makers use animals in enclosures, or hired animals, for a lot of the footage that then may get portrayed as "the wild." It's not a simple business.

I applaud the increase in nature programming. I've waited a long time to see commercial television reach the point where even a few networks are willing to pay attention to the planet and the wonderful things that inhabit it. But I think that a lot of these programs reinforce in us some old tendencies.

They make us feel that we don't have a good photograph unless we "fill the frame"—get close enough so that the whole picture is loaded with an animal. They make us expect more or less constant action out there, when in reality most animals spend almost all their time doing stuff that, when we do it, we consider fairly uninteresting. You can spend a lot of hours in Yellowstone watching elk, for example, before you see one in anything remotely resembling the nature program staple, the life-and-death situation.

But coming to terms with how it really is just means recognizing that the whole life of an elk is a life-and-death situation. They aren't boring even if they just stand there and eat, at least not if you take the time to wonder what they're eating, why they're eating it just now, and where they will probably be tomorrow in their year-long cycle of movement and activity and survival.

So it is with bear watching. When you go to watch a bear, you go to understand its world. You go to seek it out in those habitats that you, because you've done some homework, know something about. And when you're lucky enough to find the bear, you are watching not just it but its setting. Can you guess where it will head, from the lay of the land? Can you find the spots in the terrain that for reasons of cover and food and whatever else will most appeal to it?

And you do these things without messing with the bear's behavior, or disrupting its activities.

Having read this far in this book, you know a good bit about preferred habitats, foods, and feeding times of bears. You can apply that information to your search. Let me make a few general suggestions, and wish you well.

You might see a bear any time of day or night, but your best odds will usually be at first and last light. You might see a bear anywhere in the park, but your best odds are in places where you can scan a lot of country at once, where there are lots of meadows mixed with stands of forest. Pelican Valley near Fishing Bridge, Hayden Valley, the Antelope Creek drainage north of Mount Washburn, Gardner's Hole and Swan Lake Flats south of Mammoth Hot Springs, and the Firehole River valley along the geyser basins all meet that definition, but try any open spot where you can see a lot of acreage that has some quality or combination of qualities—succulent vegetation, other animals, whatever—that you know interests bears.

One of the most entertaining ironies of modern bear watching is that, after all the effort that has gone into getting the bears away from the roadside, your best chance of seeing a bear is still from the roads. Again, it's a lot like the fishing. What with modern park fishing regulations limiting the kill of fish, the best fishing in the park doesn't have to hide in the backcountry any more; it can come out right along the most traveled roads, and it does. It's the same with the bears. Because the roads were so often designed to travel through or along the edge of the most beautiful meadows and river valleys, they now provide you with the finest and most extensive prospects. I would not recommend that anyone, short of the most experienced bear observer, go into the backcountry in order to look for bears. It just isn't necessary.

Find yourself a good spot where you can scan a lot of country. Get there before first light, turn off your engine, and wait. When you get out of your car, don't slam the door—just push it shut; I've seen grizzly bears spooked by a car engine starting up a mile away on a still day. They know where that road is, and they know that people use it, and in many cases as the light gets stronger they will abandon areas near roads until night returns, but you can reduce the likelihood of that by being quiet. Even if the bear doesn't just run off when you make noise, even if it appears to be unaffected, you can be sure that it heard you, and that the odds are greater it will soon get restless and disappear. Perhaps the next noise will be the one that pushes it over some individual threshold of uneasiness.

You must have binoculars. I've learned from the best bear watchers I know to carry small, light binoculars and use them for scanning the meadows and treelines. The old-fashioned big binoculars, the ones that give you a backache after hanging around your neck an hour or so, are unnecessary. Once a bear or some other interesting animal is sighted, I switch to a spotting scope, which is not as mobile or as easily adjusted but has the power to bring the animal in close even if it's two or more miles away.

The spaces and distances may at first confuse or intimidate you. In some places you will be well able to identify and then observe a grizzly bear three miles away. With a good spotting scope, you can, even at that distance, tell a great deal about what the bear is doing, and at one or even two miles you will probably be able to recognize distinguishing features of individual bears, if there's even half-decent light.

Persistence is everything. Don't give up on your chosen spot until the light of day is very strong, and wait until mid-morning (or full dark) if you can.

Keep watching. By comparing the scene with topo maps, you can identify the meadows, see which ones are actually larger than they appear, and which ones follow stream courses and other natural travel routes that animals might use. You can develop a little system by which you check several meadows in a certain sequence again and again. As you do so, you will gradually start to pick out features that may help you explain the location of a bear to fellow observers.

It might seem almost counterintuitive, but look for other wildlife, especially large grazing animals. At first you might think that if you see a meadow full of elk, it's proof there must not be a bear around. But look at it this way. Those bears go everywhere in Greater Yellowstone, and the elk and other grazers simply can't stay here without being in their territory.

More important, those elk will help you find the bear. In the spring, mid-May to late June, when the elk are having calves, what you most hope to find is a meadow with several cow-calf groups here and there in it. Then you spend as much of your time watching the elk as you do watching the country. The elk will almost certainly know about the bear before you do; you'll see heads turn, bedded elk rise, ears go up, and all the other signs of an alert animal or group of animals. Look where they're looking. And, while you're waiting, you'll learn a lot about elk and what they do all day.

Once you've found a bear, there's lots to do: figure out what it's up to, where it came from, where it's going. Learn the bear.

And avoid doing things that are dumb. It's dumb to leave the roadside and head out across the meadow to get a better look or picture. If you don't get hurt by the bear (and few people do, though those few find small comfort in that), you will drive it farther from the road until nobody else gets to see it. Believe me, if you have never seen a bear far off in the wild, you probably can't imagine how strong the temptation is going to be to go out there and get a better look. Resist. Don't mess with the bear; just enjoy it.

It is not only dumb but illegal to attempt to affect the bear, or attract it, with noises. Long experience with animal behavior has led managers to consider such activities a serious form of harassment, and rangers don't take kindly to it. Whistling or shouting to get the bear to raise its head so you can get a better picture is bad manners not only to the bear but to the other people who may be watching (on the winding roads of the park, never assume you're the only person who can see the bear). Making predator call sounds, such as those of a wounded animal, or elk bugling, are even worse manners and just as illegal. Other people want to hear the real thing, and see the bear do what a bear does on its own; you are very likely to meet with human aggression, however the bear reacts. Just be polite, and be quiet. It's a lot more fun that way.

The grizzly bears are most consistently visible in these best viewing areas from the time of emergence until late June. After that, preferred foods take them into less open or easily watched country, where many of them stay for the rest of their year. But it's worth looking, especially if you're willing to do it right—getting up very early, staying up very late, and waiting—any time of the year that you can get here.

My own view, after a lot of days when I never saw a bear and a lot of others when I did, is that it's always worth the wait. It's never a waste of time to sit somewhere, even in the cold or rain or snow, looking at the Yellowstone wilderness. Something always happens. You may hear a sandhill crane, or see a badger digging a den, or watch a coyote mousing, or just soak up the peace that comes from letting a high mountain morning begin around you. You may not see a bear, but that's part of the deal in honest wildlife watching. You don't catch fish every time you go fishing, either.

Chapter 30

A Clashing of Symbols

*T*he bears of Yellowstone, like bears everywhere, have meant many things to us. In the west of 1872, when Yellowstone was established, bears were varmints of the worst kind, subject to every kind of persecution and destruction by people far more concerned with survival and settlement than with appreciation of large, free-ranging carnivores. The bears symbolized wilderness, and wilderness was in the way.

This was not an entirely negative image, though. Among hunters, the bear, especially the grizzly bear, symbolized something more romantic as well. Many late 19th-Century hunters, though they assumed the bear had to go, mourned its loss, as they saw the great western wilderness they had wandered and enjoyed symbolized in the bear's dangerous nature.

In the park's first years, the bears continued to have some of that image of evil, though because they were emerging as an important sport species, and because park defenders were starting to realize that park wildlife was important in other ways as well, killing them wholesale was a little less popular, and by the mid-1880s was outlawed.

By the 1890s, the bears had emerged as a new tourist attraction. People began to talk about the peculiar way in which bears and people could coexist in Yellowstone, and how easy the bears were to "tame," by feeding them garbage. Quickly, the bear became one of the foremost symbols of Yellowstone, perhaps as well known and evocative as Old Faithful, certainly better known than other park attractions. It also became a commercial symbol, used to advertise everything to do with

Yellowstone. Today there are countless motels, bars, and other businesses named for bears; the T-shirt trade alone must generate a huge amount.

The bear helped Yellowstone develop its own very complicated image, not so much as a place of wonder but as a place of oddness, where wild animals were well behaved, and where strange, weird things happened. By the early 1900s the bear's image transformation in Yellowstone was complete. It had changed from a monster of almost supernatural power (as portrayed by Norris in his hunting account in Chapter 24) into a kind of national toy, from wilderness personified to wilderness enfeebled. Along the way, its fame earned it a variety of literary portrayals, such as Seton's Wahb and Johnny, that further complicated the image.

The same things were happening to bears all over the country, but I would suggest that Yellowstone's bears, by virtue of their presence in a great tourist resort, their great ease of observability and their consequent fame, were one of the leading forces in shaping the American idea of the bear. It is said that a third of all Americans visit Yellowstone some time in their lives; upwards of 100 million people have been to the park. The bears of Yellowstone have had a lot of reach in our culture.

By World War II, the great Yellowstone bear show symbolized other things. To ecologists and conservationists, it had begun to symbolize the wrong way to treat wild animals. As national attitudes toward nature and wilderness matured, so did treatment of wildlife, and Yellowstone, though it treats its wildlife differently than do most other lands, often was in the forefront of helping to pioneer new views and ideas. Don't shoot the predators, don't feed the bears.

At the dawn of modern environmental movement, the bear's image became even more complex. By the late 1950s, grizzly bears were reduced to a few isolated populations in relatively undeveloped regions of the west, and were no longer any kind of threat to western settlement. They were at our mercy. That allowed America to take a more benevolent view of the situation, and the bear became one of the great modern conservationist symbols. The tragic controversy of the 1960s and later only strengthened that image, as the bear taught us again and again just what it will take to really preserve a few authentic wild landscapes.

At the same time, for people who really didn't mind wholesale development, or who suddenly found that uses to which they'd put the land for generations were suddenly unpopular, the bear became a less appealing symbol. Once classified as threatened under the terms of the Endangered Species Act, the bear became a symbol of frustration, an obstacle to freedom of choice in using public lands, and even private lands, in traditional ways. As conservationists relied on the grizzly bear's legal protection to hammer at all sorts of land uses they didn't want to see in Greater Yellowstone, more and more people got sick of hearing about grizzly bears. The bear's classification as threatened, as necessary as it was, has not been an unalloyed advantage to the bear's public image.

But for most, even among those who find their lives complicated by new laws and attitudes, the bears of Yellowstone still symbolize something positive and good and important. As a great national focus of our growing concern for the protection of the natural system upon which our lives are based, the bears of Yellowstone are a compelling symbol of responsibility. They provide us with a fairly simple example of what it comes down to; either we will care enough to save the system, or we won't.

It is still unclear just what we will do with the bear; we're not doing enough to save it, and yet we as a nation seem to have an overwhelming desire to do so. And so, for those of us who believe in all the good things that a world with free-ranging, wild bears in it can bring us, the bears of Yellowstone also symbolize hope.

Notes

Chapter 1
The Black Bear: Description

1. Some of the most helpful sources on the history and ecology of Yellowstone black bears are: M. Skinner, *Bears in the Yellowstone* (Chicago: McClurg, 1925); V.G. Barnes and O.E. Bray, "Population Characteristics and Activities of Black Bears in Yellowstone National Park." Final Report, Colorado Cooperative Wildlife Research Unit, Colorado State University, 1967; and P. Schullery, *Yellowstone Bear Tales* (Nitwot: Roberts Rinehart, 1991).

2. V.O. Barnes, "Black bear characteristics, activities, and capture methods," in O.E. Bray and V.G. Barnes, *A literature review on black bear populations and activities* (Fort Collins: National Park Service/Colorado Cooperative Wildlife Research Unit, 1967), p. 3.

3. W.S. Home, "Color change in a growing black bear," *Murrelet*, Winter 1977, p. 79; L. Rogers, "Color changes in black bears," in "Fourth International Conference on Bear Research and Management, Abstracts," ed. C. Martinka, n.d., n.p.; T.S. Miller, "Weights and color phases of black bear cubs," *Journal of Mammalogy* 44(1):129; L. Miller, "Color change in the black bear," *Journal of Mammalogy* 36(3):460.

4. Barnes and Bray, 1967, p.38.

5. E.S. Bacon and G.M. Burghardt, "Learning and color discrimination in the American black bear," in M. Pelton, J. Lentfer, and G. Folk, eds., *Bears— Their biology and management* (Morges: I.U.C.N., 1976), p. 27–36.

Chapter 2
The Black Bear: Food Habits

1. Barnes and Bray, p. 138.

2. W. Wright, *Ben, the black bear* (New York: Scribner's, 1910), p. 113.

3. O.J. Murie, "Progress report on the Yellowstone bear study," Yellowstone Park Files, p. 12.

4. J. Mack, "Ecology of black bears on the Beartooth face, south-central Montana," M.S. thesis, Montana State University, 1988; S.Q. Greer, "Home range, habitat use, and food habits of black bears in south-central Montana," M.S. thesis, Montana State University, 1987.

5. R. Poelker and H. Hartwell, *Black bear of Washington, its biology, natural history and relationship to forest regeneration*. Washington State Game Department Biological Bulletin No. 4, 1973.

6. Mack, p. 71–72. See also, K. Kendall, "Use of pine nuts by grizzly and black bears in the Yellowstone area," in C. Meslow, ed., *Bears—Their biology and management*, fifth international conference on bear research and management, 1983, p. 166–173.

7. Mack, p. 67–68.

8. A.B. Howell, "The black bear as a destroyer of game," *Journal of Mammalogy* 2(1):36.

9. B. Arnold, "Cannibal bear," *Yellowstone Nature Notes* 7(8):54; T. Ela, "A unique case of bear cannibalism," *Yellowstone Nature Notes* 34(1):7–8.

10. D. Houston, National Park Service, personal communication, 1978 and later.

11. D. Reinhart and D. Mattson, "Bear use of cutthroat trout spawning streams in Yellowstone National Park," in L. Darling and W. Archibald, eds., *Bears—Their biology and management*, I.B.A. eighth international conference on bear research and management, 1990, p. 343–350. From the mid-1970s to 1987, bear use of spawning streams around Yellowstone Lake increased at least threefold as the trout population recovered from overfishing and as the bears became familiar with this important food source.

12. A. Murie, "Some food habits of the black bear," *Journal of Mammalogy* 18(2):239.

13. G. Pritchard and C. Robbins, "Digestive and metabolic efficiencies of grizzly and black bears," *Canadian Journal of Zoology* 68:1645–1651. This 1990 article concluded that, "No significant interspecific differences in digestive or metabolic efficiencies," were observed between grizzly bears and black bears.

Chapter 3

The Black Bear: Denning

1. For information on black bear denning and weights in Montana, see C. Jonkel and I. Cowan, *The black bear in the spruce-fir forest*, Wildlife monograph No.27, and E. Tisch, "Seasonal food habits of the black bear in the whitefish range of northwestern Montana," M.S. thesis, Montana State University, 1961.

2. Besides Jonkel and Tisch, above, see also Skinner, 1925, p. 89–94; J. Mack, "Black bear dens in the Beartooth face, south-central Montana," in L. Darling and W. Archibald, eds., *Bears—Their biology and management*, I.B.A.

eighth international conference on bear research and management, 1990, p. 273–277; C. Skinner, "Some notes on the black bear (*Euarctos americanus*) from observations at Old Faithful, Yellowstone National Park." Yellowstone Park Reference Library, typescript, 1932; C. Skinner, "Bedroom life of bears," *Yellowstone Nature Notes* 10(9–10):33–35; J. Alton, "Bear observations," *Yellowstone Nature Notes* 10(9–10):35–36; and W. Kearns, "Hibernation of bears," *Yellowstone Nature Notes* 11(1–2):6–9. These sources were all of use in the following discussions in this chapter. Park naturalists made many observations of bear denning in Yellowstone between 1920 and 1950, publishing them in the park newsletter, *Yellowstone Nature Notes*, including those listed above and several others.

3. Mack, 1990, p. 274.

4. G. Folk, M. Folk, and J. Minor, "Physiological condition of three species of bears in winter dens," in S. Herrero, ed., *Bears—Their biology and management* (Morges: I.U.C.N., 1972), p. 107–125, is an important discussion of the physiology of the bear as well as the source of this quotation.

5. G. Folk, A. Larson, and M. Folk, "Physiology of hibernating bears," in Pelton, Lentfer, and Folk, 1976, pp. 373–380; G. Folk, J. Hunt, M. Folk, "Further evidence for hibernation of bears," in C. Martinka and K. McArthur, eds., *Bears—Their biology and management*, I.B.A. fourth international conference on bear research and management, 1980, p. 44–47.

6. Additional sources on black bear hibernation include J. Craighead, J. Varney, F. Craighead, and J. Sumner, "Telemetry experiments with a hibernating black bear," in Martinka and McArthur, 1976, p. 357–372; F. Lindsey and E. Meslow, "Winter dormancy in black bears in southeastern Washington," *Journal of Wildlife Management* 40(3):408–415; T. Floyd and R. Nelson, "Bone metabolism in black bears," in Darling and Archibald, 1990, p. 135–137; R. Nelson, G. Folk, E. Pfeiffer, J. Craighead, C. Jonkel, and D. Steiger, "Behavior, biochemistry, and hibernation in black, grizzly, and polar bears," in Meslow, 1983, p. 284–290; and P. Watts, "Comparative weight loss in three species of ursids under simulated denning conditions," in Darling and Archibald, 1990, p. 139–141.

7. Most of the modern studies of bear denning and related subjects do not mention the plug; it apparently is not observed with any regularity by researchers, or is not identifiable as a plug as opposed to a typical scat, or does not exist in all cases. Even studies conducted under controlled conditions, in cages and other enclosures, do not mention the plug, when some of these studies included analysis of post-denning feeding and defecation.

8. Craighead, Varney, Craighead, and Sumner, 1976.

9. Folk, Folk, and Minor, 1976.

10. Anon., "Black bear abroad in February," *Yellowstone Nature Notes* 2(1); anon., "Brevities," *Yellowstone Nature Notes* 6(11):6.

11. L. Rogers, "Shedding of foot pads by black bears during denning," *Journal of Mammalogy* 55:672–674; See also G. Kolenosky and S. Strathearn, "Winter denning of black bears in east-central Ontario," in P. Zager, ed.,

Bears—Their biology and management, I.B.A. seventh international conference on bear research and management, 1987, p. 311–312.

Chapter 4
The Black Bear: Mating and Cub Growth

1. Poelker and Hartwell, 1973, p. 77, summarize breeding ages in several areas.
2. Skinner, 1932, p. 3.
3. Barnes and Bray, 1967, p. 66.
4. Much of this discussion is based on Barnes and Bray, 1967, and Skinner, 1932.
5. J. Ludlow, "Observations on the breeding of captive black bears, *Ursus americanus*," in Pelton, Lentfer, and Folk, 1976, p. 65–69, and K. Barber and F. Lindsey, "Breeding behavior of black bears," in Zager, 1986, p. 129–136.
6. R. Sadleir, *The ecology of reproduction in wild and domestic animals* (London: Methuen, 1969, p. 205–212; A. Wimsatt, "Delayed implantation in the Ursidae, with particular reference to the black bear (*Ursus americanus*)," in E. Enders, ed., *Delayed implantation* (Chicago: University of Chicago, 1963), p. 49–76.
7. Skinner, 1925, p. 116.
8. W. Rowan, "A case of six cubs in the common black bear," *Journal of Mammalogy* 28(4):404–405.
9. Wright, *Ben, the black bear*, p. 27.
10. A. Erickson, "The age of self-sufficiency in the black bear," *Journal of Wildlife Management* 23(4):401–405.
11. C. Willey, *The Vermont black bear* (Montpelier: Vermont Fish and Game Department, 1978).
12. A. LeCount, "Causes of black bear mortality," in Zager, 1987, p. 77–78.
13. C. Pruitt, "Play and agonistic behavior in captive black bears," in Pelton, Lentfer, and Folk, 1976, p. 79–86; R. Jordan, "Threat behavior of the black bear," in Pelton, Lentfer, and Folk, 1976, p. 57–64; and G. Burghardt and L. Burghardt, "Notes on the behavioral development of two black bear cubs: The first eight months," in Herrero, 1972, p. 207–220.
14. P. Martindale, "A large family and possible adoption," *Yellowstone Nature Notes* 7(8):52; E. Ogsten, "Adoption among bears," *Yellowstone Nature Notes* 7(8):53–54.
15. Jonkel and Cowan, 1971, p. 31.
16. Willey, 1978.

Chapter 5
The Black Bear: Lifestyle

1. Jonkel and Cowan, 1971, p. 17–21.
2. L. Rogers, "Effects of mast and berry crop failures on survival, growth,

and reproductive success of black bears," *Transactions, 41st North American Wildlife and Natural Resources Conference*, 1976, p. 436.

3. Jonkel and Cowan, 1971, p. 35.

4. K. Gunther, National Park Service Bear Management Office, Yellowstone Park, personal communication, 1991.

5. W. Replogle, "Marathon swimming for black bear," *Yellowstone Nature Notes* 16(9–10):55. R. Gresswell, U.S. Fish and Wildlife Service, Yellowstone Park, personal communication, 1977.

6. L. Beeman and M. Pelton, "Homing of black bears in the Great Smoky Mountains," in Pelton, Lentfer, and Folk, 1976, p. 87–96.

7. T. Burst and M. Pelton, "Black bear mark trees in the Smoky Mountains," in Meslow, 1983, p. 45–53.

8. Barnes and Bray, 1967, p. 186.

Chapter 6
The Grizzly Bear: Origins

1. This chapter has three primary sources: B. Kurten, *The cave bear story* (New York: Columbia University Press, 1976); S. Herrero, "A comparison of some features of the evolution, ecology and behavior of black and grizzly/brown bears," *Carnivore* 1(1):7–17; and S. Herrero, "Aspects of evolution and adaptation in American black bears (*Ursus americanus* Pallas) and brown and grizzly bears (*Ursus arctos* Linne) of North America," in Herrero, 1972, p. 221–231.

Chapter 7
The Grizzly Bear: Description

1. Two summaries of early European contact with grizzly bears are A. Russell, *Grizzly country* (New York: Knopf, 1967, p. 103–135, and H. McCracken, *The beast that walks like man* (New York: Hanover House, p. 41–159.

2. This discussion of bear sizes and weights is based on B. Blanchard, "Size and growth patterns of the Yellowstone grizzly bear," in Zager, 1987, p. 99–107.

Chapter 8
The Grizzly Bear: Food Habits

1. C. Servheen, R. Knight, D. Mattson, S. Mealey, D. Strickland, J. Varley, and J. Weaver, "Report to the IGBC on the availability of foods for grizzly bears in the Yellowstone ecosystem." U.S. Fish and Wildlife Service, 1986; R. Knight, G. Brown, J. Craighead, M. Meagher, L. Roop, and C. Servheen, "Final report, ad hoc committee to investigate the need and feasibility of the

supplemental feeding of Yellowstone grizzly bears," National Park Service, 1983.

2. K. Gunther and R. Renkin, "Grizzly bear predation on elk calves and other fauna of Yellowstone National Park," in Darling and Archibald, p. 329–334; S. French and M. French, "Predatory behavior of grizzly bears feeding on elk calves in Yellowstone National park, 1986–1988," in Darling and Archibald, p. 335–341.

3. In addition to those listed above, here are some other food habit publications: D. Graham, "Grizzly bear distribution, use of habitats, food habits and habitat characterization in Pelican and Hayden Valleys, Yellowstone National Park," M.S. thesis, Montana State University, 1978; G. Green and D. Mattson, "Dynamics of ungulate carcass availability and use by bears on the northern winter range: 1987 progress report," in R. Knight, B. Blanchard, and D. Mattson, "Yellowstone grizzly bear investigations: Annual report of the interagency study team, 1987," National Park Service, 1988, p. 32–50; B. Harting, "Relationships between activity patterns and foraging strategies of Yellowstone grizzly bears," M.S. thesis, Montana State University, 1985; K. Kendall, "Use of pine nuts by grizzly and black bears in the Yellowstone area," in Meslow, 1983, p. 166–173; D. Mattson, "Classification and environmental relationships of wetland vegetation in central Yellowstone National Park," M.S. thesis, University of Idaho, 1984; D. Mattson, B. Blanchard, and R. Knight, "Food habits of Yellowstone grizzly bears," Canadian Journal of Zoology, in press; D. Mattson and C. Jonkel, "Stone pines and bears," in W. Schmidt and K. McDonald, Proceedings of a symposium on whitebark pine ecosystems: Ecology and management, U.S. Forest Service General Technical Report INT-270, 1990, p. 223–236; S. Mealey, "The natural food habits of grizzly bears in Yellowstone National Park, 1973–1974," in Pelton, Lentfer, and Folk, 1976, p. 281–292; D. Reinhart and D. Mattson, "Bear use of cutthroat trout spawning streams in Yellowstone National Park," in Darling and Archibald, 1990, p. 343–350; and B. Schleyer, "Activity patterns of grizzly bears in the Yellowstone ecosystem and their reproductive behavior, predation and the use of carrion," M.S. thesis, Montana State University, 1983.

4. D. Frank, "Interactive ecology of plants, large mammalian herbivores, and drought in Yellowstone National Park," M.S. thesis, Syracuse University, 1990.

5. G. Cole, "Grizzly bear-elk relationships in Yellowstone National Park," Journal of Wildlife Management 36(2):560.

6. L. Abbie, "Grizzly and bull elk battle," Yellowstone Nature Notes 19 (5–6):31.

7. W. Rush, Wild animals of the Rockies (Garden City: Halcyon House, 1939), p. 106–107.

8. Gunther and Renkin, 1990, p. 331–332.

9. D. Condon, "The Yellowstone grizzly," Yellowstone Park Reference Library, typescript, 1956, p. 4.

10. Dale Nuss, National Park Service, personal communication, 1978.

11. S. Mealey, 1980, p. 285.

12. S. Mealey, "The natural food habits of free-ranging grizzly bears in Yellowstone National Park, 1973–1974," M.S. thesis, Montana State University, 1975, p. 66.

13. Steve French, Yellowstone Grizzly Foundation, personal communication, 1990.

14. Kendall, 1983; Mattson and Jonkel, 1990.

15. Don Despain, National Park Service, personal communication, 1989. See also D. Despain, A. Rodman, P. Schullery, and H. Shovic, "Burned area survey of Yellowstone National Park: The fires of 1988," Division of research and geographic information systems laboratory, Yellowstone National Park, December 1989.

16. W. Romme and M. Turner, "Implications of global climate change for biogeographic patterns in the greater Yellowstone ecosystem," *Conservation Biology* 5(3):373–386.

17. D. Graham, 1978, p. 23.

Chapter 9
The Grizzly Bear: Denning

1. S. Judd, R. Knight, and B. Blanchard, "Denning of grizzly bears in the Yellowstone area," in Meslow, 1983, p. 113. This paper is the primary source for this chapter.

2. J. Craighead and F. Craighead, "Grizzly bear prehibernation and denning activities as determined by radiotracking," *Wildlife Monographs* No. 32.

3. A. Pearson, *The northern interior grizzly bear* (Ursus arctos L.), Canadian Wildlife Service Report Series No. 34, p. 15.

4. T. Floyd, "Bone metabolism in hibernating bears," *Yellowstone Grizzly Journal*, Spring, 1989, p. 4. See also T. Floyd and R. Nelson, "Bone metabolism in black bears," in Darling and Archibald, 1990, p. 134–141.

Chapter 10
The Grizzly Bear: Mating and Cub Growth

1. J. Craighead, F. Craighead, and J. Sumner, "Reproductive cycles and rates in the grizzly bear," in Pelton, Lentfer, and Folk, 1976, p. 337–356; R. Knight and L. Eberhardt, "Population dynamics of Yellowstone grizzly bears," *Ecology* 66(2):323–334; H. Picton and R. Knight, "Using climate data to predict grizzly bear litter size," in Zager, 1986, p. 41–44. These sources were helpful with this chapter, as were extensive personal communications with Steve and Marilynn French, Yellowstone Grizzly Foundation, 1989–1991.

2. M. Hornocker, "Population characteristics and social and reproductive behavior of the grizzly bear in Yellowstone National Park," M.S. thesis, Montana State University, 1962, p. 77.

3. J. Craighead, J. Varney, and F. Craighead, *A population analysis of the*

Yellowstone grizzly bears, Montana Forest and Conservation Experiment Station, University of Montana, Bulletin 40, 1974, p. 14. This also is a very useful paper on the complexities and variations of reproductive rates, as well as being a pivotal publication in the grizzly bear management controversy. Litter size averages from 1973 to 1990 are from R. Knight, B. Blanchard, and D. Mattson, "Yellowstone grizzly bear investigations, report of the Interagency Study Team," National Park Service, 1991, p. 9. I must explain something about the methods for computing these litter sizes. The figures of 1.91 for 1973 to 1980, and 2.4 for 1981 to 1990, are based only on the observations of marked females. As it happens, the average litter size for all the females, marked and unmarked, is lower than that, but only the marked females are used in computing these numbers because the degree of scientific control of the sample is highest with the marked animals.

4. Skinner, 1925, p. 110.

5. Skinner, 1925, p. 117

Chapter 11
The Grizzly Bear: Lifestyle

1. The home ranges and movements of numerous grizzly bear populations, including the Yellowstone population during the 1960s when it was studied by the Craighead team, are summarized in Interagency Grizzly Bear Committee, *Grizzly Bear Compendium* (Washington: National Wildlife Federation, 1987), p. 27–46. This is an excellent publication on all aspects of grizzly bear ecology and management.

2. F. Craighead, "Grizzly bear ranges and movements as determined by radiotracking," in Pelton, Lentfer, and Folk, 1976, p. 97–110.

3. B. Blanchard and R. Knight, "Movements of Yellowstone grizzly bears," *Biological Conservation*, 1991, 58:61.

4. Ibid., p. 62–63.

5. R. Knight, Interagency Grizzly Bear Study Team, personal communication, 1991.

6. D. Mattson, "Human impacts on bear habitat use," in Darling and Archibald, 1990, p. 46–47.

7. Blanchard and Knight, 1991; Mattson, 1990; B. Blanchard, "Grizzly bear—Habitat relationships in the Yellowstone area," in Meslow, 1983, p. 118–123.

8. Schleyer, 1983, and Harting, 1985, studied a variety of factors that might influence bear activities.

9. Harting, 1985, p. 49–51.

10. Blanchard, 1983, p. 119.

11. This discussion of day beds is based on R. Knight and B. Blanchard, "Yellowstone grizzly bear investigations, report of the Interagency Study Team," July, 1983, p. 35–38.

12. D. Worley, J. Fox, J. Winters, R. Jacobson, and K. Greer, "Helminth

and arthropod parasites of grizzly and black bears in Montana and adjacent areas," in Pelton, Lentfer, and Folk, 1976, p. 455–464.

13. W. Romme and D. Despain, "Historical perspective on the Yellowstone fires of 1988," *BioScience* 39(10):695–699.

14. R. Balling, G. Meyer, and S. Wells, "Climate change in Yellowstone National Park: Is the drought-related risk of wildfires increasing?" *Climate Change*, in press.

15. F. Singer and P. Schullery, "Yellowstone wildlife: Populations in process," *Western Wildlands* 15:18–22; F. Singer, W. Schreier, J. Oppenheim, and E. Garten, "Drought, fire, and large mammals," *BioScience* 39(10): 716–722.

16. B. Blanchard and R. Knight, "Reactions of grizzly bears (*Ursus arctos horribilis*) to wildfires in Yellowstone National Park, Wyoming," *The Canadian Field-Naturalist* 104(4):592.

17. R. Knight and C. Servheen, "Possible effects of a restored wolf population on grizzly bears in the Yellowstone area," in *Wolves for Yellowstone? a report to the United States Congress, Vol. ii, research and analysis*, Yellowstone National Park, 1990, p. 4–37.

18. B. Koth, D. Lime, and J. Vlaming, "Effects of restoring wolves on Yellowstone area big game and grizzly bears: Opinions of fifteen North American experts," in *Wolves for Yellowstone? A report to the United States Congress, Vol. II, research and analysis*, Yellowstone National Park, 1990, p. 4–57.

Chapter 12
The First 10,000 Years

1. A. Haines, *The Yellowstone Story* (Boulder: Colorado Associated University Press, 1977), Vol. I, p. 16–20.

2. D. Rockwell, *Giving voice to bear: North American Indian myths, rituals, and images of the bear*, (Boulder: Roberts Rinehart, 1991).

3. Haines, 1977, p. 35–154.

Chapter 13
1872–1916: The First Park Bears

1. I have explored many of these management evolutions in my book, *Mountain Time* (New York: Nick Lyons Books, 1984). Haines, 1977, covers many aspects of the history of management.

2. H. Hampton, *How the U.S. Cavalry saved our national parks* (Bloomington: Indiana University Press, 1971).

3. P. Norris, *Annual report of the superintendent of the Yellowstone National Park*, November 30, 1880 (Washington: U.S. Government Printing Office), p. 40–41.

4. The text of the 1883 regulation against hunting, which did not include

any of the major predators under its protection, appears in Haines, 1977, Vol. 1, p. 364. Philetus Norris, in his annual report as cited above, also stated that many elk carcasses were poisoned with strychnine to kill wolves and coyotes. This may have killed some bears as well, depending upon the amounts used and the timing of the poisoning; the available evidence makes it very difficult to tell.

5. McCracken, 1955; Russell, 1966.

6. J. Craighead and F. Craighead, "Management of bears in Yellowstone National Park," unpublished report, 1967, p. 7–8. This report suggests that black bear numbers "mounted rapidly as park visitation increased." It also agrees with Skinner, 1925, that when hunting was disallowed (which the report mistakenly states occurred in 1886 instead of 1883) black bears became more numerous. The Craigheads, based on their reading of early accounts, believed the grizzly bear was more common in the Yellowstone area than the black bear before 1900. My own more extensive readings of the early literature have so far left me unsure it is reliable to the extent necessary to make such a judgment.

7. G. Grinnell, "Report from the park," *Forest and Stream*, June 11, 1885. On July 2, 1885, *Forest and Stream* reported that bears were "frequently encountered" by a party on a trip from the geyser basins to Yellowstone Lake.

8. Haines, 1977, Vol. 2, p. 80.

9. Keep in mind also that the army took a very active view of its management of all park mammals; predators were still subject to frequent killing, and the death of park animals was certainly seen as a matter of routine necessity. Bears were still quite common in the west, and it is perhaps too easy to judge these killings by modern values, which place the bear much higher on the scale of important animals to protect.

10. L. Brett, *Report of the acting superintendent of the Yellowstone National Park*, October 14, 1911, p. 11.

11. Haines, 1977, Vol. 2, p. 117.

12. J. Pitcher, August 6, 1902, Yellowstone National Park Archives Box 239. A handwritten notation on the document says it was distributed again to hotel managers and others on June 12, 1905.

13. The most detailed published account of this episode appears in P. Schullery, *Yellowstone Bear Tales*, p. 55–58, a series of local reports of the attack.

14. P. Schullery, *Yellowstone Bear Tales*, p. 94–98, reprints these accounts.

15. F. Smith, *Book of a hundred bears* (Chicago: Rand McNally, 1909).

16. P. Schullery, *Yellowstone Bear Tales*, p. 59–67.

17. P. Schullery, "'Buffalo Jones' and the bison herd in Yellowstone: Another look," *Montana, the Magazine of Western History*, Summer, 1976, p. 40–51.

18. See footnote 6.

19. T. Roosevelt, *Outdoor pastimes of an American hunter* (New York: Scribner's, 1905), p. 347–351.

20. W. Wright, *The Grizzly Bear* (New York: Scribner's, 1910).

21. R. Dole, "Report on sanitary conditions in Yellowstone Park," 1914, unpublished typescript, Yellowstone National Park Archives.

Chapter 14
1916–1945: The Great Yellowstone Bear Show

1. J. Varley and P. Schullery, *Freshwater wilderness: Yellowstone fishes and their world* (Yellowstone Park: Yellowstone Library and Museum Association, 1983), review the many introduced fish species. Schullery, 1984, reviews changing policies regarding the introduction of other exotics and non-native species. G. Wright, *The evolution of science in the national parks and its impact on wildlife management* (Urbana: University of Illinois Press, in press) is a more detailed examination of the issues of research and management in the National Park Service.

2. The history of elk management in Yellowstone Park is most exhaustively documented in D. Houston, *The northern Yellowstone elk: Ecology and management* (New York: MacMillan, 1982).

3. A. Murie, *The ecology of the coyote in the Yellowstone* (Washington: U.S. Government Printing Office, 1940).

4. J. Varley, "A history of fish stocking activities in Yellowstone National Park between 1881 and 1980," Yellowstone information paper no. 35, 1981.

5. J. Hughes, "General park administration," in *Proceedings of the national park conference held at the Yellowstone National Park, September 11 and 12, 1991* (Washington: U.S. Government Printing Office, 1912), p. 193.

6. M. Skinner, "The predatory and fur-bearing animals of Yellowstone Park," *Roosevelt Wildlife Bulletin* 4(2):163–282.

7. Varley and Schullery, 1983, p. 103.

8. J. Grinnell and T. Storer, "Animal life as an asset of national parks," *Science* 1(44): 375–380.

9. B. Moore, "Importance of natural conditions in national parks," G. Grinnell and C. Sheldon, eds., *Hunting and Conservation* (New Haven: Yale University Press, 1925), p. 340–345, is an important statement of the developing attitudes about park management in the early Twentieth Century.

10. G. Wright, "Men and birds in joint occupation of national parks," in *Fauna of the national parks of the United States, wildlife management in the national parks* (Washington: U.S. Government Printing Office, 1935), p. 4.

11. G. Wright, J. Dixon, and B. Thompson, *Fauna of the national parks of the United States* (Washington: U.S. Government Printing Office, 1933), p. 84.

12. J. Craighead and F. Craighead, 1967, p. 24. G. Cole, "Preservation and management of grizzly bears in Yellowstone National Park," *BioScience* 21(16):861–862.

13. Ibid., p. 862.

14. 71st Congress, 1st Session, H.R. 1531, April 19, 1929, A bill for the relief of Margaret Constable.

15. O. Murie, "Progress report on the Yellowstone bear study," 1944, Yellowstone Park Reference Library.

Chapter 15
1946–1967: Crisis and Response

1. W. Robbins, E. Ackerman, M. Bates, S. Cain, F. Darling, J. Fogg, T. Gill, J. Gillson, E. Hall, C. Hubbs, and C. Durham, A report by the advisory committee to the National Park Service on research of the National Academy of Sciences—National Research Council (Washington: National Academy of Sciences. 1963), p. 32.

2. A. Leopold, S. Cain, C. Cottam, I. Gabrielson, and T. Kimball, "Wildlife management in the national parks," Report to the Secretary of the Interior, 1963. My comments on the report are based in part on my conversations with Starker Leopold.

3. The best book, by far, to read as an introduction to the many controversies over how best to manage the park and the surrounding ecosystem is R. Keiter and M. Boyce, *The greater Yellowstone ecosystem: Redefining America's wilderness heritage* (New Haven: Yale University Press, 1991). This book provides many of the common viewpoints, from the most protective to the most exploitative, on resource management in Greater Yellowstone. For a cross-section of views, see especially, R. Keiter, "An introduction to the ecosystem management debate," p. 3–18, D. Patten, "Defining the greater Yellowstone ecosystem," p. 19–26, J. Craighead, "Yellowstone in transition," p. 27–40, J. Sax, "Ecosystem and property rights in greater Yellowstone," p. 77–86, M Boyce, "Natural regulation or the control of nature," p. 183–208 (perhaps the single most helpful chapter in the book on the philosophical issues of management of park resources), S. Chadde and C. Kay, "Tall-willow communities on Yellowstone's northern range: A test of the 'natural regulation' paradigm," p. 231–262, and R. Keiter and M. Boyce, "Greater Yellowstone's future: Ecosystem management in a wilderness environment," p. 379–413. A brief book that reviews the development of northern range management issues is D. Despain, D. Houston, M. Meagher, and P. Schullery, *Wildlife in transition: Man and nature on Yellowstone's northern range* (Boulder: Roberts Rinehart, 1987). A very good historical overview of the overgrazing issue on the overgrazing issue on the northern range, an important companion to Houston, 1982, is D. Tyers, "The condition of the northern Yellowstone winter range in Yellowstone National Park: A discussion of the controversy," M.S. thesis, Montana State University, 1981.

A wide variety of journalists and special interest advocates have also addressed the change in management direction that occurred in the late 1960s, when the National Park Service undertook its so-called "natural regulation" experiment on the northern range and also overhauled bear, fisheries, and other resource management procedures. I especially recommend, T. McNamee, *Nature First* (Boulder: Roberts Rinehart, 1987) as a provocative statement of how Greater Yellowstone might be best managed. McNamee, a former president of the Greater Yellowstone Coalition, has also written one of the best modern books on bears, *The Grizzly Bear* (New York: Knopf, 1984), which covers not only Yellowstone but all the other populations in the lower 48 states. But perhaps the best known of these advocacy publications is A. Chase, *Playing God in Yellowstone* (Boston: Atlantic Monthly, 1986), an oddly hostile book that, for all its shortcomings as journalism, does at least offer the dubious service of gathering up every negative opinion on every management issue relating to Yellowstone Park. Chase takes the most aggressively manipulative stance on most management issues, apparently wanting to leave no element of the natural setting to its own devices; in some circles, the book's extreme position on intensive husbandry of park resources has earned it the nickname, "Laying sod in Yellowstone." The book is perhaps most effectively rebutted, in its main principles, at least, by H. Rolston, "Biology and philosophy in Yellowstone," *Biology and Philosophy* 5:241–252, an equally provocative and much calmer analysis of the issues.

Chapter 16
The Grizzly Bear Controversy Begins

1. J. Craighead and F. Craighead, 1972, p. 4.
2. J. Craighead, "Proposal for research on ecology of the grizzly bear (*Ursus horribilis*) initiated by the Montana Cooperative Wildlife Research Unit, submitted to the National Science Foundation and the National Academy of Sciences," 1960.
3. J. Craighead and F. Craighead, 1967. The Park Service's response to the Craighead report, as I summarize that response here, is distilled from W. Barmore, "Bear management recommendations by John and Frank Craighead," memorandum to Yellowstone superintendent, 1967; G. Cole, "Craighead report on Yellowstone bears," memorandum to deputy chief scientist, National Park Service, September 12, 1967; and R. Linn, "Management of bears in Yellowstone National Park, by Drs. John and Frank Craighead," memorandum from deputy chief scientist to associate director, Bureau of Sport Fisheries and Wildlife, May 21, 1968. Too often the public was given the impression that the Craighead report was dealt with only by bureaucrats, when actually the National Park Service's response was generally based on the reactions of scientists (all three of these, for example) and bear managers.
4. G. Fredine, comments in J. Craighead, M. Hornocker, W. Woodgerd, and F. Craighead, "Trapping, immobilizing and color-marking grizzly bears," *Transactions of the twenty-fifth North American wildlife conference, March 7, 8, and 9, 1960* (Washington: Wildlife Management Institute, 1960), p. 363. Mr. Fredine spoke vaguely but affirmatively about such a study while discussing the new Craighead study then just underway:

> I hope that this study is just a springboard to a long-range study of the grizzly bear throughout its remaining rnage in the United States, and although

you always appoint a committee when you need to do some work, I really think it might be a good idea for the varioust [sp.] people in the states of Montana, Idaho, Wyoming and Colorado where we still have some grizzlies to get together and exchange ideas and form a program which will yield the information that we [need].

This is obviously not a proposal for a formal interagency management approach, but it does begin to capture the spirit of that kind of breadth.

5. Cole, 1972, p. 862.

6. Linn, 1968.

7. G. Cole, "Grizzly bears," memorandum to Yellowstone superintendent, June 17, 1969.

8. J. Craighead, "Investigator's annual report," January 14, 1969.

9. J. Anderson, letters to J. Craighead, April 7, 1969, and July 9 and 20, 1970; J. Craighead, letters to J. Anderson, April 14, 1969, and June 9, 1970.

10. J. Craighead, letter to J. Anderson, April 14, 1969.

11. A.S. Leopold, letter to W. Spivak, February 10, 1975. In this letter, Starker Leopold said that, "The Craigheads offered to review for the Committee their considerable findings on Yellowstone grizzlies, but only if all employees of the National Park Service were excluded from the room." (p. 2). Starker later told me, in conversations, that he was not at all personally persuaded by the Craighead presentation; that is, though they did have lots of data, it was not in his opinion directly convincing that a fast dump closure was better than a slow one.

12. A.S. Leopold, S. Cain, and C. Olmsted, "A bear management policy and program for Yellowstone National Park," a report to the Director by the natural science advisory committee of the National Park Service, as a result of a meeting in Yellowstone National Park, September 6 and 7, 1969, p. 2–3

13. A.S. Leopold, 1975, p. 2.

14. F. Craighead, "Increasing concern over grizzly bear survival," *Jackson Hole Guide*, November 6, 1969.

Chapter 17
Regrouping

1. The Craighead position, as summarized here, is based on the material cited in the previous chapter plus these: J. Craighead, letter to Jack Anderson, n.d., received April 5, 1971; BJ. Craighead and F. Craighead, "Grizzly bear-man relationships in Yellowstone National Park," *BioScience* 21(16):845–857; J. Craighead, M. Hornocker, and F. Craighead, "Reproductive biology of young female grizzly bears," *Journal of Reproductive Fertility*, Supplement 6:447–475; and J. Craighead, J. Varney, and F. Craighead, *A population analysis of the Yellowstone grizzly bears*, Bulletin 40, Montana Forest and Conservation Experiment Station, University of Montana, 1974. Additional material is cited in the bibliography of this book. The National Park Service's position is summarized from the following: N. Reed, letter to Senator Metcalf, June 2,

1971; G. Cole, "Interim progress on 1971 bear management program," memorandum to Yellowstone superintendent, August 23, 1971; G. Cole, "Preservation and management of grizzly bears in Yellowstone National Park," *BioScience* 21:858–863; G. Cole, "Grizzly bear-elk relationships in Yellowstone National Park," *Journal of Wildlife Management* 32(2):556–561; and G. Cole, "Management involving grizzly bears in Yellowstone National Park, 1970–1972," National Park Service natural resources report no. 7, 1973. What surprised me most in the early and mid-1970s, when I first became interested in this issue, was how many journalists were familiar with the Craighead publications and were unfamiliar with Cole's, though both were publishing in the scientific literature. There was a pretty obvious presumption that only the Craigheads were able to get their scientific views published, or were the only ones with anything scientific to say. Whoever was right, the story was not done justice.

2. J. Anderson, letter to J. Craighead, February 9, 1971.

3. J. Craighead, letter to J. Anderson, n.d., received April 5, 1971.

4. G. Moment, "Bears: The need for a new sanity in wildlife conservation," *BioScience* 18:1105–1108; G. Moment, "Bears and conservation: Realities and recommendations," *BioScience* 19:1019–1020; G. Moment, "Man-grizzly problems—Past and present," *BioScience* 20:1142–1144; C. Wilber, "Incompatible species," letter to the editor, *BioScience* 20:326.

5. Fund for Animals, news releases concerning Yellowstone bear management and Fund for Animals suit, February, 1974.

6. Craighead, Varney, and Craighead, 1974.

7. National Academy of Sciences, "Report of the committee on the Yellowstone grizzlies," N.A.S., 1974. This is my source for the summary of the committee's findings.

8. G. Cole, "Comments on NAS grizzly report," memorandum to research files, September 11, 1974; G. Cole, "Requested comments on NAS report and Ted Sudia's draft memo to Asst. Secretary, Interior," memorandum to Yellowstone superintendent, October 24, 1974.

9. National Park Service, "Summary of 1974 National Academy of Sciences recommendations and measures taken as of November, 1976," Yellowstone National Park, 1976.

10. I. Cowan, letter to G. Cole, April 29, 1975. This letter occupies an odd position in the debate. Though Cowan speaks of "we" as if he is representing the committee, no formal revision of the report was ever done.

11. M. Meager and J. Phillips, "Restoration of natural populations of grizzly and black bears in Yellowstone National Park," in Zager, 1983, p. 152–158.

Chapter 18
The Greater Yellowstone Grizzly Bear

1. National Park Service, *Fishing Bridge and the Yellowstone ecosystem,*

a report to the Director, November, 1984 (Denver: U.S. Government Printing Office, 1984). This report, which contains a detailed history of the development and research efforts involving it, is the primary source for this discussion.

2. K. Gunther, "Visitor impact on grizzly bear activity in Pelican Valley, Yellowstone National Park," in Darling and Archibald, 1990, p. 73–78.

3. G. Brown, "Human use adjustment areas," memorandum to chief ranger, March 3, 1983; K. Gunther, "Bear management area program, Yellowstone National Park," Information paper no. BMO-5, Yellowstone National Park, summarizes the development and rationale of the system.

4. M. Beck and D. Junkin, "Whose park is it, anyway," *Newsweek*, June 25, 1978, p. 33.

5. R. Reese, *Greater Yellowstone: The national park and adjacent wildlands* (Helena: Montana Magazine, 1984), second edition 1991.

6. R. Barbee, "Comments on the proposed forest plan—Gallatin National Forest," Yellowstone National Park, 1985, p. 2

7. Greater Yellowstone Coordinating Committee, *Vision for the future, a framework for coordination in the greater Yellowstone area*, U.S. Forest Service and National Park Service, August, 1990. For background on the process and how it went awry, see R. Barbee, P. Schullery, and J.D. Varley, "The Yellowstone vision: An experiment that failed or a vote for posterity?" in *Partnerships in parks & preservation*, Albany, New York, September 9–12, 1991, p. 80–85.

Chapter 19
How Many Bears Is Enough?

1. G. Cole, "Management involving grizzly bears in Yellowstone National Park, 1970–1974," paper presented at the 26th annual A.I.B.S. meeting of biological sciences, Oregon State University, 1975.

2. R. Knight, J. Basile, K. Greer, S. Judd, L. Oldenburg, and L. Roop, "Annual report—1974—interagency grizzly bear study team," March, 1975, p. 33.

3. L. Roop, "The Yellowstone grizzly bear: A review of past and present population estimates," in R. Knight, B. Blanchard, K. Kendall, and L. Oldenburg, "Yellowstone grizzly bear investigations, report of the interagency study team, 1978 and 1979," September, 1980, p. 61–75. Roop said, "At present the IGBST has made no population estimates based on field data, but study team members are of the opinion that there are between 300 and 350 animals in the population. It has been stressed that these figures are not from a scientific data analysis but are a result of inductive inference from the number of animals handled and observed." (p. 65)

4. R. Knight, B. Blanchard, and K. Kendall, "Yellowstone grizzly bear investigations, report of the interagency study team, 1980," July, 1981, p. 29.

5. Ibid.

6. R. Knight, B. Blanchard, and K. Kendall, "Yellowstone grizzly bear investigations, report of the interagency study team, 1981," July, 1982, p. 51.

7. R. Knight and L. Eberhardt, "Population dynamics of Yellowstone grizzly bears," *Ecology* 66(2):331.

8. S. Herrero, *Bear attacks: Their causes and avoidance* (New York: Nick Lyons Books, 1985), p. 255.

9. H. Picton, "Climate and reproduction of grizzly bears in Yellowstone National Park," *Nature* 274:888–889.

10. H.D. Picton and R. Knight, "Using climate data to predict grizzly bear litter size," in Zager, 1986. p. 41–44; H. Picton, D. Mattson, B. Blanchard, and R. Knight, "Climate, carrying capacity, and the Yellowstone grizzly bear," in G. Contreras and K. Evans, eds., *Proceedings of the grizzly bear habitat symposium*, U.S. Forest Service general technical report INT-207, 1986, p. 129–135. What is under consideration here is not whether one factor or another is the cause of some change in litter size or carrying capacity, but the relative importance of several factors. S. Stringham, "Effects of climate, dump closure, and other factors on Yellowstone grizzly bear litter size," in Zager, 1986, p. 33–39, for example, argues that dump closures were more significant by far than climate changes.

11. D. McCullough, "The Craigheads' data on Yellowstone grizzly bear populations: Relevance to current research and management," in Zager, 1986, p. 28.

12. Ibid.

13. M. Shaffer, "Determining minimum viable population sizes: A case study of the grizzly bear (*Ursus arctos* L.)," Ph.D. thesis, Duke University, 1978; M. Shaffer, "Minimum population sizes for species conservation," *BioScience* 31:131–134; M. Shaffer, "Determining minimum viable population sizes for the grizzly bear," in Zager, 1983, p. 135–141; McCullough, 1986, p. 25; W. Suchy, L. McDonald, M. Strickland, and S. Anderson, "New estimates of minimum viable population size for grizzly bears of the Yellowstone ecosystem," *Wildlife Society Bulletin* 13(3):223–228. D. Bolger, C. Biehl, M. Sorice, and M. Gilpin, "Estimating effective population size for the Yellowstone grizzly bear population: effects of non-Poisson family size distribution and breeding sex ratio," in F. Singer, ed., *Conference on science in the national parks, proceedings, vol. 2, wildlife management and habitats*, the fourth triennial conference on research in the national parks and equivalent reserves, July 13–18, 1986. The George Wright Society and the National Park Service, 1987, p. 3–16.

14. Knight and Eberhardt, 1985, p. 333.

15. H. Picton and R. Knight, "Using climate data to predict grizzly bear litter size," abstract for 6th international bear research and management conference, February 1983, Grand Canyon, Arizona, p. 3.

16. U.S. Fish and Wildlife Service, interagency grizzly bear committee, draft, grizzly bear recovery plan, 1990.

17. D. Gaillard and L. Willcox, Greater Yellowstone Coalition, letter to C. Servheen, U.S. Fish and Wildlife Service, commenting on recovery plan; Daniel Conner, Great Bear Foundation, letter to membership, n.d. (1991) regarding bear management issues, p. 3. A tolerably good summary of

conservationist comments appeared in *The Billings Gazette*, February 20, 1991, "Conservationists oppose grizzly bear recovery plan," p. 6–B.

18. L. Metzgar, "Comments on grizzly bear recovery plan, revised draft," memorandum to conservation organizations concerned with grizzly bear recovery, n.d.

Chapter 20
Don't Feed the Bears, Again

1. Herrero, 1985, p. 248.

2. D. McCullough, "Behavior, bears, and humans," *Wildlife Society Bulletin* 10:30.

3. K. Jope, "Implications of grizzly bear habituation to hikers," *Wildlife Society Bulletin* 13:32–37.

4. M. Haroldson and D. Mattson, "Response of grizzly bears to backcountry human use in Yellowstone National Park," Interagency grizzly bear study team research report, October, 1985.

5. C. Hunt, F. Hammond, and C. Peterson, "Aversive conditioning study, 1987 progress report," Wyoming Game and Fish Department, April, 1988.

6. S. Herrero, 1985, p. 254–255.

7. J. Marti, "CBS News gets mauled," *High Country News*, October 29, 1984.

8. Ibid.

9. National Park Service, "Board of inquiry into the death of Brigitta Fredenhagen," Yellowstone National Park, September 4, 1984. In October of 1986, William Tesinsky, of Great Falls, Montana, was killed by a sow grizzly bear south of Canyon village; an investigation of the site where his body was found (with the bear still nearby) suggested that he had attempted to approach closely to the animal and was attacked.

10. R. Knight, G. Brown, J. Craighead, M. Meagher, L. Roop, and C. Servheen, "Final report, ad hoc committee to investigate the need and feasibility of the supplemental feeding of Yellowstone grizzly bears," December 5, 1983, p. 2.

11. C. Jonkel, "Grizzlies," letter to the editor, *High Country News*, June 10, 1983, p. 14.

Chapter 21
Keeping the Bears

1. M. Bean, *The evolution of national wildlife law* (Washington: U.S. Government Printing Office, 1977), p. 211–212.

2. A. Stebler, "Conservation of the grizzly—Ecological and cultural considerations," in Herrero, 1972, p. 302.

3. R. Barbee, Yellowstone superintendent, letter to Gallatin County Assistant Planner W. Johnson, March 8, 1991; R. Martinka, regional supervisor,

Montana Department of Fish, Wildlife & Parks, letter to M. Peck and R. Johnson, Gallatin County Planners, February 15, 1991; The American Grizzly Bear Project (The Greater Yellowstone Coalition, The Wilderness Society, The Sierra Club), "Alert! Alert! Alert!, proposed grizzly park threatens grizzly bears," newsletter, September 20, 1991.
    4. W. Romme and M. Turner, "Implications of global climate change for biogeographic patterns in the greater Yellowstone ecosystem," *Conservation Biology* 5(3):373–386; H. Picton, D. Mattson, B. Blanchard, and R. Knight, 1986.

Chapter 22
The Bear as Person

    1. A nice review of many of the images of the bear in human culture is P. Shepard and B. Sanders, *The sacred paw: The bear in nature, myth, and literature* (New York: Viking, 1985). The closest thing to a history of the bear in American hunting culture is P. Schullery, *The bear hunter's century: Profiles from the golden age of bear hunting* (New York: Dodd, Mead, 1988), an informal review of some notable bear hunters. The history of hunting and other blood sports has not received the attention most other aspects of bear history have.

Chapter 22
Famous Yellowstone Bears

    1. E. Seton, *The biography of a grizzly* (New York: The Century Company, 1899).
    2. E. Seton, *Lives of game animals* (New York: Doubleday, Doran and Company, 1909); E. Seton, *Wild animals at home* (New York: Grosset and Dunlap, 1913).
    3. A. Allen, "Spud, the hold-up bear of Yellowstone," *American Forests,* September, 1925, p. 540–542.
    4. D. Yeager, "Bringing up Barney," *Nature Magazine* 21(1):27–30.

Chapter 24
Hunting Yellowstone Bears

    1. A. Russell, *Grizzly Country* (New York: Knopf, 1967), p. 99–100.
    2. A. Henderson, "Journal of the Yellowstone expedition of 1866 under Jeff Standifer, also the diaries kept by Henderson during his prospecting journeys in the Snake, Wind River, and Yellowstone country during the years 1866–1872," Yellowstone Park Reference Library, typescript.
    3. W. Trumbull story originally appeared in the *Helena Gazette,* but is reprinted here from N. Langford, *The discovery of Yellowstone Park,* ed. Aubrey Haines (Lincoln: University of Nebraska Press, 1972), p. 68.

4. Ibid.

5. P. Norris, *Report upon the Yellowstone National Park, to the Secretary of the Interior, by P.W. Norris, Superintendent, for the year 1879* (Washington: U.S. Government Printing Office, 1880), p. 8–9.

6. H. Albright, "Annual report for Yellowstone National Park—1920," p. 107–108.

Chapter 25
Making Themselves at Home

1. J. Douglas, "Black bear and cub under Lake Hotel," *Yellowstone Nature Notes*, March 18, 1925.

2. C. Skinner, "Some notes on the black bear (Euarctos americanus) from observations at Old Faithful, Yellowstone National Park, 1931–1932," Yellowstone Park Reference Library, typescript.

3. S. Young, *Report of the superintendent of Yellowstone National Park,* Yellowstone National Park, October 15, 1908, p. 10.

4. Mrs. F. Bieberdorf, "Bruin takes a Turkish bath," *Yellowstone Nature Notes*, May–June, 1940, p. 34–35.

5. M. Beal, "Bear caves in Norris Geyser Basin," *Yellowstone Nature Notes*, November–December, 1951, p. 72.

6. Seton, 1899.

7. T. Jaggar, "Death Gulch, a natural bear trap," *Appleton's Popular Science Monthly*, February, 1899, p. 1–7.

Chapter 25
Bears, Tourists, and Rangers:
The Eternal Triangle

1. D. Bock, "A survey of public opinion concerning the Yellowstone bear feeding problem," Research project, Colorado A. & M. school of forestry, 1953.

2. N. Reid and D. Learmonth, "Bear management in national parks," Joint Committee, United States and Canadian National Parks, 1969, p. 9–10.

3. O. Wister, "Old Yellowstone days," *Harper's Monthly*, March, 1936, p. 476.

4. F. Smith, *Book of a Hundred Bears* (Chicago: Rand McNally, 1909).

5. P. Martindale, "Close contact with grizzly bears," Yellowstone Park Reference Library, handwritten report.

6. O. Wister, 1936, p. 476.

7. M. Beal, *The story of man in Yellowstone* (Yellowstone Park: Yellowstone Library and Museum Association, 1960), p. 256.

8. H. Albright, "New orders for national park bears," *The Backlog: A Bulletin of the Camp Fire Club of America*, 1945, p. 6–7.

9. W. Kearns, "The speed of grizzly bears," *Yellowstone Nature Notes,* January–February, 1937, p. 2–3.

10. P. Schullery, 1988, p. 216–219.

11. T. Roosevelt, *Outdoor pastimes of an American hunter* (New York: Scribner's, 1905), p. 351.

12. D. Yeager, *Our Wilderness Neighbors,* (Chicago: A.C. McClurg Company, 1931).

13. One of the interesting things about this exchange is that the President of the American Human Association, Mr. Stillman, freely acknolwedged that he personally knew "nothing whatsoever about the conditions there," but that a "valued correspondent" had informed him that park officials, while caring enough to see that the bears were adequately fed with garbage during the summer, were doing nothing at all to help them through the winter. Furthermore, Mr. Stillman related, he understood that the "bears are found in an emaciated condition in the spring and that while suffering the pangs of starvation, they sometimes eat the flesh from their paws." This is interesting because it may actually relate to the shedding of paw pads as discussed early in this book, but it's even more interesting because it shows how automatically at least some portion of the public assumes that the bears, though they survived here without us for thousands of years, simply must need our help.

14. E. Roberston, "Bears and people," memorandum to West District Ranger, June 10, 1960.

15. D. Nuss, National Park Service, personal communication, 1978.

Chapter 27
Living with Bears

1. W. Hape, National Park Service, personal communication, 1978.

2 T. Roosevelt, *American bears: Selections from the writings of Theodore Roosevelt,* P. Schullery, ed. (Boulder: Colorado Associated University Press, 1983), p. 48.

3. Anonymous, "Grizzly visits snowshoe cabin," *Yellowstone Nature Notes,* November 20, 1924, p. 2.

4 M. Skinner, 1925, p. 65–68.

5. W. Hape, personal communication, 1978. Mr. Hape also is the source of the story about the skillet. He showed me a photograph of the skillet.

6. Anonymous, "Bears become bold," *Yellowstone Nature Notes,* October 31, 1927, p. 7.

Chapter 28
Camping With Bears

1. K. Jope, 1985, p. 35.

2 G. Miller, "Responses of captive grizzly and polar bears to potential repellents," in Meslow, 1983, p. 278.

3. G. Miller, 1983; S. Herrero, 1985; L. Rogers, "Reactions of free-ranging black bears to capsaicin spray repellent," *Wildlife Society Bulletin* 12:59–61; G. Miller, "Field tests of potential polar bear repellents," in Zager, 1987, p. 383–390; D. Woolridge and P. Belton, "natural and synthesized aggressive sounds as polar bear repellents," in Martinka and McArthur, 1980, p. 85–92; D. Woolridge, "Chemical aversion condition of polar and black bears," in Martinka and McArthur, 1980, p. 167–174.

4. S. Herrero, 1985, p. 149; C. Byrd, "Of bears and women: investigating the hypothesis that menstruation attracts bears," M.S. thesis, University of Montana, 1988.

5. R. Grimm, "A climbing grizzly," *Yellowstone Nature Notes*, November–December, 1938, p. 58–59.

6. F.W.C., "Bear troubles," *Yellowstone Nature Notes*, March–April, 1936, p. 9; Frank W. Childs, "Experimental use of liquid tear gas on park bears," National Park Service report, October 17, 1934.

In 1943 and 1944, O.J. Murie participated in experiments with electric cattle prods on black bears; they would scare the bear briefly, but the bear would soon return to the garbage or other food source that had attracted it (O. Murie, field notes, on file in the Murie Museum, Teton Science School, Kelly, Wyoming). He also discussed this in Murie, 1944, where he also recommended more experimentation with electrification of garbage cans and other attractants, and with dogs as possible deterrents.

Acknowledgments

By the time I completed the second edition of this book, the acknowledgment list was beginning to look like a chapter of its own. I do owe many people thanks for their help with those first two editions, and I try to express my gratitude in the second edition.

For help with this third edition, I am especially grateful to Steve and Marilynn French of the Yellowstone Grizzly Foundation for all the ideas and wisdom they've shared with me the past three years.

I also thank the other people who have been good enough to talk to my grizzly bear ecology and management class at the Yellowstone Institute in 1990 and 1991: Sue Consolo, Steve Frye, Kerry Gunther (who also helped me update the statistical tables), Steve Herrero, Greg Hood, Dick Knight, Dave Mattson, Ray Paunovich, Louisa Wilcox, and John Varley. My learning curve at those sessions was almost as steep as my students'.

Jean Donaldson made the revision possible by typing most of the second edition onto diskettes so I could work on it, overcoming any number of computer outrages along the way.

And the continued and gratifying enthusiasm of readers of the previous editions persuaded me to keep the book in print.

Appendix A

Friends of the Bear

There are many things you can do to help the bears of Yellowstone. Start by informing yourself; the environmental movement no longer can be driven by righteous indigation alone, and the more you know, the more you can accomplish.

The mainstream conservation organizations have taken a strong interest in the grizzly bear. Defenders of Wildlife, the National Audubon Society, the National Fish and Wildlife Foundation, the National Parks and Conservation Association, The National Wildlife Federation, and the Sierra Club have all helped especially. Other organizations, such as Earth First! and Fund for Animals, have also participated in the grizzly bear dialogues, but it is less clear that their activities have yet translated into anything that has actually helped the grizzly bear population. It is true that these things are sometimes hard to measure, and everybody has their own way of pitching in.

There are a few specialized organizations, however, that you should know about. I belong to and believe in all of these, and if you want a recommendation beyond that, I'll only say that I dedicated my book *Yellowstone Bear Tales* to the good work of the Yellowstone Grizzly Foundation.

Great Bear Foundation
Post Office Box 2699
Missoula, Montana
59806

Funds research and education relating to bear ecology and conservation.

Greater Yellowstone Coalition
Post Office Box 1874
Bozeman, Montana
59715

Activist umbrella organization of many conservation groups, campaigns for protection of ecosystem values in Greater Yellowstone.

Yellowstone Grizzly Foundation
581 Expedition Drive
Evanston, Wyoming
82930

Conducts behavioral research and educational programs on Yellowstone grizzly bears.

Yellowstone Institute
c/o The Yellowstone Association
Yellowstone Park, Wyoming
82190

Conducts field courses on many subjects, including about Yellowstone bears.

Appendix B

Bear Statistics

Table 1   Black bears in Yellowstone Park, 1920–1978, population estimates from various sources.[a]

Year	Supt. Annual Reports[b]	Annual Census	Wildlife Reports	Research Biologist Reports	Year	Supt. Annual Reports[b]	Annual Census	Wildlife Reports	Research Biologist Reports
1920	100	—	—		1950	360	—	—	
1921	—	—	—		1951	—	—	—	
1922	—	—	—		1952	—	—	—	
1923	—	—	—		1953	—	360	—	
1924	—	—	—		1954	—	—	—	
1925	200	200	—		1955	—	"common"	—	
1926	225	225	—		1956	—	—	—	
1927	275	275	—		1957	—	—	—	
1928	350	350	—		1958	—	"common"	—	
1929	440	450	—		1959	—	"common"	—	
1930	490	490	—		1960	—	—	—	
1931	465	500	—		1961	—	—	—	
1932	517	—	—		1962	—	500	—	
1933	525	525	—		1963	—	500	—	
1934	500	591	—		1964	—	500	—	
1935	500	633	—		1965	—	500	—	
1936	621	621	—		1966	—	500	—	
1937	520	520	—		1967	—	500	—	
1938	450	450	—		1968	—	500	—	
1939	500	500	—		1969	—	500	—	
1940	510	510	—		1970	—	500	—	
1941	550	550	—		1971	—	500	—	
1942	—	—	—		1972	—	500	—	
1943	—	—	—		1973	—	500	—	
1944	—	550	—		1974	—	500	—	
1945	450	450	—		1975	—	500	—	
1946	450	450	—		1976	—	—	650	
1947	—	360	—		1977	—	650	—	
1948	360	—	—		1978	—	650	—	
1949	360	360	—						

[a]Note comments in text on the relative reliability/unreliability of the various early estimates. Most were crude, based in part on sighted animals.
[b]Footnote "a" in Table 2 explains discrepancies that have occurred in past reporting of these numbers from the Superintendent's Annual Reports.

Table 2   Grizzly Bears in Yellowstone Park, 1920–1970; population estimates from various sources.

Year	Supt. Annual Reports	Annual Wildlife Census	Craighead Research Team Min. Reports[b] Counts	Year	Supt. Annual Reports	Annual Wildlife Census	Craighead Research Team Min. Reports[b] Counts
1920	40	—		1946	200	200	
1921	—	—		1947	200	200	
1922	—	—		1948	—	200	
1923	—	—		1949	200	200	
1924	—	—		1950	180	—	
1925	75	75		1951	—	—	
1926	80	80		1952	—	—	
1927	100	100		1953	—	150	
1928	140	140		1954	—	—	
1929	150	160		1955	—	"common"	
1930	167	167		1956	—	—	
1931	180	180		1957	—	—	
1932	213	—		1958	—	"common"	
1933	260[a]	260		1959	—	"common"	154
1934	250	310		1960	—	—	169
1935	250	335		1961	—	—	166
1936	286–300	286		1962	—	200	155
1937	290	290		1963	—	200	177
1938	270	270		1964	—	200	185
1939	300	300		1965	—	250	187
1940	320	320		1966	—	250	202
1941	300	300		1967	—	250	175
1942	—	—		1968	—	250	181
1943	—	—		1969	—	250	195
1944	300	300		1970	—	250[c]	179
1945	250	200					

[a]The Superintendent's annual reports issued before 1934 covered the period from October 1 to September 30 of each year. In 1934 that procedure was altered so that the 1934 Superintendent's Report covered only from October 1, 1933 to June 30, 1934 (June 30 was the end of the fiscal year). This change apparently misled some previous researchers (Craighead, 1967, and Bray and Barnes, 1967) and caused their reported population estimates to be one year out of kilter with the actual year being reported on by the Superintendent (Bray and Barnes, who reported on black bears, are one year off prior to 1934, and Craighead, who reported on both black and grizzly bears, are one year off after 1935).

[b]The Annual Wildlife Reports, on file in the Biologist Office, Yellowstone Park, have had several names. They should not be confused with the "Wildlife Inventory" done by the National Park Service. The "Wildlife Inventory" listed population estimates of various animals from many different National Park Service areas, and in the case of Yellowstone was directly derivative of the Annual Wildlife Reports. Note that in a few years before 1951 the Superintendent's Annual Reports and the Annual Wildlife Reports differ on the number of bears, and that the Superintendent's Annual Reports no longer carried bear population estimates after 1950.

[c]Figures in this column for the years 1959 to 1966 are from Craighead, 1967. Figures from 1967 to 1970 are from Craighead, 1974. In Craighead, 1967, it is stated that the figures given to that date are supposed to be almost all of the grizzlies in Yellowstone. In Craighead, 1974, these figures are apparently redefined to represent approximately 77.3% of the total population of grizzlies in the Yellowstone Ecosystem.

Table 3 Grizzly Bears in Yellowstone Park and in the Yellowstone Ecosystem—population estimates, 1971–1982.

Year	In Park	In Ecosystem
1971		175[a]
1972		
1973	250–300[b]	300–400[b]
1974	254–290[c]	319–364[c]
		136[d]
		234[e]
1975	250–320[f]	237–540[g]
		301[h]
1976		
1977		
1978		312[i]
1979		
1980		300–350[j]
1981		247[k]
1982		197[l]

[a]Craighead 1971.
[b]Cole 1973.
[c]Cole 1974.
[d]Craighead 1974.
[e]National Academy of Sciences 1974—This was an estimate for the population during the period before 1970.
[f]Cole 1975.
[g]Knight 1975.
[h]Cowan 1975—This was an estimate for the period 1959–1970.
[i]McCullough 1978—This was an estimate for the period 1959–1970.
[j]Knight et al. 1980.
[k]Knight, Blanchard, and Kendall 1981.
[l]Knight, Blanchard, and Kendall 1982.

Table 4   Numbers and ratios of female grizzly bears to their cubs in observed family groups, 1959 to 1990.

Year	Females	Cubs	Ratio
1959–1966 (avg.)	15	33	2.20
1972	11	22	2.00
1973	14	26	1.86
1974	15	26	1.73
1975	4	6	1.50
1976	16	30	1.88
1977	13	25	1.92
1978	9	18	2.00
1979	13	29	2.23
1980	12	23	1.92
1981	13	24	1.85
1982	11	20	1.82
1983	13	22	1.69
1984	17	30	1.76
1985	9	16	1.78
1986	25	48	1.92
1987	13	29	2.23
1988	19	40	2.11
1989	16	30	1.88
1990	24	57	2.38

Figures before 1973 from Cole, 1976; figures since 1974 from Interagency Grizzly Bear Study Team Annual Report for 1991.

Table 5   Total known grizzly bear mortality in the Greater Yellowstone ecosystem, including natural deaths and management removals, 1970–1990.

Year	Known	Probable	Possible	Total	Portion of Total Due to NPS Management Actions
1970	43	0	1	44	20
1971	39	3	2	44	6
1972	24	0	0	24	9
1973	13	4	2	19	0
1974	15	0	1	16	2
1975	2	1	0	3	0
1976	5	1	0	6	1
1977	14	3	2	19	1
1978	5	2	3	10	2
1979	3	6	2	11	1
1980	7	3	0	10	2
1981	10	3	3	16	0
1982	17	0	0	17	3
1983	6	0	0	6	2
1984	10	1	1	12	3
1985	11	2	0	13	0
1986	11	0	0	11	2
1987	3	0	0	3	1
1988	7	6	0	13	0
1989	2	0	0	2	0
1990	9	0	0	9	1

"Portion of total due to park management actions" includes deaths resulting from accidents during such actions, as well as deaths resulting from accidents while handling bears during research work. It also includes bears sent to zoos; though those bears did not die, they were effectively removed from the population, which amounts to pretty much the same thing as far as the population is concerned.

Statistics are from J. Craighead, K. Greer, R. Knight, and H. Pac, "Grizzly bear mortalities in the Yellowstone ecosystem, 1959–1987," a milestone report published by the Montana Department of Fish, Wildlife and Parks, the Craighead Wildlife-Wildlands Institute, the Interagency Grizzly Bear Study Team, and the National Fish and Wildlife Foundation, in 1988, and from Yellowstone Park Bear Management Office files.

Table 6   Injuries from black bears, control actions, and park visitors in Yellowstone Park, 1931–1984.

Years	Number of Injuries[a]	Number of Bears Removed[b]		Number of Captures & Transplants Per Year	Average Number of Park Visitors (Millions)
1930s	58 (22–115)	33	(2–66)	—	0.3
1940s	29 (2–89)	15	(2–55)	—	0.5
1950s	56 (38–109)	19	(6–40)	—	1.3
1960s	41 (24–69)	31	(4–85)	—	1.9
1931–69	46	24		?	1.0
1970	7	7	(1)[c]	19	2.3
1971	9	4	(2)	15	2.1
1972	5	11	(3)	34	2.2
1973	5	3	(0)	13	2.0
1974	7	3	(2)	11	1.9
1975	1	1	(1)	5	2.2
1976	4	4	(1)	13	2.5
1977	2	7	(3)	15	2.5
1978	1	1		0	2.6
1979	0	0		0	1.9
1980	0	1	(1)	0	2.0
1981	1	0		2	2.5
1982	0	1	(1)	0	2.4
1983	1	1	(1)	3	2.4
1984	0	1	(1)	0	2.3
1985	0	2	(2)	0	2.3
1986	0	1	(1)	3	2.4
1987	0	2	(2)	2	2.6
1988	0	4	(1)	5	2.2
1989	0	1	(0)	1	2.7
1990[d]	0	2	(1)	1	2.9

[a]Statistics given for before 1970 are averages for each decade, with range of yearly totals in parentheses.

[b]Statistics given are average for the decade, with range of yearly totals in parentheses.

[c]Statistics given include bears killed by human accidents, usually by being hit by cars. Number in parentheses is the non-management portion of the total.

[d]Statistics from before 1979 are from Meagher and Phillips, 1983. Statistics from 1979–1990 are from bear management office compilations.

Table 7   Injuries caused by grizzly bears and grizzly bears killed in Yellowstone Park, 1930–1990.

Year	Number of Injuries	Number of Bears Killed for Control	Year	Number of Injuries	Number of Bears Killed for Control
1930	0	0	1962	2	4
1931	0	1	1963	8	2
1932	3	4	1964	2	2
1933	0	2	1965	8	2
1934	1	0	1966	2	3
1935	2	6	1967	3	4
1936	0	0	1968	2	5
1937	0	10	1969	6	10
1938	0	0	1970	3	12 (8 others
1939	0	0			sent to zoos)
1940	0	0	1971	0	6
1941	1	0	1972	3*	8 (1 other sent
1942	3*	28			to zoo)
1943	0	0	1973	0	0
1944	0	3	1974	0	2
1945	0	0	1975	2	0
1946	0	0	1976	4	1
1947	1	0	1977	1	1
1948	7	3	1978	0[b]	2
1949	0	8	1979	2	1
1950	0	0	1980	1	2
1951	0	4	1981	2	0
1952	0	1	1982	0	3
1953	1	1	1983	1	2
1954	0	5	1984	5*	3
1955	1	5	1985	0	0
1956	0	0	1986	2*	2
1957	2	1	1987	0	1
1958	1	2	1988	0	0
1959	1	6	1989	1	0
1960	1	4	1990	0	1
1961	2	1			

*Includes one fatality.

[b]One serious backcountry injury was inflicted by a bear that may well have been a grizzly; it has been impossible to confirm the species either way, and so the injury is officially classified as caused by a bear of unknown species. This same situation was true in the 1942 death of Martha Hansen.

Statistics in this table are from Cole 1970 and Meagher 1978 for before 1978. Statistics from 1978–1990 are from bear management office records.

Table 8 Property damage cases due to bears, 1931–1990.

Year	Number[a]	Year	Number[a]	
1931	209	1961	247	
1932	451	1962	112	
1933	146	1963	278	
1934	38	1964	224	
1935	141	1965	291	
1936	34	1966	298	
1937	81	1967	284	
1938	81	1968[b]	240	(55)
1939	92	1969	199	(44)
1940	75	1970	88	(16)
1941	102	1971	52	(31)
1942	118	1972	87	(26)
1943	38	1973	32	(4)
1944	18	1974	52	(6)
1945	7	1975	27	(2)
1946	20	1976	27	(4)
1947	9	1977	31	(2)
1948	27	1978	13	(2)
1949	26	1979	7	(3)
1950	48	1980	12	(6)
1951	75	1981	18	(5)
1952	84	1982	50	(15)
1953	66	1983	14	(5)
1954	115	1984	0	(0)
1955	121	1985	11	(1)
1956	106	1986	26	(15)
1957	125	1987	8	(3)
1958	117	1988	21	(5)
1959	269	1989	9	(3)
1960	358	1990	15	(4)

[a]1931–1967, the number is the total for both species of bears.

[b]1968–1990, the first number is the total for all bears (black, grizzly, and unknown species), and the number in parentheses is for grizzly bears.

Statistics for 1931–1967 from Superintendent's reports. Statistics for 1968–1990 from bear management office compilations.

Bibliography

Abbie, L. 1942. Grizzly and bull elk battle. *Yellowstone Nature Notes*, May–June, p. 31.

Adams, C.C. 1925. The relation of wild life to the public in national and state parks. *Roosevelt Wildlife Bulletin* 2(4):371–402.

Albright, H. 1931. Letter to Joseph Dixon, November 9. Yellowstone Archives. Yellowstone National Park, Wyoming.

———. 1945. New orders for national park bears. *The Backlog: A Bulletin of the Camp Fire Club of America*: 6–7.

———. 1928. *Oh ranger*. New York: Dodd Mead.

———. 1972. Memories of the great and near-great in Yellowstone. *Montana, The Magazine of Western History* 22(3):80–89.

Amato, D., and D. Whittemore. 1988. Draft, status report on Yellowstone grizzly bear. The Greater Yellowstone Coalition.

Amstrup, S., and J. Beecham. 1976. Activity patterns of radio-collared black bears in Idaho. *Journal of Wildlife Management* 30(2):340–348.

Anderson, J. 1970. Letter to John Craighead, July 9.

———. 1971. Letter to John Craighead, July 20.

———. 1971. Letter to John Craighead, August 3.

———. 1971. Letter to John Craighead, February 9.

Anonymous. 1916. A grizzly attack in Yellowstone National Park. *Outdoor Life*, October, p. 373–374.

———. 1916. The late grizzly bear attacks in Yellowstone National Park. *Outdoor Life*, December, p. 583–584.

———. 1924. Grizzly visits snowshoe cabin. *Yellowstone Nature Notes*, November 20, p. 2.

———. 1970. Noted bear expert challenges Yellowstone Park bear policy. *Cody Enterprise*, October 7.

———. 1970. Official bemoans grizzly slaughter. *Jackson Hole News*, November 12.

———. 1978. Bear feeding would lessen maulings, Craighead agrees. *Jackson Hole Guide*, June 29.

295

Arnold, B. 1930. Cannibal bear. *Yellowstone Nature Notes*, August, p. 54.

Bacon, E.S. 1976. Curiosity in the American black bear. In M. Pelton, J. Lentfer, and G. Folk, eds., *Bears—Their biology and management*, I.U.S.N., p. 153-157.

Bacon, E.S., and Burghardt. 1976. Ingestive behaviors of the American black bear. In M. Pelton, J. Lentfer, and G. Folk, eds., *Bears—Their biology and management*, I.U.C.N., p. 13–26.

———. 1976. Learning and color discrimination in the American black bear. In M. Pelton, J. Lentfer, and G. folk, eds., *Bears—Their biology and management*, I.U.C.N., p. 27–36.

Baggley, G. 1932. Outline of method for bear control. Yellowstone Park Work Plan.

Bailey, V. 1930. *Animal life of Yellowstone National Park*. Baltimore: Charles C. Thomas.

Ball, R.E. 1976. The use of time-lapse cameras in destruction and population studies of grizzly bears (*Ursus arctos*) in the Shoshone National Forest, Park County, Wyoming. M.S. Thesis, University of Wyoming.

Balling, R., G. Meyer, and S. Wells. in press. Climate change in Yellowstone National Park: Is the drought-related risk of wildfires increasing? *Climate Change*.

Barbee, R. 1985. Comments on proposed forest plan—Gallatin National Forest.

Barbee, R., P. Schullery, and J. Varley. 1991. The Yellowstone vision: An experiment that failed or a vote for posterity? In proceedings of a conference, *Partnerships in parks & preservation*, Albany, New York, September 9–12, 1991, p. 80–85.

Barmore, W. 1967. Bear management recommendations by John and Frank Craighead. Memorandum to Yellowstone Park Superintendent, July 13. Yellowstone Files. Yellowstone National Park, Wyoming.

Barnes, V.G. 1967. Activities of black bears in Yellowstone National Park. M.S. Thesis, Colorado State University.

Barnes, V.G., and O.E. Bray. 1966. Black bears use drainage culverts for winter dens. *Journal of Mammalogy* 47:712–713.

———. 1967. Population characteristics and activities of black bears in Yellowstone National Park. Final Report. Colorado Cooperative Wildlife Research Unit, Colorado State University.

Bartlett, R. 1974. *Nature's Yellowstone*. Norman: University of Oklahoma Press.

Basile, J.V. 1982. Grizzly bear distribution in the Yellowstone area, 1973-79. USDA-FS, Intermtn For. and Range Exp. Sta. Research Note INT-321.

Beal, M. 1951. Bear caves in Norris geyser basin. *Yellowstone Nature Notes*, November–December, p. 72–73.

———. 1960. *The story of man in Yellowstone*. Yellowstone Park: Yellowstone Library and Museum Association.

Bean, M. 1978. *The evolution of national wildlife law*. Washington: U.S. Government Printing Office.

Beck, M., and D. Junkin. 1984. Whose park is it, anyway? *Newsweek*, June 25, p. 33.

Beeman, L., and M. Pelton. 1976. Homing of black bears in the Great Smoky Mountains. In M. Pelton, J. Lentfer, and G. Folk, eds., *Bears—Their biology and management*, I.U.C.N., p. 87-96.

Bennett, L.J., P.F. English, and R.L. Watts. 1943. The food habits of the black bear in Pennsylvania. *Journal of Mammalogy* 24(1):25-31.

Bieberdorf, F.W., Mrs. 1940. Bruin takes a Turkish bath. *Yellowstone Nature Notes*, May-June, p. 34-35.

Blanchard, B. 1978. Grizzly bear distribution in relation to habitat areas and recreational use: Cabin Creek—Hilgard Mountains. M.S. Thesis, Montana State University.

———. 1983. Grizzly bear-habitat relationships in the Yellowstone area. In P. Zager, ed., *Bears—Their biology and management*, B.B.A., 118-123.

Blanchard, B., and R. Knight. 1980. Status of grizzly bears in the Yellowstone system. *Proc. 45th North Am. Wildl. Conf.*, p. 263-267.

———. 1990. Reactions of grizzly bears, *Ursus arctos horribilis*, to wildfire in Yellowstone National Park, Wyoming. *The Canadian Field-Naturalist* 104(4):592-594.

———. 1991. Movements of Yellowstone grizzly bears. *Biological Conservation* 58:41-67.

Bock, D. 1953. A survey of public opinion concerning the Yellowstone bear feeding problem. Research Project, Colorado A. & M. School of Forestry.

Bolger, D., C. Biehl, M. Sorice, and M. Gilpin. 1987. Estimating effective population size for the Yellowstone grizzly bear population: Effects of non-Poisson family size distribution and breeding sex ratio. in F. Singer, ed., *Conference on science in the national parks, proceedings, vol. 2, wildlife management and habitats*, the fourth triennial conference on research in the national parks and equivalent reserves, July 13-18, 1986. The George Wright Society and the National Park Service, p. 3-16.

Brannon, R. 1984. Influence of roads and developments on grizzly bears in Yellowstone National Park. Interagency Grizzly Bear Study Team.

Bray, O.E., and V.G. Barnes. 1967. *A literature review on black bear populations and activities*. National Park Service and Colorado Cooperative Wildlife Research Unit.

Bromely, G. 1965. The bears of the southern far east of USSR. Canadian Wildlife Service translation of Russian.

Bucknall, E. 1972. Annual Wildlife Report, May 1, 1971 to April 30, 1972. Yellowstone Park Files.

Bunnell, F.L., D.S. Eastman, and J.M. Peek, eds. 1978. Symposium on natural regulation of wildlife populations. In Proceedings of the Northwest Section, The Wildlife Society, No. 14, University of Idaho.

Burghardt, G.M., and L.D. Burghardt. 1972. Notes on the behavioral development of two black bear cubs: The first eight months. In S. Herrero, ed., *Bears—Their biology and mangement*, I.U.C.N., p. 207-220.

Burst, T., and M. Pelton. 1983. Black bear mark trees in the Smoky Mountains. In P. Zager, ed., *Bears—Their biology and management*, B.B.A., p. 45–53.

Burt, W.H., and R.P. Grossenheider. 1952. *A field guide to the mammals*. New York: Houghton Mifflin.

Byrd, C. 1988. Of bears and women: Investigating the hypothesis that menstruation attracts bears. M.S. thesis, University of Montana.

Cahalane, V.H. 1947. *Mammals of North America*. New York: MacMillan.

Cahn, R. 1976. The future of the parks: II. In *Research in the Parks: Transactions of the National Park Centennial Symposium*. Washington DC: U.S. Government Printing Office, p. 213–220.

Chase, A. 1983. The last bears of Yellowstone. *The Atlantic*, February, p. 63–73.

———. 1986. The grizzly and the Juggernaut. *Outside* (January).

Childs, F. 1934. Additional notes on the hibernation habits of the black bear (*Euarctos americanus*), from observations taken in Yellowstone National Park, 1933–1934. Yellowstone Files. Mimeographed.

———. 1934. Experimental use of liquid tear gas on park bears. National Park Service report.

Cole, G. 1967. Research goals, Yellowstone National Park.

———. 1967. Craighead report on Yellowstone bears. Memorandum to Deputy Chief Scientist, National Park Service. Yellowstone Park files.

———. 1969. Elk and the Yellowstone ecosystem. Yellowstone Research Note no. 1.

———. 1969. Grizzly bears. Memorandum to the Superintendent.

———. 1971. Preservation and management of grizzly bears in Yellowstone National Park. *Bioscience* 21:858–863.

———. 1972. Grizzly bear-elk relationships in Yellowstone National Park. *Journal of Wildlife Management* 36(2):556–561.

———. 1972. Preservation and management of grizzly bears in Yellowstone National Park. In S. Herrero, *Bears—Their biology and management*, I.U.C.N., p. 274–288.

———. 1973. Management involving grizzly bears in Yellowstone National Park, 1970–1972. Natural Resources Report no. 7, National Park Service.

———. 1973. Management involving grizzly bears and humans in Yellowstone National Park, 1970–1973. *Bioscience* 24:335–338.

———. 1974. Comments on National Academy of Sciences Report. Memorandum to files, September 11.

———. 1975. Management involving grizzly bears in Yellowstone National Park, 1970–1974. Paper presented at 26th Annual A.I.B.S. Meeting of Biological Sciences at Oregon State University.

———. 1975. Natural vs. man-caused deaths of wild animals in national parks. Yellowstone Park Information Paper no. 26.

———. 1975. Population regulation and the consequences of artificially feeding wild animals. Yellowstone Park Information Paper no. 27.

———. 1976. Management involving grizzly and black bears in Yellowstone National Park, 1970–1975. Natural Resources Report no. 9, National Park Service.

———. 1978. A naturally regulated elk population. Research Report, Yellowstone National Park.

Condon, D. 1956. The Yellowstone grizzly. Yellowstone Park Files.

Cottam, C., A.I. Nelson, and T.E. Clarke. 1939. Notes on early winter food habits of the black bear in George Washington National Forest. *Journal of Mammalogy* 20:310–314.

Cottrell, L. 1925. Black bear abroad in February. *Yellowstone Nature Notes*, March 18, p. 6.

Cowan, I.M. 1975. Letter to Glen Cole, April 29.

Craighead, F. 1969. Increasing concern over grizzly bear survival. *Jackson Hole Guide*, November 6.

———. 1970. Grizzlies may be endangered. *High Country News*, October 5.

———. 1973. They're killing Yellowstone's grizzlies. *National Wildlife*, October 4–9.

———. 1976. Grizzly bear ranges and movements as determined by radiotracking. In M. Pelton, J. Lentfer, and G. Folk, *Bears—Their biology and management*, I.U.C.N., p. 97-110.

Craighead, J. 1960. Proposal for research on ecology of the grizzly bear (*Ursus horribilis*) initiated by the Montana Cooperative Wildlife Research Unit. Submitted to the National Science Foundation and the National Academy of Sciences.

———. 1969. Letter to J. Anderson, April 14.

———. 1969. Investigator's Annual Report. Yellowstone Park Files, 14 January.

———. 1971. Letter to Jack Anderson, April.

Craighead, J., and F. Craighead. 1967. Management of bears in Yellowstone National Park. Unpublished report.

———. 1971. Grizzly bear-man relationships in Yellowstone National Park. *Bioscience* 21(16):845–857.

———. 1972. Grizzly bear prehibernation and denning activities as determined by radiotracking. *Wildlife Monographs*, no. 32.

Craighead, J., F. Craighead, and M. Hornocker. 1961. An ecological study of the grizzly bear, third annual report, summary of work accomplished, 1959–1961. Montana Cooperative Wildlife Research Unit.

Craighead, J., F. Craighead, and H. McCutcheon. 1970. Age determination of grizzly bears from fourth premolar tooth sections. *Journal of Wildlife Management* 34(2):353–363.

Craighead, J., F. Craighead, and J. Sumner. 1976. Reproductive cycles and rates in the grizzly bear, *Ursus arctos horribilis*, of the Yellowstone ecosystem. In M. Pelton, J. Lentfer, and G. Folk, eds., *Bears—Their biology and management*, I.U.C.N., p. 337–356.

Craighead, J., K. Greer, R. Knight, and H. Pac. 1988. Grizzly bear mortalities in the Yellowstone ecosystem, 1959–1987. Montana Department of Fish, Wildlife & Parks, Craighead Wildlife-Wildlands Institute, Interagency Grizzly Bear Study Team, and National Fish & Wildlife Foundation.

Craighead, J., M. Hornocker, and F. Craighead. 1969. Reproductive biology of young female grizzly bears. *Journal of Reprod. Fert., Suppl.* 6:447–475.

Craighead, J., J.S. Sumner, and G.B. Scaggs. 1982. *A definitive system for analysis of grizzly bear habitat and other wilderness resources.* University of Montana: Wildlife-Wildlands Institute Monograph Series no. 2.

Craighead, J., J. Varney, and F. Craighead. 1973. A Computer analysis of the Yellowstone grizzly bear population. Unpublished mimeographed report.

———. 1974. *A population analysis of the Yellowstone grizzly bears.* Bulletin 40, Montana Forest and Conservation Experiment Station, University of Montana.

———. 1976. Telemetry experiments with a hibernating black bear. In M. Pelton, J. Lentfer, and G. Folk, eds., *Bears—Their biology and management,* I.U.C.N., p. 357–372.

Craighead, J., et al. 1971. Satellite monitoring of black bear. *Bioscience* 21(24):1206–1213.

———. 1960. Trapping, immobilizing and color-marking grizzly bears. In *Transactions of the Twenty-fifth North American Wildlife Conference,* March 7, 8, and 9, 347–363.

Crocker, F.C. 1893. After wapiti in Wyoming. In T. Roosevelt and G. Grinnell, eds., *American big game hunting.* New York: Forest and Stream Publishing Co, p. 140–154.

Darling, F.F., and N. Eichorn. 1969. *Man and nature in the national parks.* Washington, D.C.: The Conservation Foundation.

Despain, D. 1972. Fire as an ecological force in Yellowstone ecosystems. Yellowstone Information Paper no. 16.

———. 1973. Major vegetation zones of Yellowstone National Park. Yellowstone Information Paper no. 19.

———. 1991. *Yellowstone vegetation.* Boulder: Roberts Rinehart.

Dennis, B., P. Munholland, and J. Scott. 1989. Estimation of growth and extinction patterns for endangered species. Montana State University Statistics Group, Department of mathematical sciences.

Dinkel, T.R., and M.Y. Su. 1974. Aerial detection of grizzly bears in Yellowstone National Park. Final Report, National Park Service Science Center.

Dixon, J. 1929. Report of the bear situation in Yellowstone. Yellowstone Park Special Research Report. Mimeographed.

Doane, G. 1970. *Battle drums and geysers, the journals of Gustavus Doane.* Bonney and Bonney, eds. Chicago: Swallow Press.

Dole, R. 1914. Report on sanitary conditions in Yellowstone Park. Yellowstone Park Archives, typescript. Yellowstone National Park, Wyoming.

Dood, A.R., R.D. Brannon, and R.D. Mace. 1985. Grizzly bear environmental impact statement, preliminary draft. Helena: Montana Department of Fish, Wildlife, and Parks.

Douglas, J. 1925. Black bear and cub under Lake Hotel. *Yellowstone Nature Notes,* March 18, p. 6.

Egbert, A. and A. Stokes. 1976. The social behavior of brown bears on an Alaskan salmon stream. In M. Pelton, J. Lentfer, and G. Folk, *Bears—Their biology and management,* I.U.C.N., p. 41–56.

Erickson, A. 1959. The age of self-sufficiency in the black bear. *Journal of Wildlife Management* 23(4):401–405.

Erickson, A., J. Nellor and G.A. Petrides. 1964. *The Black Bear in Michigan.* Research Bulletin 4, Michigan State University Agricultural Experiment Station.

Folk, G.E., M.A. Folk, and J.G. Minor. 1972. Physiological condition of three species of bears in winter dens. In S. Herrero, ed., *Bears—Their biology and management,* I.U.C.N., p. 107–125.

Folk, G.E., A. Larson, and M.A. Folk. 1972. Physiological condition of three species of bears in winter dens. In S. Herrero, ed., *Bears—Their biology and management,* I.U.C.N., p. 107–125.

Franklin, W.S. 1913. The Yellowstone Park. *Science* 38(969):127–129.

French, S. 1991. Ursopomorphism. *Yellowstone Grizzly Journal,* Winter/Spring, p. 6–7.

————. in press. Grizzly bear attacks: Prevention and survival.

French, S., and M. French. 1990. Predatory behavior of grizzly bears feeding on elk calves in Yellowstone National Park, 1986–1988. In Darling and Archibald, eds. *Bears—Their biology and amangement,* I.B.A., p. 335–341.

————. 1989. Yellowstone bear behavior during and after the fires. *Yellowstone Grizzly Journal,* Spring, p. 1–3.

————. 1989. 1988–1989 winter kill of ungulates. *Yellowstone Grizzly Journal,* Spring, p. 8.

————. 1990. 1989: The first season after the fires. *Yellowstone Grizzly Journal,* Winter, p. 8–10.

French, M. and S. French. 1990. A case of natural mortality: The story of cub #2. *Yellowstone Grizzly Journal,* Winter, p. 1–3.

————. 1991. The baby boom of 1990. *Yellowstone Grizzly Journal,* Winter/Spring, p. 1, 8.

French, S., and R. Ward. 1991. Molecular genetics study of North American bears. Study outline.

Fund for Animals. 1974. News releases concerning Yellowstone bear management and Fund for Animals Lawsuit. February.

Gilbert, B. 1976. The great grizzly controversy. *Audubon,* January, p. 62-92.

Glenn, L., et al. 1976. Reproductive biology of female brown bears, *Ursus arctos,* McNeil River, Alaska. In M. Pelton, J. Lentfer, and G. Folk, *Bears—Their biology and management,* I.U.C.N., p. 381–390.

Graham, D. 1978. Grizzly bear distribution, use of habitats, food habits and habitat characterization in Pelican and Hayden Valleys, Yellowstone National Park. M.S. Thesis, Montana State University.

Greer, K. 1972. Grizzly bear mortality studies in Montana. In S. Herrero, ed., *Bears—Their biology and management,* I.U.C.N., p. 53–66.

————. 1976. Managing Montana's grizzlies for the grizzlies! In M. Pelton, J. Lentfer, and G. Folk, eds., *Bears—Their biology and management,* I.U.C.N., p. 177–190.

Greater Yellowstone Coordinating Committee. 1990. Vision for the future, a framework for coordination in the greater Yellowstone area. Billings, U.S. Forest Service and National Park Service.

Griffel, D.E., and J.V. Basile. 1981. Identifying sheep killed by bears. USDA-FS, Intermtn. For. & Range Exp. Sta. Research Note INT-313.

Grimm, R. 1938. A climbing grizzly. *Yellowstone Nature Notes*, November–December, p. 58–59.

Grinnell, G.B. 1885. Report on the park. *Forest and Stream*, June 11, p. 1.

Grinnell, J., and T. Storer. 1916. Animal life as an asset of national parks. *Science* 1(44):375–380.

Gross, J. 1973. A computer re-analysis of a computer analysis of the Yellowstone grizzly bear population by Craighead, Varney and Craighead.

Gunther, K. 1990. Visitor impact on grizzly bear activity in Pelican Valley, Yellowstone National Park. In Darling and Archibald, eds. *Bears—Their biology and management*, I.B.A., 1990, p. 73–78.

Gunther, K., and R. Renkin. 1990. Grizzly bear predation on elk calves and other fauna of Yellowstone National Park. In Darling and Archibald, eds. *Bears—Their biology and management*, I.B.A., p. 329–334.

Haines, A. 1977. *The Yellowstone story*. Boulder: Colorado Associated University Press.

Hamer, D., S. Herrero and R. Ogilvie. 1977. Ecological studies of the Banff National Park grizzly bear, Cuthead/Wignore region, 1976. Parks Canada.

Hampton, H.D. 1971. *How the U.S. cavalry saved our national parks*. Bloomington: Indiana University Press.

Hanna, W. 1978. *The grizzlies of Glacier*. Missoula: Mountain Press.

Hape, W. 1978. Personal communication.

Haroldson, M., and D. Mattson. 1985. Response of grizzly bears to backcountry human use in Yellowstone National Park. Interagency Grizzly Bear Study Team.

Harrison, G. 1979. Are we creating killer bears? *Sports Afield*, February, 54–55, 106–108.

Harting, A.L. 1985. Relationships between activity patterns and foraging strategies of Yellowstone grizzly bears. M.S. Thesis, Montana State University.

Haynes, B.D., and E. Haynes. 1966. *The grizzly bear: Portraits from life*. Norman: University of Oklahoma Press.

Heller, E. 1925. The big game animals of Yellowstone National Park. *Roosevelt Wildlife Bulletin* 2(4):404–467.

Henderson, A.B. undated. Journal of the Yellowstone expedition of 1866 under Jeff Standifer, also the diaries kept by Henderson during his prospecting journeys in the Snake, Wind River, and Yellowstone country during the years 1866–1872. Yellowstone Park Files. Typescript.

Hensel, R., W. Troyer, and A. Erickson. 1969. Reproduction in the female brown bear. *Journal of Wildlife Management* 33(2):357–365.

Herrero, S. 1972. Aspects of evolution and adaptation in American black bears (*Ursus americanus Pallas*) and brown and grizzly bears (*U. arctos Linne*) of

North America. In S. Herrero, ed., *Bears—Their biology and management*, I.U.C.N., p. 221–231.

———. 1976. Conflicts between man and grizzly bears in the national parks of North America. In M. Pelton, J. Lentfer, and G. Folk, eds., *Bears—Their biology and management*, I.U.C.N., p. 121–146.

———. 1985. *Bear attacks: Their causes and avoidance*. New York: Nick Lyons Books/Schocken.

Herrero, S. and D. Hamer. 1977. Courtship and copulation of a pair of grizzly bears, with comments on reproductive plasticity and strategy. *Journal of Mammalogy* 58(3):441–444.

Holzworth, J.M. 1930. *The wild grizzlies of Alaska*. New York: G.P. Putnam's Sons.

Home, W. 1977. Color change in a growing black bear. *Murrelet*, Winter, p. 79.

Hornaday, W. 1922. *The minds and manners of wild animals*. New York: Charles Scribner's Sons.

Hornocker, M. 1962. Population characteristics and social and reproductive behavior of the grizzly bear in Yellowstone National Park. M.S. Thesis, Montana State University.

Houston, D.B. 1971. Ecosystems of national parks. *Science* 172:648–651.

———. 1973. Wildfires in northern Yellowstone National Park. *Ecology* 54(5):1111–1117.

———. 1977. Elk as winter-spring food for carnivores in northern Yellowstone Park. Paper presented at the American Association for the Advancement of Science Annual Meeting, February.

———. 1977–1979. Personal communication.

———. 1982. *The northern Yellowstone elk: Ecology and management*. New York: Macmillan.

Howell, A.B. 1921. The black bear as a destroyer of game. *Journal of Mammalogy* 2(1):36.

Hubbard, W.P., Harris, and Seale. 1960. *Notorious grizzly bears*. Chicago: Swallow Press.

Hunt, C., F. Hammond, and C. Peterson. 1988. Aversive conditioning study, 1987 progress report. Wyoming Game and Fish Department.

Jaggar, T.A. 1899. Death Gulch, a natural bear-trap. *Appleton's Popular Science Monthly*, February.

Jenness, H., A. Erickson, and J. Craighead. 1972. Some comparative aspects of milk from four species of bears. *Journal of Mammalogy* 53(1):34–47.

Johnson, A. 1973. Yellowstone grizzlies: Endangered or prospering? *Defenders of Wildlife News*, October, p. 557–568.

Johnson, F. 1900. Bear in Yellowstone Park. *Recreation* 12(1).

Johnson, F. 1950. History of the Yellowstone bear problem. Memorandum from Acting Superintendent to Regional Director. Yellowstone Park Files.

Jonkel, C. 1975. Of bears and people. *Western Wildlands*, Winter, p. 30–37.

———. 1978. Black, brown (grizzly), and polar bears. In J. Scmidt and D. Gilbert, eds., *Big game of North America*. Harrisburg: Stackpole Books, p. 227–248.

Jonkel, C. and I. Cowan. 1971. *The black bear in the spruce-fir forest.* Wildlife Monograph no. 27.

Jope, K.L. 1985. Implications of grizzly bear habituation to hikers. *Wildlife Society Bulletin* 13:32–27.

Jordan, R. 1976. Threat behavior of the black bear, *Ursus americanus.* In M. Pelton, J. Lentfer, and G. Folk, eds., *Bears—Their biology and management,* I.U.C.N., 57–64.

Judd, S.L., R. Knight, and B. Blanchard. 1983. Denning of grizzly bears in the Yellowstone National Park area. In P. Zager, ed., *Bears—Their biology and management,* I.B.A., p. 11–118.

Kearns, W. 1937. The speed of grizzly bears. *Yellowstone Nature Notes,* January–February, p. 2–3.

Kendall, K.C. 1980. Bear use of pine nuts. In C. Martinka and K. McArthur, *Bears—Their biology and management,* B.B.A., p. 166–173.

Knight, R., and L.L. Eberhardt. 1984. Projected future abundance of the Yellowstone grizzly bear. *Journal of Wildlife Management* 48(4):1434–1438.

———. 1985. Population dynamics of Yellowstone grizzly bears. *Ecology* 66(2):323–334.

Knight, R., S. Mealey, and C. Servheen. 1987. Supplementary report to the Yellowstone ecosystem subcommittee, from task force to prepare recovery alternatives for the Yellowstone grizzly bear population.

Knight, R., and S.L. Judd. 1983. Grizzly bears that kill livestock. In P. Zager, ed., *Bears—Their biology and management,* I.B.A., p. 186–190.

Knight, R., D.J. Mattson, and B. Blanchard. 1984. Movements and habitat use of the Yellowstone grizzly bear. Interagency Grizzly Bear Study Team.

Knight, R., et al. 1974. Grizzly bear study team, first interim report. USDI-NPS.

———. 1975. Yellowstone grizzly bear investigations: Annual report of the Interagency Study Team. USDI-NPS.

———. 1976. Yellowstone grizzly bear investigations: Annual report of the Interagency Study Team, 1976. USDI-NPS.

———. 1977. Yellowstone grizzly bear investigations: Annual report of the Interagency Study Team. USDI-NPS.

———. 1980. Yellowstone grizzly bear investigations: Report of the Interagency Study Team. USDI-NPS.

———. 1981. Yellowstone grizzly bear investigations: Annual report of the interagency study team. USDI-NPS.

———. 1982. Yellowstone grizzly bear investigations: Annual report of the interagency study team. USDI-NPS.

———. 1983. Yellowstone grizzly bear investigations: Annual report of the interagecny study team. USDI-NPS.

———. 1985. Yellowstone grizzly bear investigations: Annual report of the interagency study team. USDI-NPS.

———. 1986. Yellowstone grizzly bear investigations: Annual report of the interagency study team. USDI-NPS.

———. 1987. Yellowstone grizzly bear investigations: Annual report of the interagency study team. USDI-NPS.

―――. 1988. Yellowstone grizzly bear investigations: Annual report of the interagency study team. USDI-NPS.

―――. 1989. Yellowstone grizzly bear investigations: Annual report of the interagency study team. USDI-NPS.

―――. 1990. Yellowstone grizzly bear investigations: Annual report of the interagency study team. USDI-NPS.

―――. 1991. Yellowstone grizzly bear investigations: Annual report of the interagency study team. USDI-NPS.

―――. 1983. Final Report of the ad hoc Committee to Investigate the Need and Feasibility of the Supplemental Feeding of Yellowstone Grizzly Bears. Yellowstone National Park.

Kurten, B. 1976. *The cave bear story*. New York: Columbia University Press.

Langford, N. 1972. *The discovery of Yellowstone Park*, ed. Aubrey Haines. Lincoln: University of Nebraska Press.

Lentfer, et al. 1972. Remarks on denning habits of Alaska brown bears. In S. Herrero, ed., *Bears—Their biology and management*, I.U.C.N., p. 125–132.

Leopold, A.S. 1970. Weaning grizzly bears. *Natural History*, January, p. 94–101.

Leopold, et al. 1963. *Wildlife management in the national parks—Report to the Secretary*. USDI-NPS.

―――. 1969. A bear management program and policy for Yellowstone National Park. Report to the Director by the Natural Sciences Advisory Committee of the National Park Service. USDI-NPS.

Lindzey, F. and E.C. Meslow. 1976. Winter dormancy in black bears in southwestern Washington. *Journal of Wildlife Management* 40(3):408–415.

Linn, R. 1968. Memorandum to the Associate Director of the Bureau of Sport Fisheries and Wildlife, May 21.

Little, J.R. 1974. Memorandum from Acting Regional Solicitor, NPS to Associate Solicitor, Conservation and Wildlife. Yellowstone Park Files.

Ludlow, J. 1976. Observations on the breeding of captive black bears, *Ursus americanus*. In M. Pelton, J. Lentfer, and G. Folk, *Bears—Their biology and management*, I.U.C.N., p. 65–70.

Luque, M. and A. Stokes. 1976. Fishing behavior of Alaska brown bear. In M. Pelton, J. Lentfer, and G. Folk, *Bears—Their biology and management*, I.U.C.N., p. 71–78.

Mack, J. 1990. Black bear dens in the Beartooth face, south-central Montana. In Darling and Archibald, p. 273–277.

―――. 1988. Ecology of black bears on the Beartooth face, south-central Montana. M.S. thesis, Montana State University.

Marti, J. 1984. CBS News gets mauled. *High Country News*, October 29.

Martindale, P. 1926. Bears still out. *Yellowstone Nature Notes*, May–June, p. 2.

―――. c. 1920. Close contact with grizzly bears. Yellowstone Park Files. Handwritten report.

―――. 1931. Bears during the so-called hibernation state. Yellowstone Park Files. Typescript.

Martinka, C.J. 1971. Status and management of grizzly bears in Glacier

305

National Park, Montana. *Transactions of the North American Wildlife and Natural Resource Conference*, vol. 36, p. 312–322.

————. 1974. Population characteristics of grizzly bears in Glacier National Park, Montana. *Journal of Mammalogy* 55:21–29.

Matson, J.R. 1946. Notes on dormancy in the black bear. *Journal of Mammalogy* 27:203–212.

————. 1952. Litter size in the black bear. *Journal of Mammalogy* 33:246–247.

————. 1954. Observations on the dormant phase of a female black bear. *Journal of Mammalogy* 35:28–35.

Mattson, D. 1984. Classification and environmental relationships of wetland vegetation in central Yellowstone National Park. M.S. Thesis, University of Idaho.

————. 1990. Human impacts on bear habitat use. In Darling and Archibald, p. 33–56.

Mattson, D., and R. Knight. 1991. Application of cumulative effects analysis to the Yellowstone grizzly bear population. Interagency grizzly bear study team report: 1991C.

————. 1991. Implications of short–rotation (70–120 year) timber management to Yellowstone grizzly bears. Interagency Grizzly Bear Study Team Report: 1991A.

Mattson, D.J., R. Knight, and B. Blanchard. 1985. Derivation of habitat component values for the Yellowstone grizzly bear. Paper presented at the Grizzly Bear Habitat Symposium, Missoula, Montana, April 30–May 2.

Mattson, D., and M. Reid. 1991. Conservation of the Yellowstone grizzly bear. *Conservation Biology* 5(3)364–372.

Mattson, D., and D. Reinhart. 1990. Whitebark pine on the Mount Washburn massif, Yellowstone National Park. In W. Schmidt and K. McDonald, comp., *Proceedings of a symposium on whitebark pine ecosystems*. U.S. Forest Service General Technical Report INT-270, p. 106–117.

McCracken, H. 1955. *The beast that walks like man*. New York: Hanover House.

McCullough, D. 1978. Population dynamics of the Yellowstone grizzly bear. Paper presented for the International Symposium on Population Dynamics of Large Mammals, Logan, Utah, May 25–27.

————. 1982. Behavior, bears, and humans. *Wildlife Society Bulletin* 10:27–33.

————. 1983. The Craigheads' data on Yellowstone grizzly bear populations: Relevance to current research and management. In P. Zager, ed., *Bears— Their biology and management*, I.B.A., p. 21–32.

McGee, G. 1977. *Senate Hearing before the Committee on Appropriations: Proposed critical habitat area for grizzly bears*. Fiscal Year 1977. 94th Congress, 2nd sess. Washington, D.C.: U.S. Government Printing Office.

McGuire, J.A. 1911. Camping in the Yellowstone. *Outdoor Life*, May, p. 479–485.

McNamee, T. 1984. *The grizzly bear*. New York: Knopf.

Meagher, M. 1973. *The bison of Yellowstone National Park*. Washington D.C.: U.S. Government Printing Office.

————. 1976. Summary of 1974 National Academy of Sciences

recommendations and measures taken as of November, 1976. Yellowstone Park Files. Photocopied.

————. 1977. Evaluation of bear management in Yellowstone National Park, 1976. Yellowstone Research Note no. 7. Yellowstone Park Files.

————. 1978. Evaluation of bear management in Yellowstone National Park, 1977. Yellowstone Research Note no. 8. Yellowstone Park Files.

————. 1977–1991. Personal communication.

Meagher, M., and S. Fowler. 1989. The consequences of protecting problem grizzly bears. *Bear-people conflicts—Proceedings of a symposium on management strategies*, Northwest Territories Department of Renewable Resources, p. 141–144.

Meagher, M., and J.R. Phillips. 1983. Restoration of natural populations of grizzly and black bears in Yellowstone National Park. In P. Zager, ed., *Bears—Their biology and management*, B.B.A., p. 152–158.

Mealey, S.P. 1975. The natural food habits of free ranging grizzly bears in Yellowstone National Park, 1973–1974. M.S. Thesis, Montana State University.

————. 1979. Guidelines for management involving grizzly bears in the greater Yellowstone area. USDA-FS.

Miller, G.D. 1983. Responses of captive grizzly and polar bears to potential repellents. In P. Zager, ed., *Bears—Their biology and management*, B.B.A., p. 275–279.

Miller, L. 1955. Color change in the black bear. *Journal of Mammalogy* 36:460.

Miller, T.S. 1963. Weights and color phases of black bear cubs. *Journal of Mammalogy* 44:129.

Mills, E. 1919. *The grizzly: Our greatest wild animal*. New York: Houghton Mifflin.

Mitchell, J. 1976. Bear at the brink. *Sports Afield*, January and February.

Moment, G. 1968. Bears: The need for a new sanity in wildlife conservation. *Bioscience* 18:1105–1108.

————. 1969. Bears and conservation: Realities and recommendations. *Bioscience* 19:1019–1020.

————. 1970. Man-grizzly problems—Past and present. *Bioscience* 20: 1142–1144.

Moore, B. 1925. Importance of natural conditions in national parks. In G. Grinnell and C. Sheldon, eds., *Hunting and conservation: The book of the Boone and Crockett Club*. New Haven: Yale University Press, p. 34–355.

Moore, S. 1970. Grizzly bear study ends. *Livingston Enterprise*, January 19.

Moorman, E.J. 1963. Memoirs of E.H. Moorman. *Livingston Enterprise*, various dates, February.

Morrison, E.E. 1976. *Guardian of the forest: A history of the Smokey Bear program*. New York: Vantage Press.

Morse, M. 1936. Hibernation and breeding of the black bear. *Journal of Mammalogy* 18(4):460–465.

Mundy, K.R.D., and D.R. Flook. 1973. *Background for managing grizzly bears in the national parks of Canada*. Canadian Wildlife Service Report Series 22.

Murie, A. 1937. Some food habits of the black bear. *Journal of Mammalogy* 18(2):238–240.

———. 1940. *Ecology of the coyote in the Yellowstone.* Washington D.C.: U.S. Government Printing Office.

———. 1961. *A naturalist in Alaska.* New York: Devin-Adair.

Murie, O.J. 1944. Progress report on the Yellowstone bear study. Yellowstone Park Files.

———. 1954. *A field guide to animal tracks.* Boston: Houghton Mifflin.

National Academy of Sciences. 1974. Report of the Committee on the Yellowstone grizzlies.

National Park Service. 1971. Memorandum of understanding between the National Park Service and the Bureau of Sport Fisheries and Wildlife providing for research on the grizzly bear, *Ursus arctos,* in Yellowstone National Park by the Montana Cooperative Wildlife Research Unit. Yellowstone Park Files.

———. 1971. Wilderness study, Yellowstone National Park. Yellowstone Park Files.

———. 1972. Draft environmental statement, proposed Yellowstone Master Plan. Yellowstone Park Files.

———. 1973. Yellowstone National Park: Master Plan. Yellowstone Park Files.

———. 1975. Grizzly bear management program, Yellowstone National Park, Wyoming, Idaho, Montana. Yellowstone Park Files.

———. 1984. Board of Inquiry into the death of Brigitta Fredenhagen. Yellowstone Park Files.

———. 1985. Response to Chase article "The grizzly and the Juggernaut." Photocopy.

Netherby, S. 1974. Detente with *ursus. Field and Stream,* June, p. 132–135.

Nuss, D. 1978–1979. Personal communication.

Peacock. D. 1990. *Grizzly years.* New York: Holt.

Pearson, A.M. 1972. Population characteristics of northern interior grizzly bears in the Yukon Territory, Canada. In S. Herrero, ed., *Bears—Their biology and management,* I.U.C.N., p. 32–35.

———. 1975. *The northern interior grizzly bear* (Ursus arctos L.). Canadian Wildlife Service Report Series, no. 34.

Pelton, M., et al. 1976. Attitudes and opinions of persons experiencing property damage and/or injury by black bears in the Great Smoky Mountains National Park. In M. Pelton, J. Lentfer, and G. Folk, eds., *Bears—Their biology and management,* I.U.C.N., p. 157–168.

Peterson, S. 1973. Comments on the Craighead Computer Evaluation...Yellowstone Park Files. Photocopied.

Picton, H. 1978. Climate and reproduction of grizzly bears in Yellowstone National Park. *Nature* 274:888–89.

Picton, H.D., and R. Knight. 1980. Obtaining biological information from grizzly bear (*Ursus arctos horribilis*) hair. *Proceedings of the Northwest Section of the Wildlife Society, Banff, Canada.*

———. 1983. Using climate data to predict grizzly bear litter size. In P. Zager, ed., *Bears—Their biology and management*, I.B.A., p. 41–44.

Poelker, R. and H. Hartwell. 1973. *Black bear of Washington, its biology, natural history and relationship to forest regeneration.* Washington State Game Department Biological Bulletin no. 4.

Pope, S. 1923. *Hunting with bow and arrow.* San Francisco: G.P. Putnam's Sons.

Pritchard, G., and C. Robbins. 1990. Digestive and metabolic efficiencies of grizzly and black bears. *Canadian Journal of Zoology* 68:1645–1651.

Pruitt, C. 1976. Play and agonistic behavior in captive black bears. In M. Pelton, J. Lentfer, and G. Folk, *Bears—Their biology and management*, I.U.C.N., p. 79–86.

Rausch, R.L. 1963. Geographic variation in size in North American brown bears, *Ursus arctos* L., as indicated by condylobasal length. *Canadian Journal of Zoology* 41:33–45.

Reed, N. 1974. The grizzly debate, a response from Interior. *National Wildlife*, December–January, p. 16.

Reese, R. 1984. *Greater Yellowstone: The national park and adjacent wildlands.* Helena: Montana Magazine, Inc.

Regenstein, L. 1973. Letter to Nathaniel Reed, August 23.

Reid, N. and D. Learmonth. 1969. Bear management in national parks, prepared for Joint Committee United States and Canadian National Parks, by Neil Reid (NPS) and Donald Learmonth (Parks Canada). Yellowstone Park Files. Mimeographed.

Reiger, J. 1975. *American sportsmen and the origins of conservation.* New York: Winchester Press.

Reinhart, D. 1990. Grizzly bear habitat use of the Cooke City, Montana area. Interagency Grizzly Bear Study Team.

Reinhart, D., and D. Mattson. 1990. Bear use of cutthroat trout spawning streams in Yellowstone National Park. In Darling and Archibald, p. 343–350.

Reinhart, D., and D. Mattson. 1990. Red squirrels in the whitebark pine zone. In W. Schmidt and K. McDonald, comp., *Proceedings of symposium on whitebark pine ecosystems.* U.S. Forest Service General Technical Report INT-270, p. 256–263.

Replogle, W. 1939. Marathon swimming for black bear. *Yellowstone Nature Notes*, September–October, p. 55.

Reynolds, H., J. Curatolo, and R. Quimby. 1976. Denning ecology of grizzly bears in northeastern Alaska. In M. Pelton, J. Lentfer, and G. Folk, *Bears— Their biology and management*, I.U.C.N., p. 403–410.

Robertson, E. 1960. Memorandum to West District Ranger, entitled Bears and people. Yellowstone Park Files.

Robbins, W.J., et al. 1963. A report by the Advisory Committee to the National Park Service on research of the National Academy of Sciences—National Research Council. National Academy of Sciences.

Rogers, L. 1974. Shedding of foot pads by black bears during denning. *Journal of Mammalogy* 55(3):672–674.

———. 1976. Effects of mast and berry crop failures on survival, growth, and reproductive success of black bears. In *Transactions of the 41st North American Wildlife and Natural Resources Conference,* published by the Wildlife Management Institute, Washington D.C.

———. 1984. Reactions of free-ranging black bears to capsaicin spray repellent. *Wildlife Society Bulletin* 12:59–61.

Rogers, L., et al. 1976. Characteristics and management of black bears that feed in garbage dumps, campgrounds, or residential areas. In M. Pelton, J. Lentfer, and G. Folk, *Bears—Their biology and management,* I.U.C.N., p. 169–176.

Romme, W., and M. Turner. 1991. Implications of global climate change for biogeographic patterns in the greater Yellowstone ecosystem. *Conservation Biology* 5(3):373–386.

Roop, L. 1975. Grizzly bear progress report. Wyoming Game and Fish Department.

———. 1977. Grizzly bear progress report. Wyoming Game and Fish Department.

———. 1978. Grizzly bear progress report. Wyoming Game and Fish Department.

Roosevelt, T. 1893. *The wilderness hunter.* New York: G.P. Putnam's Sons.

———. 1925. *Outdoor pastimes of an American hunter.* New York: Charles Scribner's Sons.

Ross, P., G. Hornbeck, and B. Horejsi. 1988. Late denning black bears killed by grizzly bear. *Journal of Mammalogy* 69(4):818–820.

Rowan, W. 1947. A case of six cubs in the common black bear. *Journal of Mammalogy* 28(4):404–405.

Rush, W. 1928. How fast does a black bear climb? *Journal of Mammalogy* 9(4): 335–336.

———. 1939. *Wild animals of the Rockies, adventures of a forest ranger.* Garden City: Halcyon House.

Russell, A. 1967. *Grizzly country.* New York: Knopf.

Russell, C.P. 1933. A concise history of science and scientific investigations in Yellowstone National Park. Yellowstone Park Files.

Schleyer, B. 1983. Activity patterns of grizzly bears in the Yellowstone ecosystem and their reproductive behavior, predation and the use of carrion. M.A. Thesis, Montana State University.

Schnoes, R., and E. Starkey. 1978. Bear management in the national park system. National Park Service Oregon Cooperative Park Studies Unit, School of Forestry, Oregon State University.

Schoonmaker, W.J. 1968. *The world of the grizzly bear.* New York: Lippincott.

Schullery, P. 1975. The Yellowstone archives: Past, present, and future. M.A. Thesis, Ohio University.

———. 1976. "Buffalo" Jones and the bison herd in Yellowstone: Another look. *Montana, The Magazine of Western History,* Summer, p. 40–51.

———. 1978. A partnership in conservation . . . Roosevelt and Yellowstone. *Montana, The Magazine of Western History,* p. 2–15.

———. 1984. Bear myths. *Field and Stream,* August, p. 64–65, 87–88.

———. 1984. Securing the grizzly's small portion. *National Parks*, July–August, p. 27–32.

———. 1984. *Mountain time*. New York: Nick Lyons Books/Schocken.

———. 1985. Reflections on bear stories. *Safari Magazine* 11(6):78–83.

———. 1989. Yellowstone grizzlies, the new breed. *National Parks*, November, p. 24–29, 49.

———. 1989. Stopping nature's clock. *Backpacker*, October, p. 17–21.

———, ed. 1979. *Old Yellowstone days*. Boulder: Colorado Associated University Press.

———, ed. 1983. *American bears: Selections from the writings of Theodore Roosevelt*. Boulder: Colorado Associated University Press.

———, ed. 1991. *Yellowstone bear tales*. Niwot: Roberts Rinehart.

Schullery, P., et al. 1984. Fishing Bridge and the Yellowstone ecosystem: A report to the Director. USDI-NPS.

Servheen, C. 1982. A national plan of recovery. *Western Wildlands* 8(1):13–15.

Servheen, C., R. Knight, D. Mattson, S. Mealey, D. Strickland, J. Varley, and J. Weaver. 1986. Report to the IGBC on the availability of foods for grizzly bears in the Yellowstone ecosystem.

Seton, E.T. 1899. *The biography of a grizzly*. New York: The Century Company.

———. 1909. *Lives of game animals*. New York: Doubleday, Doran and Company.

———. 1913. *Wild animals at home*. New York: Grosset and Dunlap.

Shafer, C. 1985. Land conversion and human density influences on the movements of the grizzly bear in the greater Yellowstone ecosystem. Interagency Resources Division, National Park Service, Washington, D.C.

Shaffer, M.L. 1981. Minimum population sizes for species conservation. *Bioscience* 31(2):131–134.

———. 1983. Determining minimum viable population sizes for the grizzly bear. In Meslow, p. 133–139.

Shepard, P., and B. Sanders. 1985. *The sacred paw: The bear in nature, myth, and literature*. New York: Viking.

Skinner, C. 1932. Some notes on the black bear (*Euarctos americanus*) from observations at Old Faithful, Yellowstone National Park. Yellowstone Park Files. Typescript.

Skinner, M. 1925. *Bears in the Yellowstone*. Chicago: A.C. McClurg and Company.

———. 1925. *The Yellowstone nature book*. Chicago: A.C. McClurg and Company.

———. 1927. The predatory and fur-bearing animals of Yellowstone Park. *Roosevelt Wildlife Bulletin* 4(2):163–282.

Smith, F.D. 1909. *Book of a hundred bears*. Chicago: Rand McNally.

Smith, J. 1913. The Yellowstone Park. *Science*, June 20, p. 941.

Sparrowe, R. 1968. Sexual behavior of grizzly bears. *The American Midland Naturalist* 80(2):570–572.

Spencer, H.F., Jr. 1955. *The black bear and its status in Maine*. Maine Department of Inland Fisheries and Game, Division Bulletin 4.

Stebler, A.M. 1972. Conservation of the grizzly—Ecological and cultural considerations. In S. Herrero, ed., *Bears—Their biology and management*, I.U.C.N., p. 297–303.

Stokes, A.W. 1970. An ethologist's views on managing grizzly bears. *Bioscience* 20(21):1154–1157.

Stonorov, D., and A.W. Stokes. 1972. Social behavior of the Alaska brown bear. In S. Herrero, ed., *Bears—Their biology and management*, I.U.C.N., p. 232–242.

Storer, T. and L. Tevis. 1955. *California grizzly*. Berkeley: University of California Press.

Suchy, W.J., et al. 1985. New estimates of minimum viable population sizes for grizzly bears of the Yellowstone ecosystem. *Wildlife Society Bulletin* 13(3):225–227.

Thompson, B. 1934. Letter to Max Bauer, Yellowstone Naturalist, September 3.

Thompson, T. 1942. Grizzly bears get food. *Yellowstone Nature Notes*, May–June, p. 33.

Tisch, E.L. 1961. Seasonal food habit of the black bear in the Whitefish Range of northwestern Montana. M.S. Thesis, Montana State University.

Trefethen, J. 1975. *An American crusade for wildlife*. New York: Winchester Press and the Boone and Crockett Club.

U.S. Executive Order 11507. 1970. Prevention, control, and abatement of air and water pollution at federal facilities. February 4.

U.S. Fish and Wildlife Service. 1982. Grizzly bear recovery plan. USDI-FWS.

———. 1990. Grizzly bear recovery plan revision number 1. USDI-NPS.

Van Wormer, J. 1966. *The world of the black bear*. Philadelphia: Lippincott.

Walker, R. 1975. Memorandum to Director, U.S. Fish and Wildlife Service, entitled Grizzly bear management program Yellowstone National Park. Yellowstone Park Files.

Weaver, J. 1978. The wolves of Yellowstone. Natural Resources Report no. 14. National Park Service.

———. 1986. Of wolves and grizzly bears. *Western Wildlands*, Fall, p. 27–29.

———. 1986. Grizzly bear habitat: Classification and mapping. A report to the Interagency Grizzly Bear Committee. U.S. Forest Service, Missoula, Montana.

Wickelgren, I. 1988. Bone loss and the three bears. *Science News* 134:424–425.

Wilber, C. 1970. Incompatible species. *Bioscience* 20(6):326. Letter to the Editor.

Wilkinson, T. 1989. GYC report says more protection needed to save embattled bruin. *Greater Yellowstone Report*, Winter, p. 6–7, 17.

Willey, C. 1978. *The Vermont black bear*. Vermont Fish and Game Department.

Wills, L. 1975. Two agencies criticized about grizzly bear kills. *Bozeman Daily Chronicle*, November 2.

Wister, O. 1936. Old Yellowstone days. *Harper's Magazine* (March 1).

Wooldridge, D.R. 1980. Chemical aversion conditioning of polar and black bears. In C. Martinka and K. McArthur, eds., *Bears—Their biology and management*, B.B.A., p. 167–173.

Worley, D., et al. 1976. Helminth and arthropod parasites of grizzly and black bears in Montana and adjacent ranges. In M. Pelton, J. Lentfer, and G. Folk, *Bears—Their biology and management*, I.U.C.N., p. 455–464.

Wright, G., J. Dixon, and B. Thompson. 1933. *Fauna of the national parks of the United States*. Washington D.C.: U.S. Government Printing Office.

Wright, G., and B. Thompson. 1935. *Fauna of the national parks of the United States: Wildlife management in the national parks*. Washington D.C.: U.S. Government Printing Office.

Wright, W. 1910. *Ben, the black bear*. New York: Charles Scribner's Sons.

———. 1910. *The grizzly bear*. New York: Charles Scribner's Sons.

Yeager, D. 1931. *Our wilderness neighbors*. Chicago: A.C. McClurg Company.

———. 1933. Bringing up Barney. *Nature Magazine* 21(1):27–30.

Yellowstone Park. 1970. Proposed criteria for transplant or disposal of problem bears. Yellowstone Park Management Plan.

———. 1977. Bear management operational plan. Yellowstone Park Files.

———. 1982. Final environmental impact statement—Grizzly bear management program. USDI-NPS.

Zunino, F. 1981. Dilemma of the Abruzzo bears. *Oryx* 16(2):153–156.

Index

Abruzzo National Park, 182
aggressiveness, 77, 232–234
Albright, Horace, 103, 109, 224
American Association for the
    Advancement of Science, 104
American Forests, 203
American Humane Association, 229
anal plug, black bear, 20
Anderson, Captain George, 93–95, 123, 124
Anderson, Jack, 117, 118, 125, 133, 135, 139,
    142–143
Antelope Creek, 249
anthropomorphism, 26
appearance: black bear, 9; grizzly bear,
    42–44
Army Corps of Engineers, 212
Army Quartermaster Corps, 98
Astringent Creek, 187
attacks, of bears, 96–98, 106–108, 113, 140,
    152, 187, 245
Audubon Society, Murie Chapter, 188

Barbee, Robert, 161, 164, 181
bark as food: black bear, 12; grizzly bear,
    55
"Barney," the black bear, 203, 215
basement-denning, black bear, 214–215
bathing, black bear, 33
Beal, Merrill, 216
*Bear Attacks, Their Causes and
    Avoidance* (Herrero), 185, 243
bear monitor system, 150
bear traps, 230, 231
bear watching, 248–252

Bears in the Yellowstone (Skinner), 108
Beartooth Mountains, 18, 19
begging, by black bear, 100, 101, 148
berries as food, for black bear, 13
Berryman, Clifford, 130
Biography of a Grizzly, The (Seton), 203
Blanchard, Bonnie, 74
Book of A Hundred Bears (Smith), 96
Bridger-Teton National Forest, 157
Bureau of Sport Fisheries and Wildlife,
    133, 134

Cain, Stanley, 127
cambium, as black bear food, 12
climate: as influence, on bears, 73–74, 176;
    of Yellowstone, 87
Cole, Dale, 193
Cole, Glen, 49–51, 125, 135, 138, 140, 144–
    146
coloring, of grizzly bear, 42
Committee on the Yellowstone Grizzlies,
    The, 143, 146
conflict, grizzly bear, 114–132
Constable, Margaret, 106
copulation: black bear, 24; grizzly bear, 63
courtship: black bear, 24; grizzly bear, 63
Cowan, Ian McTaggart, 143
Craighead, Frank, 116, 129, 130, 141, 188
Craighead, John, 114, 126, 189
Craighead Research Team, 42, 44, 58, 63,
    64, 66, 69, 79, 115–132, 133–138, 142–
    148, 168–179, 186
cub development, black bear, 26–27
cub diet: black bear, 26; grizzly bear, 65

cub enemies, black bear, 28
cub size, black bear, 25, 29

Death Gulch, 217–218
denning: black bear, 17; grizzly bear, 57–61
denning body functioning: black bear, 19, 21; grizzly bear, 60
denning length, grizzly bear, 60
denning preparation: black bear, 18; grizzly bear, 57–60
denning sites: black bear, 18, 19; grizzly bear, 58–60
description: black bear, 7, 16; grizzly bear, 41–44
diet, bears, 125
Dole, Robert, 101
Douglas, Joseph, 214
dumps. *See* Rabbit Creek Dump, Trout Creek Dump, and specific topics, such as Craighead Research Team, food habits, and garbage

Eberhardt, L. L., 171
Ecological Society of America, 104
ecological preservation, 112, 113
Ecology, 171
embryonic delay: black bear, 25; grizzly bear, 64
Endangered Species Act, 156, 157, 165
enemies: black bear, 35; grizzly bear, 78, 82
Environmental Impact Statement, 165

famous Yellowstone bears, 202–206
fat storage: black bear, 17; grizzly bear, 57
feeding, of bears, 182–190, 219–227
feeding range, grizzly bear, 70–76
fighting, black bear, 33
Firehole River, 249
fires of 1988, 79–81
fish eating, grizzly bear, 45, 54
Fishing Bridge, 152–154, 249
food habits: black bear, 11, 17, 30–32, 33; grizzly bear, 45–56
Ford, Gerald, 228
Forest and Stream, 91–92
Frank, Douglas, 47
Fredenhagen, Brigitta, 187
French, Steve, 41, 191, 238

French, Marilyn, 191
Fries, Major, 212
Frost, Ned, 212
Fund for Animals, 142

Gallatin National Forest, 157
garbage, as food for bears, 93–95, 100, 105, 106, 118, 120, 122, 123, 173–177, 183, 221–223
garbage cans, 148
Garder's Hole, 249
gestation period, black bear, 25
Glacier National Park, 113, 140, 184
Good Sam Club, 154
Graham, Dean, 55
Grant Village, 152–154
Great Smoky Mountains, 34
Greater Yellowstone area, 161
Greater Yellowstone Coalition, 160
Greater Yellowstone Coordinating Committee, 161
Greater Yellowstone Ecosystem, 2, 46, 71, 150, 161, 163, 168, 182
Greater Yellowstone: The National Park and Adjacent Wildlands (Reese), 157–159
Green Mountain National Forest, 193
Grizzly Bear, The (Wright), 101
Grizzly Bear Management Areas, 155
Grizzly Bear Recovery Plan, 165
group territoriality, black bear, 32

Hanna Barbera Productions, 203
Hansen, Martha, 106
Hape, William, 234
Hayden Valley, 249
Henderson, A. Bart, 208, 211
Herrero, Stephen, 172, 182, 185, 241, 243
hibernation, 19
Hofer, Elwood, 232
homing ability: black bear, 33; grizzly bear, 75
Hornocker, Maurice, 63
hot springs, 215, 216
human perception, of bears, 199–201, 253–255
Hunting With the Bow and Arrow (Pope), 212
hunting: of bears, 91–92, 166, 207–213; prohibition, 93

insects as food: black bear, 14–15; grizzly bear, 53
Interagency Grizzly Bear Committee, 167, 178, 188
Interagency Grizzly Bear Study Team, 42, 44, 46, 47, 56, 58, 61, 64, 69, 71, 73, 74, 75, 80, 142, 145–147, 151, 154–155, 159, 167, 169, 177, 187, 191

Jackson Hole Guide, 129
Jaggar, T. A., 218
"Jesse James," beggar bear, 100, 203
"Johnny Bear," 203
Jones, C. J. "Buffalo", 98
Jonkel, Dr. Charles, 188

killing, of bears, 130, 131, 135, 138, 139, 140, 143, 145, 146, 148, 183
Knight, Richard, 82, 143, 145, 171–179, 191

land management, 149–164
Langford, Nathaniel, 210
Leopold, A. Starker, 111, 127
Leopold Report, 111, 116, 119
life span: black bear, 10; grizzly bear, 42
lifestyle: black bear, 30–36; grizzly bear, 69–83
litter size, black bear, 25
Lives of the Hunted (Seton), 203
Livingston Enterprise (Montana), 92

Mack, John, 18, 19
Madison River system, 1
male promiscuity, black bear, 23–24
Mammoth Hot Springs, 1, 93, 249
management, of bears, 106–108, 110–113, 116–132, 135, 165, 168, 180
Martindale, Philip, 222
Mather, Stephen, 103, 109
mating and cub growth: black bear, 23–29; grizzly bear, 62–68
mating promiscuity, grizzly bear, 62
Mattson, David, 56, 71
May, Roger William, 187
McCullough, Dale, 173–174, 183
Meagher, Mary, 100
Mealey, Steve, 53, 159
meat eating, of grizzly bear, 45, 47–54
minimum viable population, bears, 177
Mintzmyer, Lorraine, 162
Mission 65, 109

Missouri River, 1
Montana Cooperative Wildlife Research Unit, 115, 116
Mount Washburn, 249
Mountain Time (Schullery), 112
Murie, Olaus, 108

National Academy of Sciences, 142, 143, 149, 168
National Park Protective Act of 1894, 95
National Park Service, 51, 100, 101, 103–104, 108–110, 112, 115–117, 119, 132, 133–148, 152–154
National Park Service Act of 1916, 102, 104, 156, 157
National Zoo, 232
Nature, 173
Newsweek, 155
Night of the Grizzlies (Olsen), 140
Norris, Philetus, 91
nursing, by black bear, 25–26
Nuss, Dale, 230
nuts as food: black bear, 12–14; grizzly bear, 53–55

Old Yellowstone Days (Schullery), 100
Olmsted, Charles, 127
Olson, Sigurd, 127

parasites, grizzly bear, 78
Pearson, Albert, 60
Pearson, H. A., 92
Pelican Valley, 249
Picton, Harold, 173, 178
Pitcher, Major John, 95
Pope, Saxton, 212
population, bear, 92, 100, 104, 118, 131, 135, 137, 139, 144, 146, 150, 154, 168–182, 193
post-denning period, black bear, 21–22
pregnancy, black bear, 18, 24, 25, 32
protection, of bears, 149, 150, 156, 157,160

Rabbit Creek Dump, 128
reproductive systems: black bear, 32; grizzly bear, 62
Robinson, Elbert, 231
Rocky Mountains, 19, 82, 88
Roop, Larry, 132, 187
Roosevelt, Theodore, 100, 106, 227–229, 231

rubbing trees, black bear, 33
Rush, William, 50

safety, 236–247
Science, 96, 104
senses, of black bear, 9
Servheen, Christopher, 82
Seton, Earnest Thompson, 203
shedding, by black bear, 7–8
Shoshone National Forest, 157, 159
Simpson, Alan, 154, 188
size, of black bear, 8–9
Skinner, Curtis, 215
Skinner, Milton, 233
Smith, F. D., 96
Snake River system, 1
sounds: of black bear, 36; of grizzly bear, 79
Southwick, R. E., 96
speed: of black bear, 10; of grizzly bear, 42
"Spud," the black bear, 203
Sununu, John, 162
Swan Lake Flats, 249

teeth: black bear, 12; grizzly bear, 44
territoriality, black bear, 31, 33
tree climbing, black bear, 34, 39
tree markings, black bear, 34
Trout Creek Dump, 76, 127–129
Trumbull, Walter, 209

U.S. Calvary, 90–91
U.S. Department of Agriculture, 167
U.S. Department of the Interior, 167
U.S. Fish and Wildlife Service, 103, 114, 142, 154, 165, 189
U.S. Forest Service, 142, 161–162
U.S. Geological Survey, 101
Ursus americanus, 37

Ursus arctos, 37, 40
Ursus etruscus, 37, 40
Ursus thibetanus, 37

Varley, John, 189
vegetarian, grizzly bear as, 47, 53, 55
Virginian, The (Wister), 221
Vision, 161–163

Wahb, 203
Walker, Harry, 140, 141
Washburn-Langford-Doane expedition, 209
weight gain, black bear, 17
Welch, Frank, 98, 211
Wild Animals at Home (Seton), 203
"Wildlife Management in the National Parks" (report), 111
wildlife protection, 103–104
Wildlife-Wildlands Institute of Missoula, 189
Winster, Owen, 221, 223
wolves, 81–83, 163
Wright, William, 101
Wyoming Game and Fish Department, 131, 189
Wyoming Outfitters Association, 188

Yancy's Hotel, 232
Yeager, Dorr, 203
Yellowstone Grizzly Foundation, 41, 44, 46, 48, 51, 57, 63, 66, 75, 191, 238
Yellowstone Institute, 156
Yellowstone Lake, 54
Yellowstone Park Act of March 1, 1872, 89
Yogi Bear, 205
Young, Arthur, 212

zoos, 93–95, 129, 135, 195, 248

About the author. . .

Paul Schullery is the author, co-author, or editor of many books, including six about Yellowstone and four about bears. He has been involved in Yellowstone issues for twenty years, since he first worked in the park as a ranger-naturalist. His articles and essays have appeared in many publications, including *BioScience, Country Journal, The New York Times Book Review, Outdoor Life, Encyclopedia Brittanica Year Book of Science and the Future, National Parks,* and *Gray's Sporting Journal.* He has served on the Council of Advisors of the National Parks and Conservation Association, and is an adjunct professor of history at Montana State University. In 1990 and 1991, he conducted the grizzly bear ecology and management class at the Yellowstone Institute. Paul lives and works in Yellowstone, where he spends a lot of time looking for bears.